The Secrets Business

Other Books by the Author

BONDAGE
THE SEARCH FOR AIR SAFETY
FIRE

THE
SECRETS BUSINESS

Stephen Barlay

Thomas Y. Crowell Company
Established 1834   New York

"BOSTON PUBLIC LIBRARY"

First United States publication 1974
Originally published in Great Britain under the title *Double Cross*

Designed by Ingrid Beckman

Manufactured in the United States of America

ISBN 0-690-00290-4

Library of Congress Cataloging in Publication Data

Barlay, Stephen.
    The secrets business.

    1. Business intelligence.   I. Title.
HD38.B245 1974   658.4'7   73-18266
ISBN 0-690-00290-4

2   3   4   5   6   7   8   9   10

In memory of Bobi

Contents

Introduction

IN THE EARLY 1960's, a magazine asked me to write about industrial security. I did some research, spoke to some specialists and several industrialists. Even with my scanty knowledge about what was vaguely termed industrial espionage, it soon struck me how little topflight executives of major concerns knew about the subject and, what was worse, how lightly they seemed to treat this obvious menace. I tried to find out more about it and turned to scores of private detectives—an almost natural choice for the uninitiated, which includes the executive who seeks security advice or wishes to receive some otherwise unobtainable information.

This latter part of the task appeared to be amazingly easy. One private detective after another freely told me about his experiences, mostly on the defensive side although admitting, occasionally, a few offensive assignments. After a while, however, it was impossible not to notice the perennial pattern of their stories, which were based on a handful of much publicized court cases, and seasoned, cooked, and embellished to individual taste. Eventually I learned that the overwhelming majority of these "cases" and the personal role of my informers were sheer invention. What made them rush to talk to me was simply to grab publicity wherever possible. Their motive was plain; clients would more readily bring their marital and other problems to the detective who handles highly confidential and sophisticated industrial jobs than to a mere snooper whose bread and butter are earned from unsavory bedroom scenes.

The choice of the uninitiated is understandable; private detectives are often regarded as the tip of the iceberg, with the mass of business intelligence lurking down in the depths of darkness. The real picture is that of an inverted iceberg. The vast expanse of not very harmful activities floats in full daylight—the really hurting tip remains invisible.

It was at a fairly early stage of my research that I had to choose between two possible courses: either to try to expose a few, possibly minor cases of espionage in full or to attempt to fathom all those murky waters with the expediencies of corroborating evidence and becoming an unenviable confidant of crooks. Hoping that it would serve a useful purpose, I opted for the latter, although I recognized that the morality of this decision might remain questionable.

Although in several cases I had to give strong assurances that I would change the names of people, firms, and even industries, in the course of my investigation I often tried to analyze why many of these successful, wealthy, and powerful intelligence operators talked to me. There is no complete rational explanation, but there are a number of reasons, and these emerged clearly and repeatedly throughout the seven years of building up personal contacts.

François Levine, a French "business consultant"—they all love and hide behind euphemisms—provided my first major break. He gave me the detailed account of a case involving two executives who work for a well-known Greek shipping magnate. He assured me that their boss never questioned and knew nothing about the source of their useful information concerning a rival, and that they used it only to enhance their stature and gain promotion within the organization. I shall never forget this Frenchman's concluding remark: "I think I've given you enough to go and sell an interesting article about the case. But if you really mean to understand what's going on and on what scale, it may pay you in the long run to keep it to yourself and use it as some guidance." I took his advice, resisted the temptation, and a full eight months later, he was the first to give me some introductions that snow-balled around the world.

Today I know why he talked to me originally. In a roundabout way, unwittingly, I was to help him discredit one of his competitors in a minute circle of friends and enemies. I am aware of the fact that he was not the only one who used me.

Many such "business consultants" and "marketing special-ists" simply welcome the opportunity to talk about their work and achievements to someone, anyone, as long as they feel admired and know that their secrets are safe for one reason or another, like the lack of strong evidence that would stand up in court against a heavy libel suit. Their burden of anonymity and unmentionable triumphs is never alleviated by the political spy's patriotism, sense of duty, comradeship, or occasional indirect recognition; they work for themselves and profit is their sole motive. They wield real power, but few enjoy the role of the *éminence grise*. They can never hope to be recorded in the annals of heroism. They can never brag about their deals and influence to their children. They can show off the fruits of their cover business (the only way to legalize their profits), but that is not their elixir.

A "business efficiency consultant" said to me in Washing-ton, "It's like a big lump of raw onion in my throat that I can't tell my wife, 'Honey, you know why the stock of that big electronic company is suddenly going up? You know why? Because I, little me, gave them the key to the winning bid for a contract in Germany.' And you want to know something? My wife even believes that I learned to fly and bought an airplane only because it's more economical to go that way to Chicago where I have some business interests."

A few people I made talk by methods I am not ashamed but certainly not proud of, and toward the end, there were others whose professional pride was hurt; I had approached so-and-so but not them—why?

It was obvious from the start that several of even my best contacts would try to show off with the aid of outright lies or "borrowing" cases from one another. Because of that, I am using only those that are supported by some further evidence and corroboration.

This frequently wasteful basic research and the application of the "first interview—be selective only afterward" principle were, however, quite inevitable because my months of reading newspaper and business-magazine files and practically all available books on the subject in the United States and Europe produced only background material against which to evaluate my own findings.

I often had to turn to original sources, even when examining the few, already much publicized, court cases, because all parties concerned were usually anxious to keep on-the-record details to a minimum.

It would be most gratifying now to compile a long list of acknowledgments to the several hundred contacts, informers, industrial security agents, counterespionage specialists, detectives, economic intelligence officers, to lawyers who gave me access to confidential files on espionage cases that had been settled out of court, and to the business executives who permitted me to read limited sections of their information and security records, and to thank them all for their invaluable help—except that few if any of them would be thankful in return for a printed expression of indebtedness.

Apart from those who authorized me to use direct quotations from them in the book, most people in the *secrets business*—the goodies as well as the baddies—use secrecy as the best air conditioner for their natural habitat of darkness where anonymity is a prerequisite of success on either side.

This peculiar atmosphere, the characters I met, and the exotic settings in which some of my encounters took place, might give the impression to the skeptical witness, like myself, that this is the real-life world of James Bond. The only sobering difference that must be remembered is that here the adjective "real-life" mostly means legwork instead of ingenuity, the shifty eyes of the fox instead of the lion's steady stare, and greasy palms instead of steely fists.

1

Declaration of War

THE SKY WAS LOW and London-gray, sealed firmly like the lid of a pressure cooker on Heathrow Airport. Soon to bathe in the alluring artificial glow of the departure lounge, shivery autumn faces emerged from coaches and cars. In the year 1971, it was a good day for minor criminals and semiscandalous divorcées; their court cases had been squeezed out of the newspapers that were still reverberating the heat of the first British mass expulsion of 105 Russian diplomats for commercial espionage.

Special Branch officers, however, could begin to relax; the Tupolevs flying "expulsion specials" had all gone. Services were running on schedule; perfunctory passport inspection melted into endless blinking in slow motion; passengers dashed through breathlessly to delve into duty-free goodies; a "Mr. Khrmmmmmmmm, sorry, Mr. Krhmmmmm from Zambia" was urgently required at the information desk; the megaphone girls never ran out of calls, warnings, and recognition of self-importance; and the Paris shuttle departure was not yet even announced.

Two tall men of the nondescript City-gent breed alighted from a well-matured Bentley, quite aware of the fact that one cannot simply "get out" of a machine like that. It is likely that no one paid any attention to them. That is if we discount a man of dull, sky-bound gaze whom they passed at the door; another who stepped out of a blue Cortina behind them; and a keen plane spotter who directed a pair of powerful 10 x 50 binoculars toward the middle-aged woman driver as she maneuvered the Bentley into an empty slot in the open car park.

The passengers of the Bentley checked in at the aristo-cratic hand-luggage-only desk, then walked up the stairs, and settled at a table in the cafeteria without bothering to line up at the self-service counter. They conversed quietly but not too quietly in German about carefully selected trivia. A few moments later, their driver joined them with three cups of coffee. She sat impassively until the man with the silver hair left to gather a generous supply of newspapers in English, French, and German. Then she turned to the other: "One more letter, you said, sir?"

"Oh, yes."

Her notepad was bound in leather. He dictated in immaculate English without any trace of an accent. It was an apology to a well-known British financier-socialite whose dinner table is a regular watering place of the select herds that represent Big Business. Regretfully the writer had to cancel a dinner engagement due to unfortunate and un-foreseeable circumstances.

"Will that be all?"

"I guess so."

The Paris flight was called. She slipped her notes into her suede-lined handbag and was not at all sure what made her feel infinitely sad. Was it the imminent loss of a generous boss? Was it that she had a month to sell the office furniture and dispose of the lease, a month's notice on full pay and another month's severance pay to help her listen to the "yes,

yes, but the chairman is looking for a little less experienced (younger) person" tune of job hunting? Or was it simply that yes, perhaps she had served a traitor, crook, spy, or something like that for six years?

The two men walked to passport control. The inspector's cursory glances froze for a split second somewhere in the direction of the line behind the two passengers. He then gave them the authoritative nod of thank you. The pair had reached the final station of the air traveler's Golgotha. They stood in a corner without seeking respite at the counters of the liquor bonanza.

Soon they were in the endless tunnels to the aircraft. They passed a man of dull, shoebound gaze. Another man behind them chose not to go through the final gate. The yellow antiglare coating of a plane spotter's lenses turned and followed them across the tarmac and right up to the top of the stairs.

The three cups of coffee in the cafeteria were left untouched. Mr. Khrmmmmmmmmmm from Zambia was still being paged by a never-despairing voice. The blue Cortina happened to follow the Bentley right to the garage where the woman driver terminated the long-standing car-hire agreement.

It all added up to the case of the most civilized expulsion in the long history of undesirability. But that was not its only significance.

The two men parted company at Le Bourget. One was met by a middle-aged secretary with a Mercedes. The other, with the distinguished silver top, caught a flight to Frankfurt, where eventually I met him for coffee and cakes in the spring of 1972.

He is a "strictly political animal"—his definition—a former member of the Bundestag, who is not noted for his aversion to leaking information to the media for ready cash or political advantage. He spoke to me for reasons known only to himself.

Having vividly described the Heathrow scene, he came to the point: "OK. The German we are talking about is a merchant. Or something like that. OK? Suppose the British government was right and he did cause a lot of damage to British companies. There was talk about a couple of hundred million pounds. OK. But what did he do? He bought and sold information. These were his wares. What information? I don't know. The British government doesn't quite know either. They claim it concerned some very valuable bids on international projects and, as a result, British firms failed to win certain contracts. A loss, a major loss, may not be a national disaster even if Britain desperately wants to earn more foreign currency. But does that justify expulsion? There was no war, and he was not a spy. Not like the Commies with whom it's the done thing. They spy on us, we spy on them; there are some expulsions followed by angry diplomatic exchanges, but nobody is really sore. This case is different. OK? This man is not and has never been a German agent. He had nothing to do with our government. If he is an industrial spy or business intelligence agent, he represents only himself. He does the same as many others of other nationalities do all over the world. So he couldn't be expelled as a spy. OK."

He paused only to order more coffee to quench his indignation.

"Now then. Is he a criminal? What's the proof? Even the allegedly damaged companies refuse to say anything against him. What's his crime? What's the law against it? Everybody is buying information. If you buy the *Financial Times* or the *Neue Zurcher Zeitung*, you're buying information. Is it a crime? OK, there're more unusual ways of obtaining information.

"Take my own case. It was on an ordinary scheduled flight

to New York in the early 1950's that I first heard about the Allies' telephone tapping being used to the advantage of certain British and American firms. The occupation forces had the right to tap phones for security reasons. Yet two businessmen on the flight discussed information they had received in this way. I overheard them. Did that make me a spy? And yet this man, who has just been expelled from a friendly country does no more than that—well, most of the time. He likes parties, influential people like him; he chats them up, and he listens. OK, the British government found him an awkward customer. So what do they do? They make a confidential approach to the German government, asking our people to persuade this man to leave quietly. Herr Brandt was furious. And some of his colleagues were ready to retaliate by 'asking' British businessmen to leave and avoid Germany. But with Britain's entry into the EEC nobody wanted to—how do you say it?—rock the ship. No scandal, please; we're all helpful friends. OK? So they settle at this poor individual's expense. No official expulsion—it will also help him to save face with his friends—but he must be persuaded not to fuss and to go quietly. My disgusting job was to see to that.

"Now whether you like it or not, it's the declaration of a new war. After the two world wars and the cold war, this is the beginning of the cool war, or secret war, when private interests merge into the national interest—and the national interests clash. But that's the Reds' philosophy; everything is nationalized so any aspect of the economy is a matter of national interest and security. Except that now, in the cool war, it's not East against West, but a free-for-all, not excluding members of the Club. I mean EEC, the European Economic Club." He made no secret of it that he rather liked his joke.

I found it hard to sympathize with many of his views, and

the fate of the "poor merchant" failed to break my heart. But all that is beside the point. About the expulsion itself it seemed impossible to obtain more authentic confirmation. Not surprisingly, officials either did not know or did not want to know anything. One source with a Home Office contact obtained a glorious and strictly confidential comment of "no comment" for me. The off-the-record remark of a Special Branch officer reached me by another indirect route: "No, the case does not sound unfamiliar." A French contact had one word for my information: "Correct." When pressed, he added: "Correct in every detail." Although on other occasions he proved himself rather helpful and talkative, now he refused to elaborate.

It is rather irrelevant whether or not this alleged expulsion amounted to a formal declaration of "the cool war." It is always difficult to decide what should be regarded as the first real though unofficial act of war. But after several years of dabbling in the business-intelligence agents' twilight world where the X's in XXth century stand for the double cross, I have no doubt left that the information world war is a reality. The emphasis in espionage has shifted from the politico-military to the economic themes. It is not East against West anymore. It is also West against West, North against South, each man, each chairman, for himself, unless their combined interests coincide with those of the nation against another nation or a supranational concern.

In the times-gone pink elegance of a Frankfurt *konditorei*, that German diplomat was quite unperturbed as he spoke about this war between endless cups of coffee which were to drown his plateful of dainty cakes, more cakes, and another no less dainty one for the road. With his prediction about the days of French diplomats being expelled from Germany, Americans from Sweden, Dutch from France, and anybody from anywhere for economic espionage, he reminded me of two other completely different occasions when even the words used were similar.

The first was in Hawaii. With Barry Goodenow, a former FBI agent, I sat in his luxury apartment overlooking the full curve of Waikiki beach, and he warned against "kidding ourselves too much with business friendship in the West. Let's face it. Industrial espionage is not only a private war. It's World War III. Governments are involved; for example, we'd quite readily feed false scientific or economic information to friend and foe alike, hoping that the other's intelligence efforts will be delayed. It's a question of making the extra buck—and today, information is the commodity with the greatest profit margin."

The other occasion arose in the course of a rather unnerving cab ride around New York City. Approaching the United Nations building along First Avenue, my companion —a formidable young lady of total unfemininity with, I suspect, a punchcard for her sex organs—pointed at the flags with the rhetorical question: "So what's wrong with information peddling? Those guys in there are in the same racket. They'd pinch your thoughts if they could. They only use those flags as a cover for all those ambassadors, U.N. partygoers and other diplomatic schlemiels. Anyway that's what Mr. Kubik thinks, and he knows. He buys from them—and they're his best customers."

2

The Kubik File

KUBIK IS A PSEUDONYM, chosen by the man himself as perhaps some in joke for his friends who would recognize his somewhat cubic build. He is no Mr. Big of economic intelligence. There is no such man. If anything, Kubik is one of the scores of major operators in this field, which just about puts him in the millionaire class.

He is reputed to have sold a single "package"—the formula of a new drug, complete with marketing strategy, advertising plans, the shortcomings of the drug, and the successful presentation form to hoodwink the Federal Drug Administration—for a million dollars. His net profit was less than half that amount, after the deduction of an exotic list of expenses that included a custom-built catamaran, a villa in Capri, a block of stock in a North Sea oil-exploration venture, a cellarful of champagne, and cash as bribes; the salary of a large specially employed staff for eighteen months; and about fifty thousand dollars spent on the purchase, installation, and maintenance of electronic-surveillance equipment.

He is an elusive American with an international network of legitimate business interests, and permanent homes in four countries. Allegedly he has "a low threshold of resistance" to applying strong-arm methods—a fairly unusual feature in business intelligence.

That sums up all I knew about him—minus his identity or even pseudonym—when in December 1969 I had a weird telephone call from the stewardess of a well-known European airline.

"You remember the friend you were once so anxious to meet?"

"Yes."

"He hears you plan to go to New York in the near future."

"It's not a secret, but it wasn't exactly advertised."

"It's a small world."

I admit I was beginning to feel rather uncomfortable. If he had heard about my planned trip, he would also know about my constant interest in his affairs.

"I believe you did him a favor."

That was news to me. (It would transpire only a couple of years later that a conversation I had with a company-merger specialist had been reported to Kubik in full, including my remarks about the latest antics of a particularly loathsome sex-for-secrets operator. Apparently Kubik had some unfinished business with that operator, and he found my unintentional assistance most useful in settling the score. According to his personal code of ethics—"an aye for an aye, and a nay for a nay, what? You'll appreciate that, I'm sure"—he was indebted to me.

"Where will you be staying in New York?"

"I don't know. Not yet."

"Try the Tudor."

"Why?"

"My friend finds it handy."

"For what?"

"He didn't say."

"Will he meet me?"

"He didn't say."

"Does he want to know when I will be there?"

"He didn't ask."

At the beginning of February 1970, I checked in at the Hotel Tudor in East Forty-second Street. For two days my behavior must have looked rather peculiar. I saw a potential contact in every passerby, waiter, and policeman. When a man in the lobby asked me what time it was, I was so eager to help check his watch against mine and to offer him assistance in finding a repairer that he retreated in panic. The receptionist began to give me very odd answers when I reported to him my whereabouts at least once in every hour and asked for messages that never came.

On my third day in New York, when I returned to the hotel in the evening, I found a typed note on the floor of the room: AWAIT CALL FROM MISTER RYAN IN THE MORNING. It was a woman who phoned the next day. She introduced herself as Miss Terry-Ann. (Later she would explain that both names were "variations of Mystery Ann—you get it?" Yet another dose of what I came to identify as the cubic brand of humor.) The following morning, February 5, I was to leave the hotel at 11:15, turn right toward First Avenue, and keep walking until she picked me up in a blue Chevrolet. I watched the traffic and tried to guess which car would be hers, but eventually her transport was an ordinary cab with only one extraordinary feature—the driver. He was the only New York cabby who, with the bulletproof window that separated him from the backseat fully shut, never once attempted to engage his passengers in lengthy abusive exchanges about the city administration.

He drove around, now fast, now slowly and aimlessly, but it was not difficult to observe that he doubled back on his route several times. Was he making sure that we were not tailed? Confirmation of this intention came after about twenty minutes. He joined the line of cars snaking toward the East Side Airline Terminal; then just before we reached the area where passengers are deposited, he pulled out of line and sped away. If any driver following us had joined the line behind, he would now have to expose himself by the "coincidence" of a similar change of mind.

Until then, Terry-Ann's chatty topics were restricted to tourism and international travel. Her good fur coat, dark well-cut "business suit," diamond-and-ruby–studded watch with matching ring and brooch only emphasized her resemblance to a disastrously unsuccessful female impersonator. She began something about the dangerous slush on the streets, but leaving the terminal, she interrupted herself: "Now listen, a mutual friend of ours asked me to tell you something."

"I thought I'd meet him."

"I know nothing about that. Anyway we're not in the same business."

"What's his business?"

"I thought you knew. I have no idea. Next question."

"Sorry. What were you going to tell me?"

"Something about my business. I'm an auctioneer. I don't care what's offered for sale, I sell anything, including my hammer, to the highest bidder. Now this friend of ours thinks you might be interested in an unusual scene. I believe you could be in Bangkok on March ninth." She paused, then added, "It's a Monday."

"Oh, yes, if it's a Monday, I could be there."

She took it as a straight remark. "Good. Now I'll tell you exactly what to look for." I was to stay in one of the leading hotels, which she named, and sit on the poolside terrace at about noon. She advised me to lunch there because the food was exceptionally good. Some papers in the possession of "our mutual friend" would be auctioned there. They should fetch a price in excess of fifty thousand dollars. "Next question."

She had as much passion for her rather exotic business as a filing clerk for the alphabet. I could not resist trying to find a chink in her monotonous monologue. "Do you think it's safe to tell me all this in advance?"

Her answer was not very flattering. "Quite safe. It's been decided that there was no risk whatsoever. I'm not telling you anything that is not known to at least a dozen top industrial security experts, not to mention some executives of the firms that will be represented by bidders. If they can't do anything about it, then you haven't got a chance to upset the arrangements. Besides, if you turned up there with the police—who couldn't care less, I can tell you that—there would be nothing to find. There will be no papers, no money changing hands, and nobody there will know what they are talking about. Everybody will have some instructions—that's all. I'll tell you more, perhaps, if we meet there.

"Shall we?"

"Perhaps."

We talked for another few minutes before she dropped me at Fifty-ninth Street and Lexington. "Do me a favor," she said, "just walk away and don't look back."

Auction in Bangkok

A month later I was half an hour early on that terrace in Bangkok to make sure that I had a grandstand view. The curving amorphous pool was right in front of me. On the left was a patch of tropical garden with beach umbrellas and deck chairs. Sandwiched between the wall of the changing rooms and the far side of the pool, next to an artificial waterfall, there was room for only two deck chairs and a small garden table. The auctioneer, Terry-Ann's front man, sat there alone with a book, a long fruit-laden drink, two packs of cigarettes, and a lighter. Somewhat unconventionally, he wore only swimming trunks, and a similar attire was expected from all his clients who were to join him one by one.

The first bidder walked up to him at four minutes past noon. Formalities were observed. Their gestures made it obvious that the newcomer asked if the chair was free (I later learned that they used an introductory code), but it was impossible to overhear anything partly because of the distance and partly because of the noise of the waterfall which must have neutralized any transmitter or recording equipment hidden on the bidder's body. Both men sat with their backs to the terrace presumably to avoid the eyes of lip-readers. One could see that they spoke about something, but that only gave the impression of two strangers meeting by chance at the luxury poolside and exchanging a few polite noises. Less than a minute later, they stopped talking. The auctioneer returned to his book. The bidder sunned himself quietly for four minutes and thirty seconds, then dived into the pool, swam around, climbed out at the far end, and sat in another chair.

After a five-minute interval, a second man strolled casually around the pool. Clutching a glass of beer, after gestures of "excuse me," etc., he sat down, but this time there was no talking. The auctioneer smiled and moved his hand toward the beer, implying "Would you like another one?" No. 2 shook his head, drank up the last of the beer in his glass, called the waiter, and asked him to take his glass away. Only then did some conversation begin. No. 2 smoked one of the auctioneer's cigarettes—any other pack might have hidden some electronic equipment.

In all, I counted five bidders. No. 3 was a girl in what must have been the tiniest bikini between St. Tropez and the South China Sea. As there were plenty of more comfortable spots in the tropical garden on the left, few people would choose accidentally to sit next to that bladder-irritating artificial waterfall, but in the intermission between No. 4 and No. 5 it apparently happened. A woman in her fifties was politely but firmly turned away by the auctioneer.

After No. 5, a waiter called the auctioneer to a poolside telephone. He then returned to his seat, and a second round of barefooted pilgrimage began. Now there were fewer formalities, and it went at some speed. They were putting in their final maximum bids. No. 2 did not even bother to return. The girl swam to the edge of the pool, attracted the auctioneer's attention, said something, and swam away. The auction was over. It had taken eighty-five minutes. I had already ordered lunch, but I was not to have it. Terry-Ann appeared. In a provocative summer frock she looked even less appetizing than I remembered.

"I want to talk to you, but I also want to show you something. Coming?"

I started toward the waiter, but she stopped me. "I've already told him not to bother with your lunch." A taxi was waiting. I tried to ask questions, but Terry-Ann would not talk about anything but cockfighting. She was extremely excited. "We're going to a private house. It's the real McCoy. You'll see, none of this tourist stuff. Steel-tipped beaks, metal claws, and all. To the death. You can bet there, too. You got cash? It's the only place in town where they won't take American Express."

There was nothing to it—just relax and wait. She would say what she wanted to in her own good time. We reached the outskirts of Bangkok, near the river Chao Phraya. A smallish bare room was bulging with people. Hardly enough space for the cocks to fight. A sickening smell everywhere. The walls were oozing blood. An apathetic little man mopped aside the remains of the losers from time to time. Spurs were carefully retrieved.

"Come on, kill 'im," Terry-Ann urged a heavyweight bird in a frightful whisper. "The papers fetched seventy-five thousand," she added in the same breath. "Plus my commission. I get 10 percent from the buyer—kill 'im!—ten from the seller. The one who put in the winning bid has had a phone call by now. He or his principals can name the town on a scheduled route of a certain European airline where they want to collect. That's my boy!" The loser looked a complete mess. But even the winner would put anyone off poultry for a long while. "Delivery by one of the crew on the flight. The papers are sealed in a carton of duty-free cigarettes. Delivery, that is, after confirmation of advance payment in full."

"Switzerland?"

"Something like that. It's not a Swiss monopoly."

Another pair of fighters was paraded. Betting was heavy. Terry-Ann was anxious to back the winner. She swore she could kiss him. I was not sure he would let her. When, at the height of the fight, she began to quiver in her utter arousal once again, I asked her about the papers themselves.

"Oh, yes, our friend sends his regards. Come on! Come on! It's a revolutionary life-insurance scheme that took years to devise. Kind of package deal full of attractions and sales gimmicks which should make you want to die. It's all in the box complete with detailed advertising plans. Could be worth a packet to someone who had no market research and other costs. But our friend is a great patriot. Whenever possible, he would sell to Americans."

Again she became too absorbed in the fight to talk.

Later, when we were having a beer and a sandwich in a hotel, she casually dropped a bomb: it was the original firm, the owner, from which the documents had been, well, borrowed that turned out to be the highest bidder. It was not an unexpected or even unusual occurrence. Neither the loss nor the recovery had ever been reported to anyone—least of all, to the police. There was no mention of it in the company records. She suspected that probably a handful of executives would fork the money out of their own pockets. The victims of industrial espionage often do. The price is less damaging than the loss or the potential revelation of the lack of security that can destroy individual careers and the confidence of stockholders. "Publicity is the last thing the loser wants," she declared. "And if there is a chance to get back what's lost, you want to invite the smallest possible number of bidders against yourself. You don't want to expose the president and vice-presidents to ridicule, and you don't want any adverse effect on your stock prices. Really serious incidents will hardly ever lead to court cases."

In a world of increasingly fierce competition and dwindling profit margins, the boom in business intelligence was once described by a Pinkerton agent: "Surreptitious information gathering has become something like sex. Everyone is getting it; everyone knows that everyone else is getting it; but if you tell anyone where you are getting it, you won't get it anymore." Terry-Ann cautioned the victims of intelligence to guard their secret as if it were sodomy.

How did she contact the potential bidders? "Individually. Sort of personal selection. People we know." She would not elaborate.

What if the documents were photocopied and sold to several firms at the same time? "Could be done. Quite easily. But only once. We have our reputation to protect." She seemed genuinely upset by the innuendo.

"It may sound odd to you, but the whole transaction is built on trust. An executive at the original company received a set of photostats, so he knew that Kubik had them." (It was the first time that she had used the pseudonymous name favored by "our friend.") "The other companies wouldn't have seen it at all, but they know which of their rivals has lost them. They accept the arrangements in this case for Bangkok, so they can rest assured they can bid via a front man safely—they may be suspected but cannot be caught red-handed. And if they buy the papers, they know damn well that there won't be other copies in circulation. We're not in business for the shortsighted and risky once-and-never-again big kill. That's for amateurs."

Amateurs, Players, Professionals

Whenever she—and many of her colleagues—used the word "amateur," it sounded like the rudest possible insult. One could easily see why. Almost the entire public record of "business secrets for sale" has been built on blunders due to the greedy dilettantism of the opportunist, the man with a grudge, the upright citizen who would err just once in dire need of quick cash, and the naïve private detective who would imagine such work to be easy.

Take the case of the English university student who did part-time odd jobs for a London detective agency. In 1971, she was entrusted with an assignment to go to Grimsby, Lincolnshire, and obtain a precious formula for manufacturing titanium oxide. The secret of the process belongs to British Titan Products Ltd., which thus has a complete European monopoly. Her target—an employee willing to sell. Her budget—£150 and perhaps "more to come." So what does she do?

A stranger to this fishing center, she takes a cab, asks first to be driven to the factory, then further on, past the main gate. Sidney Martin, the taxi driver, is curious, and she tells him that she wants confidential information about something called TC41 for a London agency. "As a taxi driver I am not really interested in what TC41 stands for," he will eventually recall in court. He promises to find her an informant—and warns the company.

The sequence of later events is no less farcical. Philip Swinburn, an executive of the firm, poses as potential traitor, and she offers him the majestic £150 right away. While many women with their ingeniously devious ways often succeed at this game, our Mata Hari of Grimsby comes directly to the point—why, she even has a list of questions for her quarry! He needs time. She understands. It all seems to be in the bag. Three quarters of an hour later they have further discussions about her proposals—on the telephone. It "so happens" that a second executive is listening in on an extension line. Yes, the reward will be £150 and more to come, although she has no cash with her. No, she does not know who her clients are or how much they are ultimately prepared to pay. Would she be "friendly" if an executive visited her in her boarding-house? No; she prefers to invent a high-ranking police officer for a husband who, she claims, would not like that.

Although with magnificent British understatement it was recognized that the secret process would have been of "distinct advantage" to any rival, the agent and her master could only be charged with conspiring to obtain confidential information by corruption, and with offering £150 as a bribe. On the first count, they were fined £100 and £1500 respectively; on the second, a nominal one pound fine was imposed on them both. They appealed the amount. It is perhaps interesting to note that in an American case, information about a titanium oxide process was valued by Du Pont at fifteen million dollars.

Amateurism is no less blunder-prone on the selling side. This is how two incidents in the soap war among detergents giants turned into a soap opera.

In 1964, a British advertising agency man, a former prospective Parliamentary candidate, got hold of some "red-hot" advertising and marketing plans belonging to Procter and Gamble. The information was said to be worth £750,000. He wrote a letter offering it all for sale to the London office of Colgate-Palmolive, his victim's closest rivals. He then telephoned a Colgate executive who informed the police and the victims. (Probably it does not apply to this case, but the security departments of major companies are often suspicious of "offers out of the blue," which may be, and sometimes are, misleading fakes designed by their rivals as traps to expose them to damaging scandals.)

The schemer, not inappropriately called John Brand, was now led on. He asked for only three thousand pounds, and the "buyer" agreed. He left a batch of documents at a post office—later collected by the police—and sent the rest, as instructed, by taxi to a Mr. Scott at the Carlton Tower Hotel. Finally he named the place where the money in one pound notes was to be left. He went to pick up the promising parcel, but instead, he was picked up by the police. He was sentenced to thirteen months in jail.

Meanwhile, back at home base in the United States, Eugene Mayfield, a junior advertising executive of Procter and Gamble, earning twelve thousand dollars a year, offered his firm's top-secret 188-page budget and sales promotion program for a new toothpaste to—well, but of course, to Colgate. Although his wares were worth only a million dollars "to any competitor," a sum then about half as much as Brand's, he hoped to collect twenty thousand dollars, about twice the amount of Brand's target, for his effort. He was pleased to hear that Colgate found this reasonable. He then devised a foolproof scheme. The sale was to take place in a lavatory at Kennedy Airport. He and the firm's representative occupied adjoining cubicles. Once the doors were locked, he instructed the buyer to take off his trousers, put the price into the pockets, and push it through the gap under the partition. The man from Colgate, no longer attired exactly *comme il faut* for a chase in public, had to wait while Mayfield exchanged the money for the papers and returned the trousers. However fast the buyer could dress, the still anonymous Mayfield needed still fewer seconds to submerge in the crowd outside. Except that Colgate had called in the police who were there waiting for him.

Like many other cases I have studied, this episode amply illustrates the inadequacies of the law. Mayfield got away with a two-year prison sentence—suspended.

Was his fee rather overambitious? A much more professional German commented: "Not really. It all depends on the circumstances. You have to calculate the value of what you sell, its value to the buyer, your risk, time input, actual expenses, general overhead, effects of inflation, and local level and increase of living costs. Otherwise they won't treat you as an equal in business."

If one realizes that the American drug industry alone gambles with $300 million on research each year; that the American Cyanamid Company spent $24 million on the development of tetracycline antibiotics only to be robbed of vital formulae, sample cultures, and a sales potential of $250 million by a now well-known international ring; and that, as Richard M. Greene, Jr., quotes in his book *Business Intelligence and Espionage*, astronomical figures are estimated to be the annual loss of the American drug industry through stolen trade secrets; it becomes easy to understand what difference it can make that a secrets-for-sale proposal comes from a professional—or from an amateur.

A classic case to illustrate this point has emerged through a combination of various sources. To appreciate it fully, three factors must be remembered: (1) that desperate competition in pharmaceuticals nourishes a subculture of secret deals; (2) that the majority of companies believe that if one avoids and exposes espionage, others will do the same; and (3) that honest employees still outnumber dishonest ones, and therefore professionals never offer their services at random—they know which executives of which companies may be willing to buy.

In 1962, a London chemist of Parke-Davis, the large pharmaceutical firm, had a strange telephone call from the representative of "an agency supplying technical information." Although the caller claimed that what he had would certainly be useful to Parke-Davis, his technical knowledge proved to be somewhat sketchy when answering more specific questions. The chemist was suspicious that it might be a hoax, but then the caller began to display intimate knowledge of a competitor and its products, and mentioned the magic word *Aldomet*. This then new antihypertensive, which contains methyldopa, was a breakthrough in the treatment of high blood pressure. The chemist reported everything to his superiors, who in turn promptly informed Morson's, the rivals concerned, a British subsidiary of Merck, Sharp & Dohme. Allegedly a Merck executive took an immediate dose of Aldomet and remarked: "It's a good thing we spent three million dollars on the development of this stuff. Right now I can do with a lot of reduction of blood pressure."

Three Merck executives flew to London within a few hours. Judging from the manner of that initial phone call and the reference to an "agency," it seemed likely that they would have to deal with a professional espionage ring. Not wishing to take chances, they were authorized, it is claimed, to spend up to twenty-five thousand dollars on buying their own secrets back. ("They would have cabled the office for more, a lot more, if necessary, I can tell you that," was Terry-Ann's comment when we talked about the case in Bangkok.) Parke-Davis were most helpful. When the man called them once again, they arranged a meeting in the Russell Hotel, near the British Museum, and their representative took five hundred pounds in cash with him to hand over as a first instalment. And that is when the man made a grave error: he named the sum of fifty pounds as his price for the invaluable, undoubtedly authentic, confidential flow sheets of Aldomet. A substantial part of his game was up. There was no more danger that if this agent were arrested, a major international outfit would sell photostat copies to some ambitious and unscrupulous researchers employed by other companies. After some brief haggling, his price was even beaten down to thirty pounds. Instead of the money, he was soon to receive a six-months prison sentence for his amateurish endeavor. He was a disgruntled former process worker at Morson's; his regular absenteeism had earned him the sack.

Amateurs do occasionally cash in on some godsent opportunity if they are lucky enough to lay their hands on something important and to stumble onto the right market. Their safest shortcut to the jackpot is, however, to become players and work as ad hoc informers or regular retainers for organizations that operate under some legitimate cover.

In 1964, at a Washington security conference, a speaker claimed that industrial espionage had already risen to a sophisticated level, and that buying information from established rings was the quickest way to obtain trade secrets. Since then, the most enterprising dealers have established themselves so well and with such a vast volume of turnover that they can ignore the comparatively meager rewards of a commissioned job.

Vincent Carratu, head of a Manchester-based investigation and security organization, with a great deal of international and Scotland Yard Fraud Squad experience behind him, told me: "Sure, some private detectives and others make quite good money on assignment work. But the real pickings are left to the specialists. They have a network of contacts in all the big public companies, research centers, and most competitive industries, and they can afford to pay small weekly retaining fees to currently useless people for years—knowing that eventually they may come up with something useful. Then they go to town on it. They know their market, so they can literally sell to the highest bidder—and it is surprising how high this can get." He found that most of these "information centers" were based on the European continent.

My own research has led to the conclusion that indeed, major "clearing houses for information" flourish in Stockholm, Amsterdam, and Düsseldorf. A French auctioneering venture is directed, for some obscure reason, from a private address in Annecy. (Is it due to the nearness of the Swiss border, a refuge to some known industrial spies?). Yet the bulk of the richest pickings are handled in New York and Hong Kong by two, possibly three, companies that maintain considerable liaison, if not cooperation. These firms select their targets, finance "research," and work on spec. Amateurs and single-handed operators, as well as smaller agencies, also sell their wares to them because nobody else can achieve the prices they get. I was told about several items of information that had changed hands more than five times before being offered to the first potential buyer who could actually make use of it.

Despite all that I had discovered about their talent for organization, the meticulous planning and the resultant simplicity and smoothness of the Bangkok auction were absolutely stunning. Terry-Ann was delighted to hear that. In an obviously good mood she started to say something, but I was never to hear the end of it. She looked at her watch and stood up to go. "What's today? Monday? Oh yes, then it's the—how do you pronounce it?—Rajadamnern Stadium—Thai boxing, of course. You want to know something? They kick. They can kick you in the throat as easily as in the crotch. Isn't it marvelous?" The vision made her very impatient, but she remembered a message from Kubik. "He thinks he's paid his debt. Quits. Right?"

"I still want to meet him."

"I'll tell him."

She did not bother even to wave good-bye. Eight months later I heard she was dead—killed in a road accident, hit-and-run driver. With the cases I had already seen, it was beginning to look like an occupational hazard of this trade.

Death in San Francisco

Ray Mory was another car-accident victim—so they say. A few people suspect it was suicide. His widow knows it was suicide, but she claims it was, in fact, murder—by Kubik.

When I first met Mory in Singapore's Beach Road, we perched on well-worn little stools in the street, thoroughly fumigated by the Malay stall keeper who was preparing satay for us. It was mid-April 1965, and I was doing research for my book on modern forms of the sex slave trade. Mory, an American of Hungarian extraction, was involved in a racket of smuggling gold in rough canvas "James Bond" jackets (worn under the shirt) to India, where prices were high and the demand insatiable. What exactly his role was I never knew, but he seemed to have a great deal of money. While I was in Singapore, the police caught two carriers with the pockets of their James Bonds laden with gold bars. But Mory was left in peace, and he was not upset; I heard that he might be a police informer. Whatever else he was, he proved himself a most useful contact—for the humble reward of a glass of beer over which we swapped a few stories about Puskas and other old time favorites of Hungarian football.

We met again by chance six months later, in the Sahali, described as a "cafe" by blatant glorification, in Tangier's Escalada Sidi Hosni. He was utterly and totally broke, and a friend he was with gave him 150 dirhams—about ten pounds at that time. He introduced his friend as an FBI agent who might be useful to me in my research. They then spoke in no complimentary terms about a man of unforgettable name, Tom Asquare, who appeared to be responsible for Mory's recent misfortunes.

Almost a year later, I was talking to an English "security adviser," an uncouth small-time crook who showed genuine compassion for the wretched businessmen who resorted to his advice. I was told he had his ears to the ground, and I found that it showed. How he could hear anything through those layers of filth was a mystery. Toward the end of our brief conversation he mentioned "the lucky bastards who make the real money." He named Tom Blockley for one. "Boy, he's got it made for him. Never heard of him? Blockley, alias Kubik, alias half a dozen other names. Must have a legit one, but that I don't know."

Kubik was a name I began to hear more and more frequently.

In November 1967, I called on Mory's FBI friend in New York. He told me that Mory was back in California because he had stumbled onto some very profitable import business:

"You ought to see him now. Big car, big house, big everything; even the Swiss girl he imported and married is big. And, it's all aboveboard, I tell you that."

We met again in 1968. He said that Mory had "had some ups and downs" but had come out on top and traveled frequently to the Far East. "He met up with Asquare once again, except that the guy now calls himself Blockley. Tom Blockley. A smuggler, I think."

This FBI agent telephoned me in London at the end of the summer of 1971. Mory was dead. Car accident. Probably suicide. His widow had moved back to Switzerland, was living under her maiden name, practically in hiding. Some newspapers were after her. I told him I was just then going to Geneva. Could I look her up? "No, but she might phone you if you give me the address where you'll be staying."

Mrs. Mory called me in Geneva, and we arranged to have dinner at the Aux Armeurs. She was big all right. Her car had a Lausanne registration number. She said she hired it. I did not believe that: she appeared to be altogether Americanized in her table manners and bejewelled spectacles, but remained Swiss to the core.

"What was Ray's business?"

"Imports."

"What line?"

"All sorts."

"From where?"

"Far East."

"Hong Kong?"

"Hong Kong, too."

For a while he was doing exceptionally well. He then began to choose various goods that he thought he could sell in San Francisco, and had them manufactured in Taiwan, Hong Kong, or sometimes Japan. Then one day he ran into Tom Asquare in Hong Kong.

"Probably Asquare sought him out," she claimed. "Ray never liked him."

"Asquare? Is that what you said?"

"Yes. You know, what's-his-name—Blockley. He killed Ray."

"How?"

"He hounded him. Once they met he never got off Ray's back. Ray even stopped going to the Far East himself."

"How could he import goods without seeing them first? Did they send him samples?"

"No. He had the prototypes made in the States, sent them to, say, Taiwan, and they delivered the product."

"What sort of goods?"

"All sorts. Household gadgets, then toys, some clothes, and later watches."

"Who made the prototypes?"

"I don't know."

Then, apparently, Asquare-Blockley caught up with him once again. That marked the beginning of endless difficulties: deliveries were delayed; small Chinese factories that worked for Mory refused to take his orders; and "once the police department got on to him because they suspected that Ray's prototypes had been stolen from other American firms, but that was, of course, sheer nonsense." Mory then invested all his money in a smallish factory in Hong Kong because through his contacts he knew he would win a very large contract on which he had bid. He failed to get the job partly because a hitherto unknown competitor put in a vastly better and totally uneconomical bid—and partly because his factory burned down. He was convinced it was all Asquare's doing. The insurance did not cover all his debts. He tried to revive the business, but none of his former associates wanted to know him. His wife was not used to the poverty that hit them. He was ashamed.

"He once told me," she said in a flat tone, "that his only remaining ambition was to look after me well. He wished he was dead so that I could collect the insurance. I didn't take him seriously enough. The day after that, he ran into a brick wall at high speed. He was not drunk—that, we know. He had never been a careless driver, and I never saw him speed. The police said, and I thought, that it looked like suicide. It seemed the life-insurance company would not pay up.

"Then one day a thickset man came to see me. He said he was a friend of Ray and wanted to help. I should not worry about the insurance. Strings would be pulled."

Soon the insurance company did pay up. She was never to say publicly that it might have been suicide or that he had reason to kill himself. Apparently the stranger's string-pulling coincided with some moral support and character reference from J. Edgar Hoover, then head of the FBI.

"Only after I had already moved to Switzerland did I hear that the stranger who visited me in San Francisco was probably Asquare," she added.

"Asquare . . . Blockley . . . did Ray ever mention the name Kubik?" I ventured to ask.

"Once or twice. The same man, I believe."

Mrs. Mory could not complain about the variety of Kubik's names. Mory himself had lived under an assumed one. "Sounds more American, good for business," he used to explain.

Why did Kubik hate Mory so much? And if he did, why would he help the widow? Sentimental, he certainly was not. Pity? Not in character. Sexual attraction? Hard to imagine that he would fall for this rather plain homely woman in her fifties. His own peculiar code of honor was the only possible explanation. I was becoming more and more eager to hear about it from himself one day.

As for Ray Mory's career, the enigma is not insoluble. He was probably an FBI informer while his profession was first smuggling and later copying of products—a cozy line of business based on the theft of trade secrets.

3

Copycats

KAM LUANG CANNOT BE DESCRIBED as a particularly talkative man. When we were introduced in a private room at the Golden Crown, an excellent restaurant in Nathan Road, Kowloon, he was playing Mah-Jongg. He noted my presence with a cursory half smile and bow. During dinner, between Sauté Black and White Mushroom and Shark's Fin with Crab Meat—the second and third courses—I asked him if he knew Ray Mory. After the sixth course—Double Boiled Pig's Tongue and Whelk—was served, he slowly turned to me and said "Perhaps." Not wanting to appear too keen, I waited with my next question until the seventh course, Stewed Garupa (probably grouper) Fish in Brown Sauce, arrived. Did he know Kubik? Instead of answering, he topped up my glass of brandy (a vessel quite ordinary in size if holding water) several times. I kept talking to others, peppering my sentences with remarks that, I hoped, would impress Kam Luang. Apart from two introductory telephone calls from contacts well ahead of my arrival, a few names to look out for, more names to drop casually, and a current price list for some "phoneys" (imitations of well-known brands) were my passport to certain circles in Hong Kong. Still no answer from

Kam Luang. Where had I gone wrong? Why did he suspect that my "passport" was a forgery?

We had already munched Almond Cream with Dumplings, and those who had been less greedy than I, were now gulping down some Fancy Cakes, the thirteenth and last course on our specially prepared menu. The conversation around the table was slowly dying—we sipped our tea in the exhausted silence of the well-fed. At long last, Kam Luang spoke to me for the second time: "No. I don't know him."

My heart sank.

"But then," he added quite poker-faced, "I don't know others like Asquare or Blockley either."

The party was breaking up. He asked me where I was staying. I had already been warned that some of the people I might meet would feel more at home on the Kowloon side. So when I named the August Moon Hotel, there was an imperceptible nod of approval.

Next morning he called at the hotel, and we went for a long walk. Most of his conversation consisted of brief, crisp questions. What sort of garments were my line of business? What did I think of Japanese workmanship? Did I prefer Japanese watches to Swiss makes? Did I think that restrictions on the gold trade were having a beneficial effect? He was still probing. Lingering suspicion was, in fact, his natural aura which was to accompany us every time we had one of these peripatetic conferences. He began to accept that the purpose of my visit was to get quotes for various counterfeit goods, but even sought assurance that my alleged "cover"— journalism—would stand up to a police investigation if something went wrong with my deals. Yet I had to be patient with all that subtle, persistent grilling; he was protecting himself as well as my ostensible mission.

Kam "Mr. Fixit" Luang, as some people call him, is a kingpin in the shaky, suspicious, unreliable, but tremendously powerful machinery of the copycats—the international net-work of a multimillion business that reproduces and markets any goods of household brand names fast, in unlimited quantity and astonishingly good quality at prices slashed to a fraction of the original.

The secret of their success? Relatively cheap labor, vast resources of know-how and skilled work force, plenty of spare production capacity, access to surreptitious and above-board shipping at competitive rates, and above all, strong links with sources that can supply key items of confidential information. This latter ingredient elevates the copycats of Hong Kong, Taiwan, Japan, and South Korea to heights of pecuniary advantages hardly ever enjoyed by the rabble of ordinary imitators, counterfeit artists, design pirates, and perpetrators of patent infringements. For this is what ensures that they choose the most profitable wares for copying, that they can market them with surprising safety, and that their timing is excellent: they can frequently flood the shops with their copies while their unsuspecting victim still struggles with the teething troubles of the early production runs.

As the boom seems to last and last, and working opportuni-ties multiply, inevitable wage increases and new attractive side benefits of employment begin to affect the traditional cheapness of labor—a phenomenon also suffered by Japan. The copycats, however, remain unperturbed. "It is true that more than half of the population is under twenty-one, better educated and more demanding than the older generations," a Hong Kong government official explained, "but then most of our businessmen work with minimal overheads. They do not employ armies of Rolls-Royce–conscious bureaucrats, people who only extend their lunchtime with every salary increase. Then they have practically no original research, develop-ment, or even designing done here. Most of it is done by their overseas competitors for them." And, one could add, many of these traders also enjoy the full benefit of costly marketing and advertising campaigns—paid for by their victims.

The result? I was offered Japanese counterfeit Parker pens for twenty-five cents and secondary Hong Kong copies of these for nineteen cents each. Digital and other expensive models of "Seiko" watches (copies of the Japanese original which is backed by heavy advertising) were available for a give-away wholesale price ranging from twenty-two to twenty-seven American dollars to include delivery to—which meant smuggling into—any country. (A Seiko executive visiting Hong Kong once exclaimed: "But this imitation business is utterly immoral!" Coming from a Japanese businessman, whose compatriots though not colleagues still excel at the art of product copying, this remark demonstrates the power of the Chinese copycats.)

The list of frequently pirated goods is practically endless. Many American and British cosmetic and medical products; French textiles and clothes; Japanese, American, German, and British toys; French and British cigarette lighters; car accessories, cameras, and electrical goods of numerous origins; Swiss watches; drinks including scores of famous brands of whisky, brandy, and liqueurs; stamps of many nations often with the special "first day" of issue postmark—these are but a few of the most popular and lucrative merchandise for copycats.

Much of this Eastern trade was initiated and remained dominated by an odd bunch of international crooks. A few Germans were the first arrivals of a Western influx to enrich local talent with impressive technical skills and ideas. In the early 1950's, these came direct from Germany where they feared prosecution or limited promotion prospects because of their Nazi past. They carried mixed sets of true and false documents showing ostensible or de facto appointments as representatives of German and South American firms. In

Singapore and Hong Kong, with local financial backing, they started lucrative design piracy of popular products. The finish, name, and wrapping resembled the original very closely. They were soon joined by veterans of the French Foreign Legion, and then the venture branched out to counterfeit weapons, arms, and gold smuggling.

In the 1960's, a new important element appeared on the scene: nonpolitical American deserters from the Vietnam War. Their Mafia contacts in the drug trade and ideas like the production of counterfeit bonds guaranteed their welcome, but their biggest success came with the introduction of "advance pirating"—theft of prototypes or of information to produce exact copies under the true trade names, which were stockpiled or even distributed ready to appear on the market simultaneously with the much advertised original. These imitations were so faultless in appearance, and sometimes even in quality, that they became known in the trade as "genuine phoneys."

One of the Americans, reputedly an ex-colonel in the Army, has the cover job of chief executive in a Singapore-based shipping company, where he is, in fact, a partner. He lives in true millionaire style with a private jet—the basic status symbol—at his command. No commercial espionage service is said to be in the top international league until it begins to get assignments from him.

I had the pleasure of meeting only his bodyguard, a most remarkable character with a Portuguese mother and Chinese father from Macao. He is small, slim, with the wrinkled sour face of a lemon, totally insignificant and most unbodyguard-like, but he is known to be a garrote artist and "quite passable" as a killer with several other weapons. He claims to have left Macao when it "became impossible even to strangle someone without prior approval from Chairman Mao." He wears the tool of his trade, a one-fourth inch nylon rope with a spring-wire base, around his neck. A heavy bronze cross, a mighty weapon at the end of the rope, keeps dangling on his ever-shifting chest. His unnerving habit is to finger this rope like worry beads.

He and his boss are heavily involved, I believe, with the current immense razor-blade copying operation, conducted from two centers, based on detailed inside information from the victim company. Allegedly the information included the original sources of steel, wrapping paper, and printing ink, so that the copycats' supplies could be obtained if not from the same manufacturers at least to those specifications.

For the European center, the entire machinery of a now defunct blade manufacturer was purchased at scrap-metal prices. Once it was set up in Belgium with distribution centers in Italy, the European, Middle East, and African markets were soon flooded. Due partly to severe cost cutting, the copies were slightly imperfect, but still genuine "phoneys" because the general public would never notice the two differences the experts spotted. One was that the name and trademark were just printed on the copies while the print on the original blades, using an acid base, was finely etched into the surface. The other flaw was in the inner wax-paper wrapping: the real products of this world-famous brand were held in dead-center position by four vaseline dots, but the imitators never bothered to buy the modern gadget to put those dots on each blade at the end of the production line.

"Who would ever examine the wax paper or the blade surface with a fingernail before having a shave?" my informant, a marketing specialist of the company, said in despair. "The only clue to tell the customer that something must be wrong with his favorite blade is that the fake will already sort of fray, lose its sharpness, and draw blood by scratching when he could still reasonably expect better performance from his favorite brand. Most users won't notice even that. And if they do, they'll only blame us, the legitimate manufacturers, for letting our standards drop. Then they may even desert us!"

This final point explains why he, like the copycats, was not too keen to publicize the existence of fakes in connection with the name of his company. He was afraid that suspicion would spread and undermine the regular users' faith in the product.

Toward the end of 1972, investigators tipped off the Belgian police who raided the factory and arrested several men on the premises. A cleanup operation is progressing slowly in Italy and Africa, but the copycats' Far East center is still flourishing. That factory concentrates on edging its way into the victim company's huge American outlet, estimated at one in every ten razor blades sold there. The procedure of setting up this business was very similar to that in Belgium, but it had to overcome an additional problem: How to get millions of blades through American customs without exposing their illegitimate source?

For that purpose, a small Chinese export business was purchased. This firm had a few minute but genuine and regular American orders for a cheap, hardly known make of blades. These properly licensed export orders were now inflated. Under a layer of the shoddy blades, the cartons were packed with the famous "phoneys," and deliveries began—but never fast enough. Consignments were sold in advance to shops and stores that did not ask too many questions when "stock-reducing cut-price" blades were offered to them.

I asked Kam Luang about the blade business. No, he knew nothing. "Could you tell me something about it?" I did.

"Yes"—he nodded—"it makes sense. The originals are sold for fifty-six U.S. dollars per thousand in the States, while the phoneys go for eleven fifty a thousand." Which is a pretty quick and accurate assessment from a man who had just heard about this business for the first time.

Some people indicated to me that Kam Luang and an American were partners in these deals. I do not believe that. Kam Luang is a fixer, with an unpredictable price for everything. He reminded me of the delightful old kosher restaurateur I used to know in Budapest, who would charge fifteen forints for a dinner for four with wine, but perhaps ten times that amount for a plate of soup or two hundred forints for a bottle of soda water, according to his mood and whim of the moment.

The sort of operation Kam Luang would be likely to undertake was well illustrated when I bluffed that I could see a ready-made market for a new camera. It was, I claimed, still on the drawing boards of an internationally known German manufacturer. There was no reaction on Kam Luang's smooth parchment face, but less than twenty-four hours later he told me that my information was not quite up to date: "That camera is, in fact, approaching the production stage. So if you're interested, you'd better hurry up."

He then told me what he could do for me: introduction to a German business consultant who had a man on his regular payroll inside the target firm to obtain first all the specifications of the camera and later the name, the pricing, the marketing and packaging details; arrange a meeting with a man who could set up production, farming out the various parts to small factories, so that only the final assembly line would be in immediate danger should there be a successful investigation; bring me together with a marketing specialist who had access to numerous outlets but would start with Hong Kong, Singapore, and Fiji, and with a second production man to look after, eventually, the copying of boxes, leaflets, and other printed material, including the usual guarantee documents; and finally, if necessary, he would personally introduce me to a financier who was ready to match my investment pound for pound at a not too excessive rate of interest. Kam Luang would not want to be part of the deal. He would charge a flat fee of forty thousand Hong Kong dollars, worth then almost three thousand pounds.

He appreciated that I would first have to consult the syndicate I pretended to represent, and he never brought up the subject again.

This was in 1970, when Ray Mory was still alive, and I was anxious to learn more about him: "I hear he is doing well with the gadgets."

"Really?"

"And that he is interested in some garments."

There was a pause. Without looking at me, he mumbled: "You're asking too many questions."

"That wasn't a question."

"No." Another long pause. Then, "I don't remember things I hear about other people. Do you?"

It was impossible to touch a friendly chord with Kam Luang. His impassive mask of a face would not reveal even his age—to me he looked anywhere between thirty-five and sixty-five.

We had a beer in the now stale and fusty Luk Kwok Hotel, the original of the once so uproarious Suzie Wong bordello, then walked along the sleazy waterfront streets where the pimps seemed to outnumber the bar girls and their clients altogether, but not a single slit skirt approached us. Even when we went into a particularly foul pickup joint where Kam Luang exchanged a few fast Chinese words with the barman, not one hostess demanded from us a cherry brandy —the thimbleful of watered Coca-Cola, priced as if every bubble in it were a diamond. So was it true that my companion had an interest in Suzie-Wong running, too? It was to remain one of several unanswered questions about him.

This was the only time we met on the Hong Kong side where a good crisp smell of money penetrates even the liquid-dense smoke embracing the Eastern flesh trade. Never-sleeping Kowloon with its whiffs of opium was Kam Luang's natural habitat. He had his legitimate business there, a messy, miniature general store that accounted for his apparently frugal existence. He had a *tsai*, legal No. 1 wife, in Kam Tin, the old slum of a walled Chinese village away out in the New Territory, and, allegedly, one mistress in Macao and another in Aberdeen, the fishing center. Apart from these carefully segregated, humble luxuries, he seemed to extract no other joy from the fortune he was raking in relentlessly.

At the end of this our second walk, I asked Kam Luang for some quotes on the cost of copying a new collection of clothes for women.

He acknowledged the request with the casual nod I already knew, but then he seemed to change his mind: "Are you sure you want that?"

"Yes. Why?"

"You'd do better by sticking to cameras and things like that. It's safer."

It was the second warning I had received against the capricious fortunes of the fashion business. The first came from Herr Holz, the most humorless Bavarian I ever met. He was as solemn as a prophet of doom when he cautioned me: "Never get into ladies' underwear. It stinks."

Panty-hose War and Passion Fashion

When one thinks about industrial espionage and commercial intelligence, it is easy to make the mistake of restricting the subject to obvious and important targets like the motor industry, new drugs and chemicals, cosmetics, aviation, advertising, and inventions like instant meat, reinforced glass or video cassettes for the future choose-your-TV-program, which recur frequently, I know, in many professional spies' assignment books. If they keep such records, that is.

In the not too distant past, "fashion" meant Parisian haute couture if it meant anything to the spy for hire. And he was not just any odd snooper. He had to be not only a specialist of the whirling Paris scene and biennial adulation of the New Line, but also a specially specialized specialist of a house like Dior, Balmain, Chanel or, more lately, the YSL cult. YSL means, of course, Yves Saint Laurent. An intelligence giant of the couture microcosm severely castigated me for not recognizing the YSL symbol, although he, in turn, at the height of Lyndon B. Johnson and Lady Bird's headline-snatching Presidency, asked me what the letters LBJ stood for. But then to him headlines mattered less than hemlines, because those vital inches have earned him a vineyard with a fair-sized château.

The tremendous though artificially inflated value of this triviality—Now will the hemline really be imperceptibly below or delicately dead on or just that wee bit above the knee this year?—is still a closely guarded secret of The Collections. The security gently recedes from the three-red-line top-secret pre-preview electronic perimeters and arduous screening against cameras, sketch pads and, at least on one occasion, mind readers, to the level of comparative penetrability of the defenses surrounding the show for the Chosen Few. Even then, of course, you have to obtain a unique passport from the mighty Chambre Syndicale de la Couture Parisienne to prove at the gates of the inner sanctum that either you represent the synod of money or you are a properly anointed high priestess of fashion journalism who will truly observe the ritual fast before the Release Date—the long awaited moment for publication.

Full-time agents are well aware of these hazards and ignore the old techniques of using hidden miniature cameras, like the one built into the shoes of a "wealthy lady" who was caught clicking away with her heels, or of posing as the potential big spender who worms her way into the showroom and relies on her photographic memory in technicolor. The professionals find it simpler to buy, cajole, or blackmail information out of people. For this they must have good contacts, usually retainers, inside the selected fashion house, but the system ensures the retention of regular outlets. For example, the already mentioned château-based agent, hiding behind the vague description of "fashion consultant," has thus managed for several years to sell his news not only to copycats and manufacturers seeking "inspiration" for their new lines, but also to a fashion writer who uses the information most discreetly to maintain her own and her publishers' influence by amazingly perceptive trend assessments and uncannily accurate predictions.

Some great idols' latest revolutionary designs may now only reflect, occasionally, the lines already pioneered by the in boutiques of London, New York, Munich, or Ibiza, but that worries nobody—least of all, the spy. To much of the world it is still Paris that gives the stamp of approval to anything new, and this is what his client wants to know in advance.

Jacques Besson of the French Sûreté once estimated that espionage robbed French haute couture of up to fourteen million dollars annually. Several people I talked to put much higher figures on these losses. But they added an interesting aspect: not all the stolen information goes to copycats.

"Let's put it this way—if you manufacture cameras, you know at least in principle the way your competitor simply must be thinking. He has to try to produce better, cheaper, and smaller cameras for the mass market, refinements and even higher quality for the professionals, et cetera, et cetera. They have to buy information only if they desperately want, say, an invention their rival has.

"In fashion, it's different. There's no logical trend, no inevitable development. A boy wonder, the acclaimed genius of the moment, can afford to come out with a truly way-out collection—which is frequently no more than the individual re-creation of, say, a style of the 1940's. But the rest of them must stick to the pack. None of them can afford to be left out in the cold and branded as too conservative. Information helps them to make the right decision."

The obstacles and defenses ensure not only the security of haute couture, but also the specialist spies' protection from newcomers. These, however, can turn their attention to other parts of the fashion business which, I am told, offer much greater profits and less opposition. When, for instance, I visited London designer Ossie Clark, current darling of the young everywhere, I found that it would be child's play to enter his studio and workroom, and to copy everything in sight. Strangers, scarcely known models, friends and admirers, wandered freely about the place. His home, where his wife Celia Birtwell produced her original textile designs, was no less accessible. The "money" was there, waiting to be picked up by the enterprising agent.

For the copycat and his spies, the ladies' underwear market is, however, perhaps the easiest and most profitable prey. One of the most lucrative yet ingeniously simple operations was the product of the American panty-hose war.

In 1965, the appearance of panty hose was regarded as the greatest fashion revolution since the garter.

In America alone, the current turnover of this business is approaching the $1.5 billion mark. There are more than a thousand brands, many of which are local or imported products of obscure little firms. Competition is brisk with prices ranging from fifty cents to about five dollars.

It was only in 1971 that the Hosiery Manufacturers' Association made a first attempt to introduce size standardization by taking the measurements of ten thousand women to calculate the most common weight-height combinations. By that time, a national pandemonium had begun. Women complained bitterly about false claims that certain products were "stretchable to any extent" and would provide more leg room than you get in an airplane, that "top quality" meant run-prone weave even in hose "guaranteed" "to last and last." Color descriptions were vague, and new panty hose began to sag after the first sit-down.

At the instigation of Congresswoman Leonor K. Sullivan and Senator Philip A. Hart, there was an investigation by the Federal Trade Commission. It discovered that many women thought there was no difference in quality whatever the price, so they bought the cheapest kind in the store. Some of the "fit-all" panty hose were found to be Japanese miniatures suitable only for American shoppers' daughters, while others, from Germany, gave college girls the idea to start a share-a-panty-hose movement.

At some stage of the panty-hose war—in 1968, I believe— one of the larger American manufacturers commissioned Jasper "Jazzy" Ford, a private detective, to investigate the affairs of a competitor who was thought to have committed a minor patent infringement. The detective drew a blank, but not in every respect. He discovered that much of the competitor's product was manufactured in Hong Kong. It was of no interest to his client, but it gave him a brash idea.

He traveled to Hong Kong, got some visiting cards and order forms printed on the spot—it is cheaper there—and then presented himself to the owner of the small factory with a likely story. He said "his firm," the client of the factory, wanted to branch out into the cheaper market. The "new range" should look identical to the old one, packed in an identical way, but its quality must be sacrificed to competitiveness. He beat the price down almost by half—after all, the factory would produce two ranges and at least twice the original quantity.

Now came the trick with the order forms: the two ranges would be handled from different centers, Ford claimed; therefore, deliveries and bills must be addressed separately to the "appropriate branch."

A month later the first deliveries arrived, and he began to undercut the original product but still with an increased profit margin. The operation ran smoothly for about eighteen months. Then complaints were already flooding the baffled victim company. An executive flew to Hong Kong, and the cause of all their anguish was discovered in five minutes.

Should they turn to the police and begin long court proceedings that were likely to lead nowhere except to closure of the factory and loss of public confidence? They got in touch with the "branch office" and met Jazzy Ford who calmly offered to "sell out" his business to his victims. The final twist was not only that the deal was made there and then, but also that the company decided to discontinue the old range and concentrate on the cheaper product alone—announcing "radically slashed prices."

I never found out how much they paid to Ford, but it certainly helped him to go into semiretirement in 1970 under a most respectable assumed name. The "semi" in his retirement is a noteworthy story in itself. Four years earlier, he had stumbled on to a sinecure—an easy, enjoyable, superbly paid part-time job that enabled him to live well without touching his capital.

Before his Hong Kong venture had begun, he used to pride

himself on the slogan that he was "the agent who never advertised" his services. There were times when he could not afford to. In more fortunate periods one client would introduce him to others.

About 1966, he met an executive of a medium-size mail-order firm that was anxious to build up its "passion-fashion" line. Could Mr. Ford help them with er—mmm—well—some information?

Naturally. Ford was most understanding. It would be just borrowed experience from an older colleague. He knew he was on to a good thing, because the success of this "undercover" trade was not to be sneezed at.

A man named Frederick Mellinger is probably the uncrowned king of this bizarre business. On his way to his first million, he originated many female confidence boosters like the inflatable bra which, according to his catalogues, gives you the unbeatable opportunity to "blow yourself up to your favourite size." Then he sells the instant curves for any part of the body, strategically holed panties and bras, calf falsies, and the bottomless foundation garments with "the living end." Mail order and some three dozen shops bring him a turnover which must be over ten million dollars a year by now.

Most lingerie mail-order houses, however, restrict themselves to the more conservative items of passion fashion—the padded bras, Baby Doll and see-through nighties that are bound to make any woman "an attractive alternative to his TV favorites" and save her marriage by bringing "the stag night right into the family home."

Ford's assignment for the mail-order house was to obtain information about the new designs of a more experienced competitor. This he did to the utmost satisfaction of the client. He even managed to bluff his way into the head office of the "opposition": he pretended to carry out a "routine check-up" on the air conditioner facing the designers' drawing boards—a truck, a pair of overalls, and a tool bag swung about with professional nonchalance, had already opened many well-guarded doors to him. It so happened that at the end of his visit, he left a small remote-control closed-circuit TV camera hidden above a centrally positioned neon-light ceiling panel. His closeups of the latest designs were much appreciated.

A year later, the designers were moved to a bigger office, so the transmission had to stop. But by that time, Ford had bribed two employees who kept up the flow of information. He even knew that his target company planned to start a business in Europe, too, and that in Munich, they had assigned the humorless but efficient Bavarian, whom I have called Herr Holz, to do some "market research" and see what competition their new branch would encounter.

Ford immediately flew to Munich and offered a modest retainer to Holz who agreed to keep him informed about every move the firm made in Europe. Holz always refused to regard the deal as a double cross, and likened the situation to a marital triangle in which everybody was happy. He even claimed he would never cause any real harm to a decent client like the American firm.

"Ja, very decent firm. Always paid the bills, even when business was bad, very bad," Holz said when he warned me against the underwear trade. "That was a great pity that they never set up in Europe in the end." But he was to profit for a long time from this association and the original assignment he had won through his unshakable conviction that all clients dote on electronic gadgets.

Holz and his inevitable assistant—a different one almost every week but always pretty and always blonde—are soberly dressed and look painfully ordinary. But when they begin the "spiel" for the client, one has the impression of staring at the de luxe Christmas display of a toy shop. The girl is usually wired up from top to toe with microphones protruding from her bra, miniature camera and wire recorder taped to her waist. Holz carries yet another assortment of electronic gadgets, including a bleeper to be fitted to cars he wants to tail. Like a well-trained magician's assistant, the girl will show the client any piece of equipment anywhere—behind a newspaper screen for modesty.

"Useless rubbish, of course," he told me, "but it impresses the client. Ja, the idea came from an American magazine."

"Do you ever use your gadgets?"

"No. Only to convince the client that I am the right man for the job. Which I am. Whatever the job."

He did impress the American mail-order firm all right. At the time he was doing "market research" for them, they were worried about leaks from their company. Some designs and promotion plans seemed to find their way to competitors. They mentioned the problem to Holz who suggested that similarities might be a coincidence: "You must not see sinister forces behind everything." He knew, he told me, that "such cool objectivity impresses the client."

He was right. The firm asked him if he could carry out an investigation in the United States. After all, he always advertised his dingy little office shared with a telephone-message service as "the modern headquarters of an extensive international network with agents all over the world."

After due consideration, he accepted the job. He knew he could rely on the services of the only American detective he had ever met—Jazzy Ford. And surprise, surprise, within twenty-four hours he could report to the client that " our man in the States has already come up with something." Ford gave him the code numbers of two designs he himself had pinched from the company.

Holz told me: "The client shook my hand and said—You

want to hear it from the tape? No?—he said, 'Herr Holz, that's German efficiency for you.' He was right. I only heard the details from Ford a month later."

The operation was "very expensive," but who would argue with such a successful agent? Ford fought like a lion against himself. Needless to say, the expenses of his aggressive operation for the other firm also shot up. "The opposition has become suspicious. We must be careful," he told them.

The copying continued without a hitch, but Ford had to produce results for the defense, too. His greatest security scoop was achieved in the old design studio where, after days of electronic screening for bugs, he discovered a remote-control camera! He even had the insolence to conduct inquiries and come to the startling conclusion that it must have been a bogus repairman who had planted it.

Then he began to devise special operations to impress both clients. He convinced, for instance, his client No. 2 that the spies of the competitor, client No. 1, must be misled by leaking a batch of fake designs and information to them. Client No. 2 was delighted with the plan. Client No. 1 then got the red-hot intelligence material—and was equally delighted. And that was not all. A few weeks later, Ford uncovered the plot. He proved to client No. 1 that they had all been duped, and produced genuine fresh information.

Client No. 2 pressed Ford to find out who had planted the camera and who was behind all the aggressive operations against them. Holz was worried about this and questioned Ford on the telephone. As usual, he recorded the conversation. He insisted that I should hear the tape, a rather dull exchange of guarded remarks, with an abruptly ending roar of laughter:

HOLZ. What if they find out?
FORD. They won't.
HOLZ. They could start action.

FORD. Perhaps against the opposition.

HOLZ. What about us?

FORD. Don't worry.

HOLZ. Easy to say. My reputation is at stake.

FORD. Don't worry. Knowing the lingerie business, I made sure
that the evidence would be too flimsy. (*Laughs*)

HOLZ. (*Over the roar*) What's so funny? What's so funny?

He told me he had banged the phone down "on that
Schwindler." That was the first crack in their partnership.
Then, in 1968, came Ford's Hong Kong venture, which he
wanted to extend to Germany. He promised to cut his
partner in if the operation succeeded. Holz made some
inquiries but never got anywhere. He then practically
blackmailed Ford to give him a cut for nothing. Ford sold out
in 1970, and Holz did not receive a penny from the deal.
Finally Holz found his favorite blonde in bed with Ford in
Chicago. Subsequently they met three times, in New York,
Munich, and London, to discuss how to end the partnership
without killing the goose that laid the golden eggs.

Nothing was yet settled between them when quite out of
the blue Holz received a letter and a check from the client:
his counterintelligence services would no longer be required.
He telephoned Ford who did not sound very surprised. They
never spoke again. But Holz made some inquiries and found
that the client had engaged a "security adviser"—Jazzy Ford,
of course.

"Why don't you sue him?" I asked only to tease him, but
Holz was most earnest about it. "I can't. The evidence, as he
said, is too flimsy. But I'll get him. I want him to know that
I'll get him. Unless he pays up. You can tell him that."

Ford refused to see me. I later heard he had retired to
Hawaii in 1972. I wonder if he is taking swimming lessons
with a block of concrete chained to his feet.

This backstabbing story of double cross seemed to support

the cynics who suggested that the industrial-espionage threat grew with the public-relations efforts of American security agencies, and that the threat and the countermeasures came from the same source, creating a "new concept of self-perpetuating growth industry." This view was referred to by W. E. Randall, Managing Director of Chubb's, the safemakers, in his contribution to a book entitled *Security, Attitudes and Techniques for Management*, but he came to the conclusion that "businessmen are now aware of the new threat." Unfortunately I have found that this is not the case. The widespread skepticism toward the problem among the higher echelons of management virtually guarantees safe conduct for the commercial intelligence agent.

I came across an excellent example of this typical attitude in Thailand. Thai silk, a magnificent product of ancient skill, represents a vital part of that country's international prestige and revenue from exports. Yet production is down to half of what it used to be before World War II. The reason—a shortage of raw material. Thailand's two biggest sources have been drying up for years, due to industrialization in Japan and to condemnation of silk as a "bourgeois commodity" in China. The government with the help of a major exporter and manufacturer, the Star of Siam company, has started promising experimental projects to increase silk production and, through it, to fight poverty in an area where several million families live on an average income of twenty pounds a year. They could increase weaving, now done in factories but still by old-style craftsmen who, for instance, depend on the length of the nail on the left thumb to guide the thread into 1750 gaps in a steel comb on the loom.

While Thailand struggles with the problem, knowing that their silk is one of the few products in the world that could be sold in any quantities without much promotion, others in Japan, Taiwan, and Hong Kong are cashing in merrily on "genuine phoneys." Yet the experts are apt to dismiss that competition out of hand.

A Star of Siam director told me in Bangkok: "The difference is too easy to spot. I know, the Japanese and others have tried to imitate Thai silk for years, but the machines cannot quite reproduce the true handicraft effect."

"As an expert, he is probably right—from an expert's point of view. But even regular buyers and importers often fail to come under that category," commented F. W. Kendall, head of the Fidelity Inspection Service, who conducts many defensive investigations in Hong Kong on behalf of the copycats' victims. He sees the utter disbelief and skepticism of the cheated and the robbed every day. And a civil servant added, "We heard rumors, or rather more than that, though without proof, that a business intelligence operation was conducted in Thailand for two years to obtain every detail of their production secrets and their markets especially in America, the biggest importer of Thai silk. Then, apparently, copying began somewhere around here, but we don't know the details."

Kendall is convinced that Hong Kong can copy anything, with or without slight alterations, but the order, specifications, and essential intelligence information generally come from abroad. "This makes our work particularly difficult. Most of the manufacturing is done by small Chinese companies. Usually their owners can barely read or write. They often accept any order without questions quite innocently, in good faith. The real villain is the exporter, but he is cautious: he hardly ever has actual physical possession of the copied goods. So how do you catch him? The factory can be closed down, but the chain of distribution remains, and the exporter can place new orders with another factory.

"Even big, internationally known companies get top-class ranges of clothes copied. They often sell them in bargain shops before the expensive originals reach New York. The espionage part of it is done by bribery. It's a way of life here. People who accept bribes to pinch samples or, say, photograph garments being cut or the patterns themselves, do not feel immoral. If anything, they think they're rather clever.

"Yet the victims refuse to believe what happens to them. A Swiss watch company was convinced about a blatant piracy case only when we produced evidence from the copy makers' wastepaper basket. It was a nasty job. All right, I don't need to stand in the street at dawn rummaging in dustbins, because here you can fix it with the cleaner companies to get certain directors' rubbish delivered, neatly packed, on your desk each morning. But some dirty secretaries even spit their chewing gums into them. I hate to do dustbin jobs, and it's about as low as I'd get, but then it might pay."

An American executive, when confronted with a copy of his company's product, suspected theft: "It's just so perfect that it can't be an imitation." It was an electrolytic paint spray gun which had taken six years to develop. It took some intelligence agents six weeks to obtain the confidential specifications and blueprints for a Hong Kong company. Kendall spent almost six months to trace the copycats and get them to pay a quarter of a million dollars damages.

The morning after my second walk with Kam Luang, I had to go to the Commerce and Industry Department of the Hong Kong government to arrange an interview about a case of design piracy that had hit a British shirt manufacturer. I was told that if I returned at half past two in the afternoon, I could see James D. McGregor, Assistant Director in charge of the Industry Division.

A few moments after I left the building, Kam Luang stopped me in the street. "A nice coincidence," he said politely without a smile. Obviously our meeting was as fortuitous as a royal visit to Fiji. He walked with me silently for about a hundred yards. I mumbled something about journalism and an article I would write about the Hong Kong government. He seemed unimpressed but assured me he would be in touch again in due course.

Later that morning, avuncular Lau Big Shang, head of the only Chinese private detective agency in the colony, casually warned me to pick my contacts with care. He kindly insisted that one of his men should photograph the two of us in front of a picture of the Chinese detectives' god. "For souvenir and protection," he said. Did he emphasize protection? With no apparent pertinence, he added, "Hong Kong can be quite a dangerous place."

It gave me something to think about on my way back to the government building where McGregor's office controls Hong Kong industry and collects data with the aid of three hundred officers. One of their duties is to investigate the more than a hundred complaints they receive each month from overseas. Only about twenty of these are usually serious; the government can prosecute local firms whose misbehavior threatens the good name of Hong Kong's industry. Design piracy, with frequent toy copying, comes under this category. Export licenses can be withdrawn; the department has the right to raid premises and destroy wares or molds if necessary. The punishment may also include a year in jail and a fine of a hundred thousand Hong Kong dollars.

"In most of these cases," McGregor said, "the local contractor doesn't even know that the orders he works on involve patent infringement or false trademarks and description. Unless, of course, he is required to put 'Made in England' or something like that on his goods. Which happens. Like in the case of the 'Double Two' shirts."

This was the case that divided Britain's Wakefield Shirt Company executives into two camps: the Skeptics versus the

Cautious—or, as they call one another off the record the Blinds versus the Worriers. The facts are here; the verdict is yours.

Fact No. 1: Minor break-in at company headquarters. The loss: some petty cash and the managing director's diary.

Fact No. 2: After eighteen months of development, the company is ready to go all out for the white shirt market with a "revolutionary new design" incorporating all previous selling attractions plus a special noncrush finish. Representatives are instructed never to leave the samples with retailers for otherwise quite normal consideration overnight. Only a limited number of samples are issued; none of the new shirts is to be in any shop before D day. Competitors are known to be interested in the product. A factory girl is questioned about it by a stranger.

Well before the company D day, there is a break-in at the factory. Thieves enter through the roof, make direct for the pressing room where goods are stacked in great quantities, and take nothing but a few samples of the new shirt.

Fact No. 3: Copies of the successful Double Two shirt appear in several countries. The quality is inferior, but they are "genuine phoneys." In Freetown, Sierra Leone, they are called "Triple Two," but otherwise even the boxes are perfect copies with only the slogan "First looks *last* with Double Two" appropriately adjusted. Price: half of the original's.

Other copies turn up in Rhodesia and Pakistan. The labels say "Made in England." The Pakistani box adds salestalk like HEAVY WEIGHT to the original. Color, style, lettering: perfect replicas. In Aden, the looks are still identical, but the name is "Double T."

By threats and pressure on stores selling the copies, the trail leads to Hong Kong, where nine thousand companies hold proper export certificates.

"We had to look through several thousand certificates and export declarations, but we soon found the suspects," said McGregor. "The manufacturer didn't even know that the trademark was registered in Britain. He was told what to produce and what label to put on. The heaviest fine was imposed, of course, on the exporter, but I don't think that anything happened to the importers in the other countries."

Kam Luang failed to get in touch with me either in the evening or in the morning following my visit to the Industry Department office. I "posted" some messages, but there was no response. The contact who introduced us in the first place answered my question with another three: "Who? Kam what? How do you spell the name? . . . No, never heard of him." But, rather pointedly, he inquired how I got on with McGregor's office. I guessed it would be no good asking him how he knew about that.

It was with considerable relief that I left this otherwise so wonderful town a few days later. Even though Kam Luang had never delivered the quotes he had promised. But if I was, let's face it, rather unnerved by perhaps no more than my own shadow, two years later I had at least the belated and modest satisfaction of hearing a key contact and mutual acquaintance say: "Kam Luang? Oh, yes. Your comings and goings frightened the dry Chinese shit out of him."

License to Cure—or Kill

This license of ruthlessness has never been issued to James Bond. It has never been the privilege of tycoon-style traders in secrets or the self-styled "real-life Bonds," in whose real life the bonds are always counterfeit and intelligence is an occupation not a mental quality. This license is the sole birthright of the drug pirates who are among the heavy-weights of the game.

Pharmaceutical piracy is mostly legitimate. Wholesale exchange of scientific information is a cornerstone of progress—and the main facility for keeping up with the Joneses in a research-based and novelty-dependent industry. "It's awfully difficult to stop all those scientists publishing everything they've got as soon as they think they've got it," said Barry Goodenow in Hawaii. "It's only human nature. They all want to be first, and they want the Nobel prize more than a whacking big but quiet cut from the profits."

Not very long ago, scientists found it most unseemly to patent their inventions because it implied greed and threatened to destroy the romantic hero image of the dedicated researcher. Sir Alexander Fleming provided the most shining example of the truly public-spirited blunder by offering his great discovery, penicillin, to mankind—and failing to "patent the processes by which penicillin was extracted," he wrote with regret in 1958. His "cardinal error" of 1928 not only meant that Britain lost a vast fortune of revenues to other countries, but also that penicillin, one of the most important breakthroughs in modern medicine, remained on the shelf without saving lives for fourteen years. Because it was free to everyone, no one was willing to put money into its development until it became an urgent wartime project for the American government and industry. The armed forces began to receive this invaluable drug only in 1943, and the disastrous postwar scarcity of penicillin inevitably led to the black market of Graham Greene's Third Man. The American invention, the method for mass production, was then bought by all countries, including Britain, at vast expense.

At the beginning of the century, Japan sent out observers all over the world "to see what nations are the greatest, so that we can be like them." In Washington, one of the

Japanese visitors came to a simple conclusion: "We said 'What is it that makes the United States such a great nation?' And we investigated and found that it was patents, and we will have patents." ° It is, of course, quite another matter that by now, the Japanese industry enjoys patent protection and, at the same time, exploits every tiny loophole in other people's paper fortresses by the art and craft of the copycat.

The morality of the patent system has provoked much controversy. While nobody holds anything against the person who patents his invention like power steering, Polaroid camera, helicopter, air conditioning, or the FM radio, to safeguard his interest, the profit motive of the pharmaceutical industry is frequently frowned upon. Perhaps it is because the industry likes to promote itself as the altruistic savior of mankind. Or because we like to see our doctor as saintly guardian of the most important creatures in the universe— us—who is not out to grab a quick buck like his protégés. Or because pharmaceutical discoveries have become such an expensive pastime that almost without exception, only face-less research centers and mammonish corporations that hardly befit our need for hero-worship are capable of achieving them.

Whatever the case, and whatever intolerable excesses might have marred the pharmaceutical businessman's reputation, that much abused profit motive has certainly proved itself a great inducement to gambling with vast sums on research. As Sir Derrick Dunlop, former Chairman of Britain's Medicines Commission, never fails to point out, "The U.S.S.R. and its satellites have not produced a single new drug of therapeutic importance." The widely acclaimed massive talent in the Hungarian drug houses is used mainly

° L. Earle Arnow, *Health in a Bottle* (Philadelphia, J. B. Lippincott Co., 1970).

for piracy to flood the export markets with excellent cut-price copies.

The most important argument against the patent system is that it may give a monopoly to a company and so encourage high drug prices and shameless profiteering. In many countries, this is, however, prevented partly by government control and partly by a built-in anomaly of the system: patents may ensure an inventor's share of the booty, but they give no proper protection. Patents are granted only if the formula of a drug or a manufacturing process is fully disclosed. The patent is then open to inspection by all.

It has often been said that the desire to swallow pills is the greatest single difference between man and animal. An American Food and Drug Administration executive has told me that "you can succeed with the sales of any tablet, whatever its therapeutic value, as long as you can print the word 'new' on the package." These are the fundamental reasons why pharmaceutical companies watch one another and the latest patents like hawks.

Honest companies have the right as well as the duty to their stockholders to maintain regular and perfectly legitimate scientific intelligence units. Once any novelty is patented, the bonanza for all begins. Research laboratories work day and night to produce some modification on the new formula—enough to warrant a new patent—and competition between newest and newestest can flare up in earnest.

It is easy to defend and attack this situation. Both have been done with vicious ferocity. The defense claims that competition breaks all monopolistic powers and lowers prices; that the additional research leads to the new discoveries and gradual improvements that have produced most of our current good drugs; and that the wide range of refinements to suit individuals offers tailor-made cures to all. "Utter rubbish" is usually the answer to this argument and to the announcement of yet another batch of new varieties. The crusaders' battle cry sounds perfectly valid: it is true that many, probably the majority, of the "latest discoveries" are only what the industry calls ME-2's—meaning, please, sir, let *me, too,* have a slice of the cake! These seven-day wonder drugs may do no more, just fractionally more or fractionally less, than the original, and may only promote confusion among doctors who find it hard anyway to keep up with the fast developments in drug therapy—but they may actually bring relief to certain patients. So where do you draw the line?

Many big companies know the answer. They do not patent some secret formulae and processes or they try to rush the new drugs into production so fast that, as Dr. William Bean of Iowa University put it when testifying to the Kefauver Committee, the investment is paid for by "quick kill with the quick pill." These methods may slow down or cut out entirely the comparatively honest ME-2 pirate—but leave the field wide open to the industrial spy and those who do not even pretend to conduct "further research."

The pharmaceutical copycat, more than any other among these felonious felines, needs a production sanctuary, the skill to obtain information, the drug-manufacturing and marketing talent and know-how, the machinery to turn out the "quick pill," and the legal machinery for lasting litigation that ensures an optimum run for the "quick kill." If you conducted a careful investigation to find the ideal circumstances and fed all the essential factors into a computer to spell out the name of a country, then thousands of people all over the world would readily tell you that you were a fool to waste so much energy. The answer to the would-be copycat's prayers is Italy.

Italian legislators persistently refuse to follow international practice and do not grant patents for medicines. Under mounting pressure from other members of the Common Market, they are only too willing to flaunt their impeccable moral credentials: the benefit of life-saving compounds should be free to everybody. Well, almost free to everybody who can pay at least for the product itself but not for the vast expenditure on research and development, the largest, single cost factor in a truly new drug. They want us to find it merely coincidental that in our silent World War III, pharmaceutical piracy is one of Italy's most important secret weapons that makes quite a dent on the greatest medicine-producing countries' economy. But it seems no coincidence at all that in the greatest, best, and least-known pharmaceutical espionage and copying cases, all roads lead to Rome or Milan or Turin.

One of these ventures is now regarded as the biggest robbery on record, because it caused an estimated hundred million dollar loss to the American Cyanamid Corporation and, indirectly, to the United States—which only goes to show that the damage is not peanuts, and piracy as a weapon is no peashooter.

In the late 1950's, tetracyclines and the development of the broad-spectrum antibiotics offered the richest pickings to the pharmaceutical industry. Lederle, a division of Cyanamid, spent twenty-four million dollars on research. Italian companies awaited the outcome hungrily—and several professional and ad hoc spy rings were ready to cater to them. A disgruntled chemist, whose loyalty Lederle had failed to buy with enough cash and prospects, had all the secrets at his fingertips. He began to sell cultures and fermentation techniques to a front company that resold all to an Italian firm. Soon it led to the establishment of cover in the form of several "consultancies," the use of dozens of assumed names, wholesale double cross among competing spies, professional storage of stolen cultures and microfilming of documents, frequent jetting between America and Italy, haggling in style in private suites of luxury hotels, and most important of all, the extension of the market so that deals could be arranged with at least five companies in Italy, one in Hungary, and one in Poland. The three years' profit made by half a dozen key figures came to half a million dollars—some people reckon that two millions is the correct figure—which was not bad going considering that eventually three conspirators were sentenced to two years' and three to six months' imprisonment.

In another American case, an Italian aristocrat was implicated in the sale of pharmaceutical secrets in Rome. And even in pure patent infringement litigation, which many firms are forced to conduct incessantly, and in which espionage is not a complicating factor, Italian manufacturers and wholesalers of many nationalities who handle their products appear as defendants with ominous frequency. For example, Beecham's, the British group that isolated the "core" of the penicillin molecule in 1957 and so opened the way to tailor-made semisynthetic penicillins, suffered very serious losses of royalty income to Italian rivals' pirated products. Although Beecham's initiated yet another legal action, redress by the courts is so slow that the copycats can normally rely on long periods of free trading.

All this is not to say that Italians are the sole beneficiaries of pharmaceutical piracy and espionage. A "consultant" who had obtained the secret of a Merck drug swindled at least one Swiss, one British, one French, and probably some other companies by selling them the formula as his own invention for about a million dollars. When the truth came out, these innocent companies, who had acted in good faith, lost their investment. Merck's damage was estimated at twenty millions. Or, for instance, when the American Pfizer's suspected unauthorized leaks of confidential information, it paid sixty thousand dollars to John Broady, king of the American private wiretappers, to conduct a security investigation and tap the phones of several employees and legal advisers. He found that it was a rival American company, also selling tetracycline, that interfered with Pfeizer's effort to patent its own product. (It is, of course, another matter that Broady then went ahead, and apparently without any request or authorization from Pfeizer, tapped the competitor's and buyer's telephones, too.)

Such cases, however, do not alter Italy's unique position. In the course of my investigation, on two separate occasions, I was told by French and British business intelligence operators that several members of Italian trade delegations and some junior staff of the larger Italian embassies render regular services to the drug industry. They send legitimate market intelligence reports, purchase early samples of new products, pinpoint promising research projects, and help to spot struggling, dissatisfied, or excessively career-conscious employees of foreign companies. This was later corroborated by some executives of British firms.

It has never been suggested to me that these diplomats are directly involved with espionage, bribery, or other forms of corruption, but the implication is clear that they open up many avenues for the industry's agents, especially when introductions are arranged in the alluring atmosphere of embassy receptions. Unfortunately this undiplomatic diplomacy is becoming a standard weapon of the cool war and, as we shall see, involves more and more governments in the battle among industrial giants.

In the light of all the potential profits and a practically national effort, I was rather surprised to hear in Italy that a successful man known in the trade simply as Fabrizio had quit the intelligence business. Allegedly he went mad. He gave away most of his money to charity and informed on many of his colleagues. Which would explain why he keeps to himself—or rather makes sure that nobody can get at him.

I exerted some not too gentle pressure on a mutual "friend," at that time on the staff of the Hotel George V. I knew some details about this man's unsavory past which would be insufficient to lead to a court conviction but might be plenty to make him unpopular among his fellow traders in prostitution. Through him, eventually, I found out about Fabrizio's reasons for quitting, but to appreciate his decision, I first had to examine briefly what a senior German civil servant at the Bundesministerium für Jugend, Familie und Gesundheit described to me in Bonn as "the built-in risk factor" in pharmaceutical copying.

This risk is twofold. The first part is in the purity and efficacy of the copied drug. Due to inaccurate information or lack of care, the product may be disastrously below the quality expected from the original. By the time a doctor who has prescribed it realizes why a patient is not responding well enough to the treatment, it may be too late to do anything about it.

A typical example occurred in Britain in the mid-1960's, when a cut-price tetracycline preparation for pediatric application was imported from Italy. These drops, stocked by most druggists, were prescribed for young children and babies suffering high temperatures in, say, pneumonia. In Birmingham, where drugs were tested regularly, this medicine was found to have only three quarters of the alleged normal strength. The danger was obvious, and the government had to order the withdrawal of the entire batch. The Ministry of Health then tried to restrict the imports of antibiotics by granting contracts only to the original patent holders.

That was, however, only a temporary solution. In the early 1950's, important new medicines had flooded the market. In the late 60's, many of these basic, standard drugs—although not the brand-name ones—began to run out of protection by the expiration of their patents. "That's why the 1968 Medicines Act had special significance in this respect," Sir Derrick Dunlop told me. "We had plenty of low-priced drugs coming in from Poland, Hungary, and Italy, and it was vital to see that these complied with the requirements of the British Pharmacopoeia. But before the Act, we had no right to check their quality and purity. Now the new licensing and inspecting system helps to increase public safety."

Unfortunately systems and standards differ from country to country, and while some efforts are duplicated or triplicated, others are omitted leaving loopholes for disaster. Even within the EEC, it is expected to take "many, many years" to work out some uniformity of control.

One of these loopholes is, in fact, at the root of the second "built-in risk factor" that thrives on piracy. It is the lack of fast and accurate world-wide reporting of iatrogenic (drug-induced) diseases and undesirable side effects. Much, though far from enough, has been done to facilitate the early spotting and recognition of dangerous symptoms and trends. The patent holder, however, has some advantage: at least in the more advanced countries, he is usually the first to hear about complaints and suspicions. If he is honest, he will immediately pass all such information on to other companies that manufacture his drug under license—but not to pirates.

Traders in secrets, professional business-intelligence operators, have never been noted for petty scruples and ethical considerations. The risk factor is "just one of those things" to them. Attention to such details is not an ingredient of their professionalism.

Fabrizio was no exception. He always prided himself on working the same way as the big drug companies: he studied the statistical list of leading causes of deaths, like research directors, when choosing new projects for investigation. This was his professionalism. And this is how, in common with most big drug research centers, heart disease with the associated problem of obesity and the popular Western appeal of weight reduction became the field of his chief interest.

In the course of his "inquiries," he heard about a comparatively small, new, and go-ahead company—Chemie-Grünenthal. I was told that he "established contact with" (bribed) an employee "on spec," and soon learned about experiments which led to the chance discovery of a by-product with sedative qualities.

The substance, named K17, was the future thalidomide.

Like its discoverers, Fabrizio foresaw its promise to a sleeping-pill-crazy society. At a time when most others had not yet even realized that there was a bandwagon to jump on, and even before the Thalidomide Symposium was held in December 1955, he sold his information to two Italian firms, which, however, shelved it all until sales in Germany really began to soar in the late 1950's.

Apart from being a fantastic nonaddictive sedative, the new wonder drug offered perfect safety even to babies. It began to outsell all its competitors and became known as Germany's No. 1 baby-sitter. Patients in hospitals, sleepless expectant mothers, swallowed it merrily night after night. It then appeared in combination with other drugs against migraine, asthma, neuralgia, aches and pains and flu. Its future looked bright. Fabrizio sat back and congratulated himself.

While British, Swedish, Canadian, Spanish, and Portuguese companies negotiated sole licensee rights for their respective countries, while an American company tried in vain to fight government objections to rushing into full-scale production, the copycats were fast off their marks. Two Japanese firms copied the drug, and one of them actually marketed it until the license for Japan was sold by Chemie-Grünenthal.

In Italy, there were no formalities. Although, as Herbert Wartensleben, head of the German firm's legal department, told me, the license was never sold to that country, no less than seven Italian companies began to churn out thalidomide straight or in combinations. As usual, most of it was exported.

Fabrizio was once again miles ahead of the pack. His hunch was that a successful research outfit with a big winner in hand might have something else up its sleeve. He went to sleepy, patrician Stolberg, near the Belgian border, where the Chemie-Grünenthal company seemed to be the apple of the locals' eyes. Some "personal background research" on his contact enabled him by about late 1959 or early 1960 to administer a not too subtle mixture of cash inducement and blackmail.

The flow of information coming from Stolberg was most disappointing. Fabrizio was not interested in rumors of dangerous side effects of thalidomide and company efforts to suppress complaints. It was not the kind of stuff his customers were eager to buy. The only chance ever for industrial espionage to save lives was lost.

In 1961, allegedly, a horribly malformed child was born in Fabrizio's family. It was, of course, regarded as a shame, a disgrace, a punishment meted out by God, and the baby was duly hidden from everybody outside the family. Only a few months later, the real cause of the wave of deformities became known, and the scandal began.

It was never fully clarified how much of the early side effects had been reported to the license holders in various countries, but these could and did at least ask for explanations and reassurance from Chemie-Grünenthal. This facility was not available, Fabrizio realized, to the pirates. Apparently much of the thalidomide compounds sold in Brazil as late as mid-1962, six months after the full horror story had become world news, was still of Italian origin.

According to my informant, that was when "Fabrizio went mad"; he took it upon himself to look after three thalidomide children for the rest of his life. At the time of the German trial he was said to be forcing his Stolberg contact to provide Prosecutor Havertz with confidential information.

In September 1971, I attended an international pharmaceutical symposium in Geneva. One evening I mentioned this case to an Italian chemist. He said he did not know and would certainly avoid any dealings with people like Fabrizio. But he ended the conversation with a cynical smile and a question:

"Are you suggesting that industrial spies ought to provide proper after-sales service?"

I have singled out a few areas where copycats make fortunes, but in fact, there are no limitations to "genuine phoneys." All sorts of chemicals come high on the endless list of successful imitations, with items like new cigars, handbells, aviation instruments, lipsticks, racing tires, and nail polish indicating the range.

Much of the prerequisite information comes in the form of stolen documents and samples—the rest is made to walk right into the copycat's office. The latter is the method used in the darkest corners of the business jungle, where several times "headhunters" have asked me: "Why bother with the brainchild when you can get the brain itself?"

4

Brainhunters

Docket No. 27
Re: 312/MOG:LM/Paris
Filed: 26/10/69 Brussels

". . . and then suspect No. 5 proceeded to pinch my private parts so hard that I was obliged to give him a push by which act, falling on the floor beside the bed, he noticed the Philips Type El 3302A/15G serial number 6262727 tape recorder in its badly concealed position. . . . see film and tape enclosed. . . ."

This cool fragment of imitation police language comes from a detailed report, submitted by a "female operative," to the Brussels branch of an American "confidential investigations organization" which likes to be known to its few select clients as CIO. Although her style of masterly hypocrisy could not disguise the feeble effort to create an air of respectability, it did help to seal the sad fate of "Suspect No. 5."

On the enclosed film, she fluttered about in the nude with a quite remarkable lack of talent for acting, and her well-worn body failed to produce the bounce she endeavored to achieve with the aid of the high-quality springs in her bed. That a reasonably handsome, allegedly "world-wise senior executive" fell for it at all only demonstrated the blinding effect of mere availability.

The worst part of the package was the tape, also enclosed, of course. I heard her groan, and I heard her coo, and it sounded painfully unconvincing that "this sudden burst of sexuality" which had swept her into his arms could only occur in "Pareeeee." Yet, apparently, her partner never suspected that her irresistible eruption of emotions was as spontaneous as an Apollo moonshot.

When I first heard about this odd affair and its immediate background, "surveillance on five men at the Paris motor show," I did not recognize it as a significant piece of a jigsaw I would eventually manage to glue together with the aid of a dash of inspiration, a few drops of perspiration, and a huge drum of good luck.

Now that I try to muster the fragments of information in chronological order, I must restrict my account to reporting only the substance of events, one battle in the cool war, while letting the participants get away with it all. In accordance with the conditions imposed by my contacts, and being aware of long libel suits looming large over each word, I have, once again, changed the names of countries, firms, individuals, and even the traceable serial number of the tape recorder in the quoted report. I am permitted, however, to say that this international operation concerned the emergence of a fast-growing firm that was to capture a sizable share of the market in several countries' motor car and allied trades.

April 1969

Triad Instrumentations had already established so many branch outfits that only a few people knew which of these would be the operational center of the new marketing onslaught. Triad Inc. in America, Triad GmbH in Germany, Triad Co. Ltd. in Britain were still empty shells, but the board had already decided the basic staff requirements. They needed mostly marketing men, specialists in each country with "relevant experience" in the specific trade, and production ideas men working, presumably, for competitors.

A junior executive was now appointed as Paris-based recruiting officer to draw up a list of potential applicants. He lasted only three weeks. His end came when a Triad director was gently reminded at a London cocktail party that "poaching on competitors' staff could be a double-edged weapon." The director agreed with the principle, and everybody smiled. Two days later the news began to spread that an "overambitious" junior executive had acted "in a manner incompatible with Triad standards." He was demoted without further ado.

May 1969

Mr. S., a more tactful man, took up the Paris appointment. His brief was exactly the same as his predecessor's, but he had been warned emphatically that "we must not upset the trade and although it's absolutely vital to get the best possible brain for each job, we don't wish to be accused of staff enticement."

Twenty-four hours later, he was in Brussels, at the European head office of XYZ Partners, a large executive recruitment agency with not too carefully disguised management-consultancy affiliations. (Some management consultants seriously damage the reputation of their trade by giving biased advice. They seek to persuade clients to buy computers, office equipment, or even furniture only from manufacturers who pay a high commission to or even own the consultancy, and they also act as scouts or as a front for headhunters.)

Mr. S., with the substantial weight of a good introduction and the Triad name behind him, was received by a director and a senior research consultant—the polite name for a headhunter—and the briefing was a little formal but friendly and perfectly ethical. The Triad directors' careful warning that it was essential to protect the good name of the company was duly impressed upon the consultant who told me some eighteen months later:

"You could tell that the guy was green and nervous, so I had to help him along. I had to know how desperate his firm was and how far we were really supposed to go. I mean you know what this business is like—not at all what it ought to be—so what can I say? Here was a good client, and we were fighting for survival. It's a jungle where only the fittest will survive, if you know what I mean."

What he meant was that at the end of the briefing session, he asked his client if there were any objections to "modern, aggressive recruiting techniques." The answer was "No, of course not, but naturally we cannot endorse anything unethical." Naturally. The lack of endorsement protected Triad. Otherwise the agency received a carte blanche for action, ranging from diligent scrutiny of reference hooks to holding a gun to a desirable applicant's head.

The buck was immediately passed to André Rillon, a Chicago-trained Belgian consultant, who was junior enough to be "severely reprimanded" for carrying out his actual orders if something went wrong.

Mid-May 1969

The search for suitable executives was already in full swing. Rillon and his assistant leafed through reference books and received a computer printout from the company's own international executives' register which, XYZ Partners never failed to point out, contained the names, qualifications, brief career history, present position, in most cases the salary, some personal and family details of almost a quarter of a million people "all in the over $12,000 but mostly over $15,000 per annum bracket."

Although the "quarter of a million" may well be an exaggeration, it is true that such registers with something like fifty thousand names in each are the bread and butter of legitimate staff consultancy and general business intelligence. Apart from trade reference books, the business pages of newspapers and specialist periodicals are an essential source of information for compiling and updating the lists. New appointments and promotions in members-on-the-move columns are carefully noted, and the conscientious search consultant never fails to investigate why somebody has been promoted, retired, fired, and so forth. Even agencies opposed to underhand methods may use private detectives to check the movement of key personnel.

By the end of May, the selected lists began to shrink to

manageable lengths. Rillon, a smooth, sober, subservient dream of a private secretary, was in over-all charge—"probably because from Brussels it was easy to maintain regular liaison with the client," he told me with an apologetic gesture of skyward palms—but now he could begin to farm out parts of the work to branches in the various countries.

"Caution is always the key to these assignments," he explained, "and this was particularly true in this case. The motor industry, instrument, light fittings, and accessory trade is riddled with suspicion and quite rightly so. It's a cutthroat competition using a great deal of industrial espionage— which of course isn't our line. Security measures are very, shall we say, far-reaching, and one can easily lose many influential friends by attracting undue attention. It is, of course, understandable because the stakes are high. A new model is a multimillion gamble. A man who knows many secrets, plans, and company strategy, a good designer, advertising or marketing specialist, is worth a fortune to a competitor and many times that in damages to the company which loses him.

"If the man is connected with R & D (research and development), the damage can be even greater. Perhaps you are familiar with the trade in information about the development of the Wankel engine, electric battery and fuel cell driven cars, a new rustproofing technique, antipollution technology, and attempts at platinum replacement."

I encouraged him to tell me more about these, but he refused to elaborate. Perhaps I could ask his superiors, he suggested.

What he said about the car industry in general was perfectly true. A French agent who, I knew, would handle any kind of espionage and to whom packing a gun was as normal as having a handkerchief in his pocket, once refused an exceptionally well-paid American assignment because, he told me, "If I wanted to take that kind of risks I'd rather go around kissing the ladies in a cholera ward."

As far back as May 1, 1960, the *Los Angeles Times* reported that "the auto industry operates one of the world's largest espionage setups outside of government circles." Their agents knew what competitors had on the drawing boards for two or three years ahead. In 1966, Mercedes lost almost ten million Deutsch-Marks because stocks in the hands of 156 dealers throughout the world became virtually obsolete when photographs of a new model appeared in the press: customers canceled their orders until the new line would become available after the Frankfurt motor show.

In 1969, Dr. G. Amore, the Turin public prosecutor, filed industrial espionage charges against the director general and thirteen other key employees of a subsidiary of Alfa Romeo. Allegedly, they had conspired to steal all the production details of the new Fiat model 128, then still on the drawing boards. Dr. Amore claimed that the conspirators bribed Fiat employees with large cash sums and better jobs in order to obtain two thousand production cards for copying.

The notoriously slow grinding of Italian justice took four years to make some progress—and created a farcical situation. The two automobile manufacturers had forgotten their squabbles by 1973 when, in an atmosphere of true friendship, they were already cooperating on several levels and collaborating in the construction of a major plant to produce commercial vehicles in Rio de Janeiro.

I have now been told that "Fiat would not wish to press charges against Alfa Romeo concerning that indiscretion in 1969." The law, however, is that charges already preferred by the prosecutor cannot be withdrawn. In order to avoid causing embarrassment to a colleague and bad publicity to the trade, the two sides are now trying to find legal means to preserve a united front.

To counter the hazard of what is politely called "indiscretions," several big companies go to amazing lengths. Most of them make sure that their test tracks for new designs cannot be overlooked from anywhere outside the well-guarded perimeter, and some maintain aerial surveillance ever since new General Motors models in a walled yard had been photographed from a helicopter. Several motor companies' counterintelligence sections are said to be so active, particularly in America, that they can chart a senior employee's problems and ambitions, and predict his job-changing intentions well in advance.

Rillon's cautious approach to the job therefore made good sense. "In the first place, we always hope that the ideal solution will be possible. We advertise the job, the best man applies for it, and the client accepts him. It could be as simple as that. But experience shows that especially with the more senior appointments, like these for Triad, we run into all sorts of difficulties. For example, many of the top executives don't ever read the ads. And quite rightly so. They can expect to be approached. Job offers crop up at dinner parties or on the golf course. Another problem is that they don't answer the ads even if they read them because they find it a humiliating move and they're afraid of exposing themselves to gossip that may reach their employers. It usually does.

"In this case, I asked my colleagues in the relevant countries to run a few test ads with a P. O. box number to see what sort of applications we'd get. The response was most disappointing. Mind you, senior people are particularly wary of this anonymous type of ad. But at this stage I was anxious not to expose our client's expansion plans to publicity."

Did he conduct bogus interviews?

"No, that's mainly done by people in intelligence who

want to find out about the applicants' jobs, plans, work conditions. As I told you, we're not spies."

A little spying, however, became inevitable.

June 1969

It was now obvious to Rillon that he could not count on finding the ideal solution: "I had to try the next best thing, which is to see if any of those on my short list were unhappy with their jobs, salary, prospects, or life in general. Frustrated people are more likely to respond to direct personalized offers. The senior partner in Thorndike Deland Associates once told the *Harvard Business Review* that most firms never realize that a man must be unhappy or dissatisfied with something in order to think about leaving. That's my bible."

To find the unhappiest best applicant Rillon needed "outside help." This, however, had to be authorized by one of the partners.

"Once it was OK'd, I could give the assignment to an international outfit that does occasional credit and other background investigations for us," he said.

"C.I.O.?" I tried to make it sound casual. I knew that C.I.O. had a European center in Brussels, and it seemed a sensible guess.

"Yes—you know them?"

It worked. I had to be quick to exploit the fact that Rillon was, at least momentarily, impressed by my inside information. "Sure. In fact they told me a few things about the case." Which was not true. I had no idea at the time that the Paris motor show report had anything to do with Triad.

"Then I won't bore you with unnecessary details. Tell me what you want to know."

"As much as possible. I want to hear it from you. For the sake of accuracy."

Rillon obviously liked to be known as a man of precision and good memory. Just a pinch of unadulterated flattery made him want more. I thought gratefully about a friend who had built a very remarkable career in government on the simple principle that "you cannot flatter a man too much—if nothing else, he will want to believe you—but it doesn't work with women, who will only suspect that you're trying to bed them even if they are seventy-five."

From that moment, Rillon treated me as a real confidant. He went well beyond his brief in talking to me and gave me some unauthorized details. At one point, later on, he realized his mistake, but then he had to rely on me not to create an awkward situation for him within his organization.

We chatted about Landau, the Austrian who ran the European operation of C.I.O. and could organize investigations in several countries simultaneously.

"I called in Landau, and within a week things were under way," Rillon said. "I just wanted the usual background checks on some people, and filling in the gaps in our record. It's amazing how many firms now treat directors' and executives' salaries as top-secret.

"Toward the end of the month, there was a minor exhibition for the trade in Chicago where, I knew, Triad would have a stand. That was a good opportunity. We listed everybody who visited the stand because these had a professional interest in Triad, and I wanted to see if any of them were missing from my selection. We found three, in fact, and Landau's men ran a check on each. One of the three was a guy called Frank Fairmont. I never heard of him, and I found no reference to him in the motor trade publications. Eventually we tracked him back to electrical household appliances, where he had held a very senior marketing position and was still regarded as a brilliant, original thinker. This was strange. Why wasn't his joining his present employers ever announced? Had he been forced by some error or circumstances to take a third-rate job not worth announcing?"

With the triumphant smile of a magician at a children's party, Rillon produced a thick folder from his desk.

Mr. Fairmont, here was your life, including details you must have long forgotten. There were about fifty pages of reports. Photostat copies of documents, including the contract for his current job (it cost a mere fifty dollars to obtain from a secretary), his official credit rating, his bank balance for the last two years, a police CR report giving him a clean criminal record, a playground interview with his children, aged nine and twelve, saying that "Mummy always shouts if Dad is late in the evening," details of a court case that had cleared him of a charge of dangerous driving, photographs of his house and family and car, a report from a "market researcher" describing the interior of his home with a rough evaluation of his living standard, and other papers including detailed charts of how the family had spent several weekends.

Rillon mentioned these while he was looking for a brief transcript from a tape recording. "This was taken at the beginning, when we had no idea what his job could be and nobody a Landau agent dug up would tell us," Rillon said.

The agent then tried the simplest old device. He telephoned Fairmont's company, a potential major competitor of Triad. He knew that Fairmont had not yet arrived at the office. The operator put him through.

"Mr. Fairmont's office."

"Hi, this is Jack Smith here. I want to talk to Frank, please."

"He isn't in, sir. Can I help you? I'm his secretary."

"I know, honey, I remember your voice. And I'd rather talk to you than to Frank, but it can't be helped. When do you expect him?"

"He won't be in for about a week."

"Oh, yes, I remember now. He mentioned some trip—what was it?"

"Sweden?"

"That's right. The Swedish deal—"

"Ah, well, that's what he's doing right now."

"Pity he didn't take you with him. Or is it all that hush-hush?"

"It is, I suppose, but we couldn't leave the office empty. Both his assistants are with him anyway."

"Both, you said?"

"Yes, but his deputy is here. Would you like to talk to him?"

"His deputy? No, honey, I'd better wait for the old man. I'll ring him in a week or so."

"He'll call me tomorrow. I'll tell him you want to talk to him. Jack Smith, was that the name?"

"That's right, honey. That's what I said."

This was a significant lead. Fairmont had not been demoted to some obscure position: he had a deputy, two assistants, and a confidential assignment to Sweden. (The news of a pending Scandinavian deal was pure bonus.) Further inquiries were justified. It soon emerged that Fairmont had some rather revolutionary marketing ideas, and he had been given a high-powered, not exactly secret but inconspicuous, backroom job to prepare a major European sales campaign.

When he returned from Sweden, one of Rillon's American colleagues telephoned him. The name of XYZ Partners was a good enough introduction, and the consultant held a useful trump, one of the basic tools of the trade. He knew that people loved to give advice—it cost them nothing and made them feel important—so it was only advice he asked for.

The consultant could not name his client, of course, but explained that he had to find a man who . . . , and out came a long list of qualifications, age, and other requirements that added up to a faultless description of Fairmont himself. Rather shamelessly, he spelled it out: "Somebody like yourself, sir, a real whiz kid, who could practically write his own contract."

Unfortunately Fairmont did not go for the bait. Perhaps he was happy with his job. Perhaps he was, as the consultant's report said, "too much of a worldwise man to fall for an old trick like that, but he promised to let us know if he could think of somebody for the job."

Worldwise. The not very common adjective struck me. I was sure that somebody had recently used it when describing a man to me. An odd coincidence.

August 1969

The recruitment for Triad was progressing well in all countries. There were some difficulties with a reluctant French research and development engineer. He had been seen visiting a firm near Paris, and it was suspected that he might be negotiating a move there instead of accepting a Triad job in America. This possibility had to be eliminated first. He was kept under constant surveillance, and when he visited that firm again, an agent "clarified" whom he had seen there and reported that "any intention of changing jobs could be ruled out." The report to Rillon gave no details of the agent's method of "clarification," but this kind of operation is not very complicated.

Irving Shumbord, a New York private detective, gave me a good example. He was working on a counterintelligence assignment in a case of industrial espionage that involved a break-in, theft of drawings and various plans, and sale of information by employees. His job was to watch two men and report whom they had seen on a visit to New York. One day he followed the pair to a building, shared an elevator with them, and saw that they got out on the seventeenth floor, where all the rooms were occupied by a well-known office equipment manufacturer. All he had to do now was to wait in the street until the two men left the building, return to the lobby on the seventeenth floor, and ask the receptionist urgently where he could find the two visitors whose names he knew. She kindly phoned around and was told that they had seen Mr. A. but went on to see Mr. B. Eventually the last man they saw told her that the two men had already left. Shumbord pretended to be sorry that he had missed them— he had gained all the information he needed.

In the French engineer's case, once Rillon knew that the man was not negotiating for another job, a little gentle pressure could be applied. It "so happened" that at a reception a few days later the engineer's wife met a friendly woman who talked incessantly about the "fantastic opportunities just coming up in America" and about a job with Triad her boyfriend was after. Presumably the wife returned home and began to nag her husband about why he did not apply for a fantastic job like that. Rillon thinks that the husband then boasted to the wife that the Triad job was, in fact, available to him but that he was not interested. Whatever happened that evening, the French engineer signed the contract the following morning.

More than two dozen appointments had already been made by Triad who were very satisfied with Rillon and the services of XYZ Partners. Several other applicants were only waiting for the final stamp of approval. There were still some loose ends, and the partners suffered some embarrassment when a French public relations man they had strongly recommended, turned out to be a major figure in a corrupt advertising scandal, but on the whole, only two vacancies continued to give Rillon sleepless nights. For these jobs, two Americans from Rillon's lists were the first choice, and Triad obstinately refused to consider anybody else although both men were most reluctant to respond to any approaches.

One of these was a California whiz kid with the reputation of a supersalesman who could persuade a corpse to stock up with shampoo because hair keeps growing in the grave. The other was Fairmont.

"I tried to explain to S., Triad's Paris man, that it was no good if their No. 1 choice for a job was not willing to apply. For even if he was made to accept, he would never really care about the work," Rillon told me. "Triad refused to understand that a firm like ours couldn't risk its good name on making an outright offer, promising heaven on earth, to these men. What if they reported it to their employers? We could be branded with unprofessional conduct; we'd invite sneering publicity; and we, as well as our client, could be sued for enticement of staff and even for trying to get confidential information through quite brazen headhunting.

"S. advised me to run a series of tailor-made ads. You know the system. You find out what papers your target reads, guess what trade publications he must see regularly, advertise the job with exactly his qualifications and specially attractive features that you know will appeal to him. You offer more and more every week, turn down all other applicants, and wait until he's hooked. But in these two cases, I knew it wouldn't work. We had already gone a bit beyond that. Just how far did S. really want to go? That was my problem when he asked a completely unexpected question. He wanted to know how I could help him to find out the expiration date of an American government contract with one of his competitors. I said I didn't know, it was not our line; but after consultation with one of the senior partners, I told him I could arrange a meeting with Landau. He might be able to help."

Landau did help. He discovered that this contract was a most confidential affair because there had been no competition for it; only this one firm had ever been asked to submit a bid, and its details were unknown even to most of the senior company executives. It seemed hopeless to bribe someone like a vice-president, but Landau was indefatigable whenever a new client with a fat purse appeared on the limited horizon beyond his thick glasses.

Although this particular operation was not part of the Triad headhunting affair, it is a good example of the simplicity and cunning ingenuity with which some agents, like Landau, penetrate tight defenses.

One of his U.S.-based men reconnoitered the company offices and returned with some apparently innocuous incidental information. A full list of this, including all the names of outside contractors like the office cleaners was examined by C.I.O. men. Landau, who received a copy, picked out two items from the report. These told him that there was an internal telephone in the main entrance lobby for visitors, and also the name of the contractor whose uniformed staff cleaned and disinfected every telephone in the building twice a year. It was no problem to obtain one of these uniforms.

On the last Friday afternoon of the month, at 3:35, a telephone-cleaner girl entered the main lobby, said a cheerful hello to the starter, cleaned the visitors' phone in three minutes, then took an elevator to the president's floor. Nobody stopped her. As the elevator door was closing, she just caught a glimpse of a well-dressed young man who was asking the starter if he could phone somebody in the building. He was directed towards the sparkling clean visitors' set.

At 3:39, the operator put through an internal call for a visitor to the company's document library. The visitor, speaking in one of those futuristic see-through bubbles, could not be overheard. He introduced himself as Mr. L., one of the company's vice-presidents, and demanded with great self-assurance the expiration date of a government contract. He was asked to wait a moment.

At 3:41, a telephone-cleaner girl entered Mr. L.'s vice-presidential office. She chatted to the secretary while cleaning the phone.

Also at 3:41, the document librarian was worried. He had to tell the waiting "Mr. L." on the phone that although he was on the list of people entitled to access to this particular document, it was against the regulations to give any details on the telephone. The vice-president was very kind; it was most reassuring to know that confidential information was handled by such a conscientious man, and the librarian would be in trouble if he gave out dates just like that. No, the correct procedure was for the librarian to call the vice-president's office and give the information to his secretary.

"Yes, sir, can I have your number, please?"

Mr. L. now lost his temper. Did the librarian need a nursemaid for every phone call? Couldn't he ask the operator or look up the list? He replaced the receiver with a bang and left the building.

At 3:43, the phone rang on the desk of vice-president L.'s secretary. The telephone-cleaner girl picked up the receiver and was on the verge of getting the confidential information, but a most efficient secretary insisted on taking the call herself. She made a note of the message, just the date her boss himself had apparently asked for. The telephone-cleaner was, of course, standing next to her and managed to read the date on the notepad. While the secretary checked with Mr. L. and discovered that the stupid librarian must have made some mistake, she finished her job and left without any hurry.

In this way, Landau gained an unsurpassable introduction to Triad.

September 1969

Apart from the two troublesome vacancies, Rillon had filled all the Triad jobs. He had suggested five top men, but judging from Triad's unscrupulous interest in that contract expiration date, Rillon guessed that his client would want to do almost anything to get the two Americans. How far would his own company be prepared to go to please the client? A senior partner advised him that if Triad insisted on trying to do more than XYZ had already done, they should talk to Landau, whom Triad now knew and trusted and who might be able to use a "more direct" approach.

Rillon told me: "S. liked the idea. I gave him a full set of duplicates of our Fairmont and other files, and suggested that the coming Paris motor show might provide a good opportunity to make the approach because all five men were likely to be there."

It was only then that I recognized the connection between the Triad affair and one of several cases Landau had mentioned to me much earlier. The "worldwise" Mr. Fairmont had not been particularly worldwise in "Pareee" when that film and tape recording was made.

Landau is one of those people who are frequently underestimated. He wears very thick glasses; he is small and ulcerously slim, and can produce a slight stammer that gives him time to think while people are feeling sorry for him. He does not mind being patronized by clients; it is good for business. At some stage in his career, he was a detective in the Tyrol for about six months. From those glorious days he has retained a touch of dry police manners and some passing remarks that tend to depict the Innsbruck police force as the perfect mixture of Scotland Yard and the Sûreté, which again goes down well with clients. But as a final trump he can easily conjure up a complete change of gait, posture, and manners that would qualify him to star in the third act of an Agatha Christie thriller—the master detective who knows it all. This was the part he played when we met for the first time, in 1970.

I asked him about C.I.O. Did it stand for Confidential Investigations Organization?

"Yes, I suppose so," he said with the patient smile normally reserved for the occasion when one does not know the answer to an inquisitive child's question. "We quite like to be known by that name, so I suppose you could refer to us like that."

"Isn't that the real name of your outfit?"

"No. Not really."

"Then what is it? Can you tell me?"

"No, I can't. Not that I don't want to, but you see, there isn't any real name. No offices, no cover, no listed phone numbers, no printed stationery, and of course, no accounts. Which has its advantages."

"But you must have files. You've already mentioned a 'Docket No. 27' and some reference numbers."

"Yes. Files we have. Safely stored, you might say."

There was a long gap between our first and second meetings. Later I heard from various people that he did quite an extensive checking on me. Our second meeting was very brief; he asked me to arrange an introduction for him in

Australia. This I did, and eventually, he got in touch with me in London. He said he would be glad to show me some interesting items, if our privacy could be ensured. I offered to rent a hotel room for a couple of hours, but he preferred to visit me in my home. I only had to make sure that the children would not burst in at the wrong moment.

Landau arrived like a traveling circus. He set up his film projector and tape recorder, and played the film and the tape I mentioned earlier. It was then that he told me about the history and background of "Docket 27."

October 1969

Landau's assignment at the Paris motor show was "to keep five representatives, (*names*) of the . . . and . . . companies under observation and establish if they were likely to get into any compromising situations. . . ."

The vague and ethically worded brief implied, however, a great deal more to Landau. He originally claimed that this job came to him "second hand"—meaning that it was not necessarily an assignment from the five representatives' employers who, Landau and many security men would argue, were perfectly entitled to know what their staff was doing.

"We assigned two male and two female operatives to the job," he said, puffing away at his pencil-thin, half-chewed cigar in the corner of his mouth. "We kept a round-the-clock surveillance on all, but with two of the suspects—I mean the representatives—we failed to produce positive evidence.

"The third consumed a great deal of alcohol in the company of one of our female operatives, who at one point began to search for a lighter in her handbag. As a very large roll of Swiss francs in the handbag was, she claimed, in her way, he obliged by holding it for her for a minute. We managed to photograph him with the money.

"The fourth suspect was successful in seducing our female operative No. 2"—Landau made a helpless gesture with his hands—"and in her room, concealed film and sound recording of the event was effected.

"Subsequently the man introduced his friend and colleague, suspect No. 5, to our operative, and a visit was arranged for him, too. This man arrived a little too early, when our operative was still engaged in checking a spare tape recorder which she, very carelessly, pushed under the bed."

Then came the slapstick love scene during which suspect No. 5 got carried away, and the ominous pinching led to the push which was, as Landau put it, "a little unwise." Due to the discovery of the machine under the bed, she was attacked by her furious lover, "but she was saved by our male operatives who broke in posing as hotel detectives. They took photographs, of course. Having seen that there was no tape in the recorder and that his suspicions were totally unfounded, the suspect apologized to our female officer—I mean, operative—and peacefully left."

I asked Landau what use would be made of his report. He suddenly lost his report-writing vernacular:

"I don't care a damn! To blackmail them or to fire them—it's none of my business."

He blamed erring husbands and "greedy bastards" for their potential misfortunes. In a long stream of predominantly four-letter words he gave his rather unflattering opinion of the world.

Rillon of XYZ Partners told me, however, what happened. "Suspect No. 3" was the Californian supersalesman. When he saw the photograph of himself with the female operative, and when he was told that the girl, giving him the money, was a

Triad employee, he recognized that "he would have to make an awful lot of explanations to his superiors." He then found the attractive conditions of the Triad offer irresistible and changed his job.

"Suspect No. 5" was Fairmont. When he watched the film, he broke down. Then, apparently, he decided that he was prepared to lose everything but his marriage and self-respect. He resigned from his executive position and disappeared with his family. It is thought that they moved to Canada where he accepted a very insignificant office job. His wife's hysterical jealousy was well known to Triad from the earliest background investigations, and Rillon reckoned "it was quite decent of Triad and Landau not to track them down and confront her with the film out of sheer spite."

Since then, the extensive Triad operation has begun. Two of its initial achievements are, I believe, that one competitor has suffered considerable losses and that another has had to close down a plant, making seven hundred people redundant.

One file of this repugnant affair has not yet been closed. Rillon and Landau conduct a merciless vendetta, I suspect, against one another. At our last meeting, when I decided to stir things up a little, Rillon changed his usual mild tone and claimed that Landau had messed up the Paris assignment, and therefore Triad refused to pay the fee due to XYZ Partners. He also accused the Austrian of having "double-crossed everybody by selling information to a third party and by making false claims that XYZ Partners were directly responsible for his dirty work." When, after that, I met Landau once again for the last time, I conveyed the message and listened to the counteraccusations.

According to Landau, he never had any direct dealings with Triad; the job came to him second-hand via Rillon. Triad refused to pay his very considerable expenses in full, and XYZ Partners supported Triad in this, although he paid

Rillon a handsome fee as a private commission (vehemently denied by Rillon, of course), and it was XYZ or Rillon himself who sold the information to a third party, double-crossing Landau himself and the client.

It did not make much difference what the full truth about these details was. But their squabbles revealed their ulterior motives, leaving an ugly dent on my newly acquired faith in flattery as an interrogation technique—perhaps only I, the flatterer, was flattered by the success of "making" Rillon talk.

Born Free to Betray?

In August 1964, *The New York Times* dealt with American companies' growing "concern at the increasing theft of some of their intangible but most valuable assets—trade secrets." It reported that much of the espionage was done through hiring knowledgeable employees from competitors.

The already quoted *Harvard Business Review* inquiry found that the overwhelming majority of executives claimed they themselves would never hire a competitor's staff in order to obtain information, even though in their opinion 32.7 percent of their competitors would do it "rarely," and an additional 37.8 percent would do it "occasionally, frequently, or regularly."

Harold Lipset, who operates an extensive investigation service, told me in his spacious, electronic-gadget-packed home-cum-headquarters on fashionable Pacific Heights in San Francisco:

"Headhunting is the most legitimate form of direct indus-trial espionage. In a free society, as long as people are permitted to move from job to job, you can't stop this practice. There's nothing to stop a free man using his skill and experience in the service of a new employer—even if this sometimes amounts to betrayal of trade secrets."

These three comments clearly show how serious and widespread the problem is, although admittedly I have come across only a few such extreme cases as the Triad affair. As in every business intelligence operation, it is difficult to decide where to draw the line between aggressive recruiting and disguised headhunting policies.

The ebullient head of a London-based international information service told me: "We get a few requests to find out details of people's contracts with their employers, but most firms can do it for themselves. I know an American computer firm that has a team of about a dozen men, each paid well in excess of £10,000 a year plus generous expenses, to travel all over the world to exhibitions, lectures, symposiums, and chat with delegates at the bar, pick up useful bits of information, and spot specialists who could be approached with an offer or encouraged to apply for a job."

Keen recruitment or headhunt?

Genuine, legitimate advertisements for staff appear in the papers. The promise that applications will be "treated in the strictest confidence" may give a clue—particularly if the job is in a field where there are only a few competitors—that the firm is most interested in their competitors' already well-trained personnel, perhaps a knowledgeable, ambitious, and dissatisfied second-in-command.

Wanted: "Electronics Engineer, aged 28–35, with selling experience in electronics, preferably communications. Overseas experience and fluency in one or more foreign languages."

Wanted: "Deputy sales director with at least five years executive experience in selling [name of goods] to hospitals and nursing homes. . . ."

Wanted: "Director of Data-Processing Services—Europe

—circa £8,000 p.a." To get this top-level appointment, it is necessary to have "administrative experience in the European environment. . . . A minimum of eight-years close association with computerized systems and an outstanding degree of achievement in the management of a large data-processing organization are essential." Nothing will be disclosed to the client of the advertiser, a management consultant, without prior permission.

Keen recruitment or headhunt?

The methods of the search for staff may help to answer the question. In the Triad case, these revealed blatant headhunting techniques. The same is true about the approach used by an American executive placement consultant who would encourage or actively help a "target" to incur serious debts and then make an irresistible offer on behalf of his client. (The FBI, I understand, has been building up and dropping cases against him for several years because it is usually impossible to prove the connection between the mounting debts and the godsent opportunity to repay them.)

What is expected from a new employee? This is what most executives regard as the $64-question, but even the most straightforward and honest answer will not spell out the difference we seek. For although practically all companies obstinately cling to the belief that staff loyalty is their best defense against industrial espionage, they feel perfectly entitled to the full benefit of all the knowledge, ability, and special experience of a new man, who will indeed be willing to give them everything including his current loyalty.

"You can't help it," said Barry Goodenow, the ex-FBI agent in Hawaii. "When a top-management man moved from General Motors to Ford, the Thunderbird suddenly came out looking very much like a Pontiac, at least in several of its features. Yet this was not a question of industrial espionage or deliberate headhunting with the purpose of stealing ideas. It's simply the case of a man being offered a better or more suitable position or conditions more to his liking. He brings, of course, his own design ideas with him. He can't change his way of thinking, can he?"

With this argument, one could perhaps reduce the problem to "a matter of intention"—an often intangible, immeasurable, and unprovable legal commodity. Why was a man hired? Obviously to enhance his employer's business efforts. So when such a conflict comes to a court battle, the judges have an unenviable task and may have to fall back on examining methods and likely damages.

Headhunting may be found to be illegal, even without any intention of espionage. Ronald Getty, son of oil millionaire Paul Getty, "improperly enticed employees and agents" of Labo-Industrie, a French firm. Sued and convicted in a Paris court, he was given two suspended sentences of three months each and a £230 fine. In a cross-action at the same time, his firm—Veedol-France—sued M. Vacher, president of Labo-Industrie, for enticing his employees. This, too, resulted in a conviction: M. Vacher got a suspended sentence of thirteen months.

Ultimately the intentions of espionage and unethical headhunting are too difficult to prove in most cases. The majority of court actions on record deal only with the protection of a firm and its secrets from employees who go to work for competitors or become competitors themselves by starting their own businesses. Even in this respect it is hard to get legal protection because of the variations in circumstances.

In America, "legal remedies are available to fight employee pirating," said Harvey C. Smith in a lecture on competitive intelligence at the Twelfth Annual Marketing Conference of the National Industrial Conference Board. Principles "have been established in our law courts" that ". . . in hiring an employee from a competitor, absence of wrongful intent is not enough. The hiring company has an obligation to prevent use or disclosure by the employee of the secrets of his former employer."

A Union Carbide employee used the company secrets to start his own firm manufacturing "synthetic star sapphires." His former employer sued him successfully. Colgate-Palmolive hired a chemist from Carter Products. Carter obtained a ruling against the chemist using his knowledge about the Carter process of making pressurized shaving soap. In most such cases, court action followed after estimable damage had already been inflicted by a former employee and a competitor. But a Du Pont case against a senior research assistant and the American Potash and Chemical Corporation set a precedent of preventive court injunction. When the scientist answered an advertisement to join the other company, Du Pont claimed that his knowledge of secrets was worth fifteen million dollars, and the judge granted them a temporary injunction against the man's taking his new job.

A British manufacturer of diamond phonograph needles failed to obtain temporary injunctions restraining the chairman's daughter, now a director of a new rival company, from using its "trade secrets." Although she and her husband used to work for her father, the judge ruled that enough had been published about the art of diamond stylus making to enable the couple to start their own business without the secrets obtained in their previous jobs. He also found that they were not obliged "to refrain from soliciting such customers of the plaintiff company as they can remember" because the market was very limited and it would be practically impossible to find alternative customers. (At the time of writing, a permanent injunction is still being sought.)

A fine point of the law was argued in *The Times* in August 1970: "Experience is to be distinguished from information";

an employee must be free to take advantage of the training he received and the general knowledge he obtained about his trade in his job; otherwise he would be reduced to slavery. Trade secrets, however, belong to the employers. "The performance of prodigious feats of memory, such as mentally listing customers' names for future reference is just as culpable as, though less easily detectable than, secreting a written list for future use."

Many firms now try to protect their secrets by signing complicated binding contracts with their executives and sometimes even other employees to restrain them from disclosing or using confidential company information after they changed jobs. Most of these contracts are hard to enforce because they may cripple an employee's work prospects altogether. This weakness is often countered by the inclusion of a mere "holdover" clause under which an executive agrees not to work for a competitor for a year or more after the expiration of his contract. By that time, his special knowledge may become too obsolete to make his services attractive to others.

Like governmental precautions against traditional military espionage, companies can achieve the comparatively highest level of security from headhunters by the introduction of the "must know principle"—no one should be told more about plans, policies, research targets, manufacturing-process secrets, and other confidential information than the absolute minimum he must know to perform his duties. Unfortunately this system is not always practicable. Spies frequently need no more than a detail, a launching date, or just one new additive to an old chemical compound—information that cannot be withheld from the headhunters' chief target area, the higher echelons of management and research.

On a national scale, all this could accumulate economically disastrous consequences. Britain, with her perennial crisis, frequently stop-go economy, tremendous brain power, inventive and original thinking, and truly open scientific spirit unmatched by industrial investment and marketing effort, has been the most painfully obvious example for two decades. In the early 1960's, systematic American headhunting reached such lamentable proportions that the expression "brain drain," now a standard part of international vocabulary, was coined, I believe, by Peter Fairley, then of the *London Evening Standard.*

Britain was not the only victim of the brain drain. There was an outcry in several European countires, including Germany which lost almost 10 percent of her young university-leaving élite to America each year. The Swiss Federal Institute of Technology likened the trend—the annual loss of a fifth of the young scientists and engineers—to the disastrous effect of the "blood drain" in the Middle Ages when Swiss youth left the country to serve abroad as mercenaries. In December 1967, when George Douglass of the American Careers Inc. went to Paris to recruit more young Frenchmen, *Le Monde* dubbed him Mr. Brain Drain and warned that the prospects he offered could be gleaming for individuals but gloomy for the country.

Although the scientific migration list was topped by Swiss, Norwegian, and Dutch brains, Britain was perhaps the hardest hit because her research expenditure amounted to a much greater part of the gross national product than that of any other European country, and because heavy concentration on two promising fields, aviation and nuclear power, created a happy international headhunting ground. Several staff consultants found it sufficiently profitable to specialize on courting, seducing, and engaging for competitors anybody who had made the slightest contribution to the success of British aerospace research and technology, including feats like the discovery of the jet engine. This keen recruitment campaign continued until the very last moments of the American aviation boom.

The specialists, who were attracted only by the cash and promotion prospects, never thought about betraying anybody, least of all their own country. But it was inevitable that they should take with them many secrets that were, in fact, a national asset. This was particularly true of those who worked on new, better, and cheaper ways of nuclear-power production in which Britain was a world leader. In the first two stages of development, this undisputed success remained almost totally unexploited, with only two contracts to build nuclear power stations abroad, one for Italy and one for Japan. Excuses, or rather explanations, were easy to find. Anthony Wedgwood Benn, as Minister of Technology, recognized that the scientific value of the results had overshadowed the practical significance for too long, perhaps because research was seen as a kind of morale-boosting substitute for Britain's lost empire.

By then, however, the opportunity for the first nuclear empire was also being lost. The Americans were late starters in this field, but when they moved, they went ahead with admirable determination and speed. The two giants, General Electric and Westinghouse, were ready to spend liberally, to start production on a big scale, and to market even at an initial loss. The shortcut to experience was, of course, headhunting.

Research on a prototype "fast breeder" reactor at Dounreay, in Scotland, was already proving the viability of yet another new system, the foundation of a second potential nuclear empire for Britain. Because it was "damn fast and breeding like a rabbit," and because it created energy while virtually reproducing itself, ending each cycle with more fuel left in it than at the start, it was once described to me as the only perfect substitute for the "best business principle" of a

Jewish joke about prostitution: You have it . . . you sell it
. . . and you still have it.

Headhunting therefore became so vigorous that a *Daily
Telegraph* leader concluded: "There are elements of industrial espionage certainly in Westinghouse's advances and
inevitably Dounreay scientists would take with them some
know-how of much general value."

Since then, as Anthony Sampson so gently put it in his
book *The New Europeans*, the American corporations "are
now pushing ahead with fast-breeder reactors—with some
help from the British brain drain." They have sold licenses to
several countries, including Germany and Italy, and exported
or licensed almost two dozen reactors outside the United
States.

Today all is not yet lost for the financial success of the
British effort. For the first time, nationwide plans are drawn
up for worldwide sales. The Dounreay project is still keeping
the lead—just. The Russians are already running neck and
neck with them; the Americans have cut the lag to a couple
of years at most; Japanese and German research are catching
up fast, and France, about to overtake Dounreay, plans to
build the first commercial test reactor in 1975, at least a year
ahead of the others. Apart from yet another great opportunity, Britain now stands to lose far more in cash stakes than
ever before: disregarding the value of potential sales, the
actual investment is already well in excess of a thousand
million pounds.

On the brink of a new nuclear energy era, however, there
is a new menace from headhunters. There has been a recess
in American recruitment—and in the aviation industry,
British firms have made some feeble efforts to reverse the
brain drain and regain the lost manpower—but several
European staff consultants are busily lining up Common
Market clients for British brains and secrets.

The free movement of labor within the Common Market is supposed to result in two-way traffic. But in practice, the result is a natural flow of workers from areas of unemployment and lower pay toward the comparative Canaans. There is no reason to believe that it will be different with scientists, engineers, and business executives. Landau in Brussels, two private detectives in Germany, and now inquiry agents in London have told me that they already do "preliminary searches" for European staff consultants who hope to start an eastward brain drain from Britain.

What brings this plan into the realm of an actual menace is the fact that the preliminary conditions that were essential for the brain drain of the 1960's, still exist in Britain. Intellect has remained a socially undervalued commodity. The report of the Royal Society, issued in 1963, has retained its validity in talking about scientific "backroom boys" who feel they are "on tap but not on top" and lack encouraging prospects. The abundance of skill and capacity for original research is continuous—and continues to be underpaid.

And now the brightest British executives and industrial managers will also become sitting targets for the headhunters. That their average actual take-home pay lags well behind that of their counterparts in Germany, France, and some other European countries, as well as America, Australia, and South Africa, can be explained away to some extent by the differences in living costs and fringe benefits, such as company cars. But a recent *Survey of Executive Salaries*, carried out by the Inbucon-AIC Management Consultants, has revealed (at twenty-five pounds a copy) that British managers are becoming comparatively poorer and poorer because their salary increases just about keep pace with the cost of living and their meager bonuses are slowly eroded, while they enjoy far fewer and shorter holidays than people on the Continent. After living costs, rising everywhere, were taken into account, it was found that in 1971, for instance, the average executive's net gain was 13.4 percent in France, 9.2 percent in Germany, 1.8 percent in Ireland, and 0.5 percent in Britain.

If and when the new cross-Channel migration begins, nonmalicious betrayal of valuable secrets and a great loss of national assets will be the order of the day. Loyalty? Loyalty to country and company as a basis of security? Remember Mr. "Brain Drain" Douglass: "Young scientists and engineers"—and, one may add, executives—"are no longer faithful to their employers, but to their profession." Which is one way to put it.

5

"Prince Philip Tipped Me Off"

THIS RATHER STARTLING STATEMENT came from Landau who repeated it at least three times in the course of our meetings. On each occasion, he gargled with the words like a sleepy child in his evening prayer—he could rattle it off at high speed with ease, but found it difficult to slow down and dictate it to me. Whenever I stopped him, he had to start again from the beginning.

"Our physical resources have dwindled, but the intellectual capacity of our scientists and engineers is as great as ever, and it is upon their ingenuity that our future prosperity largely depends."

Landau, who seemed to go through tongue-breaking agony each time he had to say "ingenuity," claimed if Britain could depend on this, so could he: "It was a real eye-opener when the Prince told me that, because it showed up one of the best targets—Britain."

"You mean *he* actually told *you?*"

"You know what I mean. He didn't come to tell me, but when I heard the words, it was as good as a royal audience."

Out of curiosity I checked the quote and found it to be correct. It was taken from a presidential address to the

British Association in Edinburgh. Ignoring Landau's personalized interpretation, does this straightforward, patriotic statement make the Duke of Edinburgh an unwitting scout for industrial spies? In a way, yes. Pinpointing targets is the first stage and so an essential part of any business intelligence operation. It is, therefore, inevitable that any publication or authoritative statement will be duly noted and catalogued by everybody interested in a particular field. Most of this work is, of course, perfectly legitimate by any standard.

Prime targets are usually listed under two headings: *subjects*, which are vitally interesting to intelligence agents in any trade; and *trades*, which are probably most exposed to espionage by the demands of truly cutthroat competition.

The basic *subjects* were once named by Peter Hamilton, author of a book on espionage and subversion in industry, as information on research and new sources of materials, merger plans, marketing intentions, and details of tenders. Probably one ought to add several others, like advertising campaign plans, policy for prices and expansion, take-over maneuvers, general financial status and the likelihood of new investment, management structure, changes in staff, wage negotiations, staff morale, company efficiency, internal problems causing, for instance, delays in delivery, government contacts, orders, export contracts, product specifications, just to mention the most obvious subjects. From these, the range moves toward more specific areas for the more refined uses of intelligence, like the collection of any relevant data that will help a firm to measure its own efficiency, costs, production, progress, etc., in the mirror of a competitor's achievements.

Another example is the balancing act between research and marketing, the determination of the right moment for a multimillion gamble on a new discovery. Carbon fibers and battery-driven electric cars are typical of such problems.

The company that invests fast on a vast scale and begins

mass production of, say, supersonic airliners before the competitors wake up will have the market to itself and will establish a strong perhaps even unassailable position. But if, in the meantime, other companies continue research and find cheaper production methods and better designs for lower operating costs and the protection of the environment, those who have delayed their move can now invest in a wiser way resulting in increased competitiveness that the firm first on the market cannot match without a complete alteration of its production plants. Therefore it is not only a duty but a question of survival for each management to know how far their competitors have progressed in research and final decision-making, and recognize the exact market conditions.

François Levine, a French "business consultant" summarized it: "Everything that is relevant data for management decision in a given situation must be on the intelligence target list." Richard Green's book quotes a definition by Litton Industries Data Systems Division which warned its staff that competitors would be most interested in the secrets of the Four P's—Plans, Performance, Prices, and Problems. (Roy Ash, Litton's president, a strong supporter of this view, was appointed by President Nixon as the Cabinet-level director of the Office of Management and Budget.)

When one moves beyond this general Four-P rule and the main subjects, the potential target list for an individual company becomes practically endless. I once saw the business intelligence records of a major, internationally well-known corporation in the engineering industry. The files were catalogued under almost four hundred headings. Each of these was divided into a libraryful of index titles which, in turn, led to further subdivisions of thousands of entries. Needless to say, every big and small competitor, supplier, potential purchaser, had a file down to details of research, staff, policy past and present, and so on. Such a mammoth intelligence department may be required to know everything and have all details on tap at any moment, although the mass of data will sometimes swamp and obscure the most relevant vital item. An independent professional spy outfit, on the other hand, cannot afford to maintain huge information libraries because most of this material is freely available to anyone and so unsellable through the black market of secrets.

An attempt to list the *trades* that provide the most lucrative targets has caused fervent arguments with several spies and security men in the course of my research. Ultimately, most of them seemed to agree with Hal Lipset who thought that the "top of the espionage pops must be any information that can affect the stock market, oil, any trade in the race for government contracts and politics"—the latter meaning politics as a trade. Others, judging from practical experience, will add the trades in which they handled cases of espionage. By a consensus of opinion, pharmaceuticals, chemicals, and trades relying on a constant flow of novelties, such as cosmetics and household goods, emerged as other major targets.

Retailing is a relatively new field for business intelligence operators. It all starts on a very meager scale.

If there is only one general store in a small village, the owner needs very little marketing information to conduct his business successfully. Occasionally he may visit other stores in the neighborhood for a bit of comparative shopping, but news about trends, prices, fresh ideas will be brought to him by salesmen. Apart from that, he will find out from friends and customers what the villagers need—and what they are likely to pay for it.

If a second store is opened in the village, the questions begin to breed fast like nuclear reactors. What are the prices in the other store? What is the quality of its goods? Where does it get the supplies so promptly, cheaply, and in such variety? What sort of novelty goods will it introduce? When will there be a sale? What special offers will be made? How will they be advertised? With the growing need for "competitive intelligence," the need of secrecy also increases—and the vital answers to the grocer's questions come at a premium. He cannot walk into the other store without exposing his keen interest, so he sends, say, a schoolgirl for comparison shopping. He pays her a couple of apples for the day's price list—and the trade in secrets has begun.

Unfortunately the girl will not be able to answer all his questions. At first, usually, it is a local third-rate private eye who gets the business. Later, depending on the size of the competing shops or chains, the true professionals are brought in. It is amazing how far even the smallest outfits will go in sheer desperation.

Vincent Carratu's security organization handled such a case of mini-espionage near Liverpool. A lively, jolly connoisseur of food and inside information, Carratu told me, tunneling into a mountain of venison:

"A man came to me asking that I should watch his wife. I said I preferred to watch my own wife and suggested another firm which specialized in matrimonial cases. They would keep his wife under surveillance, I assured him. But then he said that it was a case of espionage involving his wife. That was nearer my line, so I agreed to go and see him in the office at his factory.

"I was in for a shock," he said, finishing the venison in what seemed to be a single mouthful. "The factory was an old shack, and the office just a corner of it. The client invented a—let's call it a gadget, which was useful to some sectors of the transportation industry. He manufactured it himself with the help of his only colleague—the wife.

"He advertised the stuff in the trade papers, got some inquiries in response every day, and used a few moonlighting sales representatives to follow up the inquiries and visit customers in the evenings or in their spare time next day. The routine was that the reps would phone him every day between four and four thirty, and he would give them the list of addresses.

"All went well until the reps began to find that when they called at various firms and private homes, somebody had already made rival sales late afternoon or early in the morning. The rival firm, selling a similar though inferior gadget, obviously spent the money on full-time salesmen and cashed in on my client's advertising. But how did they pinch the addresses? Did the wife sell them?

"I then talked to his wife, but she seemed just as shocked as her husband. I didn't believe she could be such a good actress. I said I'd make some investigation, but my client insisted that if it was not his wife it must be a bug in his 'premises.' Some premises. I sort of laughed off the suggestion. It was a most unlikely place for a bug or anything sophisticated like that. He almost accused me of not knowing my trade. So I made an electronic sweep as a matter of routine. Clients sort of expect you to do things like that; otherwise they don't quite believe you're serious.

"To my astonishment, I found a bug in the single telephone in the office. It was a rough, most probably do-it-yourself job with a very limited range, but it worked. That afternoon we observed a girl sitting in her car outside the office for about an hour. Apart from her car radio, she had a fairly good VHF receiver, and she was taking notes whenever we had a phone call from a rep.

"I tracked her to a firm that manufactured the other gadget. My client didn't want to sue. So we went to his rivals and confronted them with evidence of sales, addresses, photographs of the girl, and the bug itself. They denied everything—but the client's sales reps had no more trouble.

"It was a pity. I mean that the client wanted to get it over with fast. At least we could have played a lovely game of feeding them with false information, and causing damage, for weeks."

Carratu conducted his investigation on a level that was both understandable and useful to the client. This, however, is not always the case. Honest market intelligence organizations often go in for the pompous euphemisms and pretentious style of professionalism by which their crooked colleagues try to achieve respectability. Barnett Sussman, a marketing consultant, recounts a story° about the manager of a small retail store who felt that local changes in population might seriously affect demands, taste, and purchasing power in the area. He desperately needed market intelligence. This is just one paragraph of the report he received:

". . . The stratified sample means indicated small enough variance to assure between-item reliability for question 7. Thus the null hypothesis holds that no significant change will take place, this statement at the .01 level of confidence."

All the poor manager needed now was the services of a decipherer who soon informed him for a large fee that no major change was to be expected.

What's Cricket?

Time and again, British executives told me that business intelligence—let alone, espionage—was not cricket. They refused therefore to consider that anybody else would resort to such despicable tactics even if the majority of the world's population never heard or cared about the game and its

° *Business Intelligence*, op. cit.

spirit. This, of course, very much strengthens the hand of those most ungentlemanly "base fellows" who are ready not only to open but also to read other gentlemen's letters. Similarly dangerous fact-blindness—or the pretense of it?—also persists in many other countries. In the haughty atmosphere where intelligence work of any kind is summarily condemned, the result is that even the most ethical and unquestionably legitimate economics intelligence operators become ashamed of their profession and begin to call their departments "information units" and "data centers."

It is, however, beyond dispute that the overwhelming majority of the best intelligence material is gathered in a perfectly respectable manner. Good military espionage is also based on this simple truth. When DST, the counterespionage agency of France, published some guidance for people in industry, warning them against careless talk, boasting to strangers, and other basic occupational hazards, it estimated that Communist agents—and some competitors from friendly, Western countries—collected nine tenths of their useful data from public libraries, trade publications, lectures, trade fairs, and other freely accessible sources.

The wartime history of espionage offers an abundance of examples. An American intelligence officer, now in foreign market research, revealed that Italian provincial newspapers helped more to prepare the Anzio Beachhead than all the parachuting agents and radio stations of the resistance and prisoner interrogation.

In Russia, a transmitter was located during the war in the home of a cripple who received no visitors and never left his bedroom. It soon emerged that the man acted only as "post office." He received daily radio messages from Moscow, but he had no idea of the sender's identity. Russian security men forced him to continue his activities, and eventually, this led them to a Japanese spy in the capital.

Surveillance of the spy began in order to discover his contacts and sources. It went on for three months without any result. The man had no meetings, no friends, received nothing relevant in the mail or on the telephone. Like the cripple to whom he sent his excellent information, he hardly ever left his home, spent most of his time reading, and generally infuriated the people who watched him with his lack of activities.

Finally, to stem the steady stream of espionage, they had to arrest him. Under interrogation he admitted everything but claimed that all his information had come from legitimate sources. He saved his neck by volunteering to demonstrate his method—in jail.

He asked for all the newspapers, technical journals, and statistical publications. Although the Russians were always extremely cautious and security-conscious about printed matter—newspapers, for instance, published only partial figures showing production increases in percentages—the agent proved that meticulous bookkeeping defeated the system. He noted, for example, that *Pravda* reported a 15 percent increase in steel output above the current plan at a Siberian plant. Three months later, *Izvestia* praised the workers of that plant for sending so many tons of plan-surplus steel to the ever-hungry armaments industry. With that, even his dumbfounded jailers could calculate the volume of production.

Today the constantly increasing free flow of data from well-known, reliable sources, with much of the published material already indexed, tends to become as much a facility for as a cause of exasperation to the intelligence officer.

A second category of information is also freely available but in an unorganized and unclassified fashion—like money in the street, all you have to do is to bend down for it, but you must know where to find it. The enormous, highly professional business intelligence units, like those in the car or aviation industry, know immediately where to look for such items. But companies without the benefit of specialist advice may be baffled by relatively simple questions.

For several years, the Coca-Cola company steadfastly refused to divulge its annual sales volume. For several years, various firms yearned to discover these precious figures. Yet throughout these years, it was all on record, open to all who cared to look it up in the files of the Securities and Exchange Commission where a vast collection of important, confidential data—required by law from all major companies—are kept for the protection of the American public and the stockholder. I once had the dubious pleasure of meeting a California-based private detective who prided himself on receiving "plenty of industrial espionage assignments." This I took with some reservations, but I could well believe him that in eighteen months he had sold this open secret about Coca-Cola to four different clients for prices ranging from two hundred to two thousand dollars.

The third, still more or less freely available group of information is the beginning of the intelligence twilight zone because it contains items that are not meant to be given away. Open ears and open eyes and a strong head for liquor are the attributes of successful operators in this field.

A standard form of inadvertent revelations is the *advertisement of vacancies*. It frequently tells tales about company weaknesses, new plans, and expansion. A series of replacements in, say, marketing jobs may show an intention to start new vigorous campaigns. The firm that wishes to appoint its first Norwegian-speaking engineer, needs to say no more about the direction of its next export offensive.

Sometimes the advertisements amount to an invitation to spies and the somewhat ruthless competitor. Only an applicant with no intention of getting the job was needed to get the full details when "a Unilever company and leaders in the field of edible fat technology" advertised its wish to extend its "interest in other sectors of the food industry." It sought an additional development manager for new products and promised a "highly competitive" salary. It was perfectly feasible that this particular company had already announced all its plans for products, but if they were still retaining any secrets in this respect, they were now publishing a clear target definition for all interested parties.

Executive placement agencies hide their patrons behind a thin veil of secrecy, but competitors often find this even more exciting than full frontal client nudity. I guess it would not have been an impossible task to discover which was the "international pharmaceutical group . . . making a major breakthrough into markets in European and Latin American countries" that wished to appoint a top marketing man via ISL Management Consultants; or to identify the "multimillion consumer goods company with factories and markets already established in many countries" which was "seeking to develop its business in the Middle East" and so, understandably, needed a young export man with fluent Arabic.

Job advertisements cannot be avoided, but perhaps it would pay many corporations to remember that the regular reader can also read between the lines—with the aid of a decent filing system.

Gossip, a not particularly reliable yet most useful commodity of the stealth trade, also belongs to this category. Sales representatives and others who frequently meet employees of competitors are taught more and more systematically to pick up incidental information from colleagues. Yet excessive training and devotion to duty may backfire, as for example, in the following allegedly true story that is spreading fast in business circles; I have heard at least three versions of it.

An American junior sales executive, fresh from a business

intelligence course, played golf with the vice-president of a competitor.

"Have you heard what happened to our research director?" asked the vice-president as they were approaching the third hole.

The younger man pricked up his ears. "No. Can you tell me?" He sensed that information was coming his way.

"Last night he was arrested. He beat his wife to death with a nine-iron."

With only his first intelligence report in mind, driven by the newly acquired "attention to detail," the junior executive blurted out the now famous question: "How many strokes did it take?"

The danger in gossip is that the information may have been deliberately planted to mislead. Unguarded remarks and boozy party chitchat "overheard accidentally" are far more reliable. An Australian operator pays a regular retainer to four or five airline stewardesses and stewards who serve first-class passengers. "It's a long haul to Sydney; drinks are poured generously; people talk freely—they bring back something useful every week," he told me.

The classic example of careless conversation with grave consequences occurred in the American motor industry. The financial damage was inestimable but might have amounted to several million dollars.

It began at a routine cocktail party in Detroit. Many people from the automobile industry were invited, and all tried desperately to avoid talking shop. It was a futile attempt. Somebody mentioned the man who was, at the time, Ford's favorite photographer. A Chrysler executive overheard a snippet of conversation. The photographer was said to be in Paris. The month was June; he might be on holiday. In June when the following year's advertising campaigns were usually prepared? It was unlikely. So what were he and Ford up to?

A telex sent the Parisian Chrysler man into action, and his report confirmed the assumption. Yes, the new Fords were being photographed at the foot of the Eiffel Tower, and Hong Kong was to be the next port of call for the photographer and the new models. Ford's advertising had obviously chosen an international theme.

Quoting from the journal of *Sales Management*, Harvey Smith said: "That year Chrysler quickly countered with an ad campaign featuring its products at landmarks throughout America—a campaign that the firm felt would take the edge off the Ford theme since most car buyers could more easily identify themselves with the George Washington Bridge than with the Hongkong Hilton."

With this we are leaving the twilight zone of legitimate intelligence and entering the gray, unmapped areas where the borders of truly noncricket industrial espionage are still indefinite with no Checkpoint Charlie to warn the traveler that from here on he will become if not an outright spy, at least an adventurer. For the grocer on an innocent comparative shopping expedition visits the competitor's premises under false pretenses. And when an executive buys a few shares of stock in each of the competitor companies, using perhaps funds specially provided by his employer, in order to receive interim reports issued only to stockholders, he obtains confidential information in an impeccable manner for a not so respectable purpose. One can just notice a touch of gray in their lily-white intentions. Cases in the "gray zone" are open to interpretation.

"Nobody has ever asked us to do industrial espionage and we'd turn it down without hesitation, but commercial investigations are perfectly straightforward, and these we take," said Londoner Colin Finlay, head of the respectable FBI (Finlay's Bureau of Investigation), as we sat in his office and crackling reports from his men kept coming in on the direct-link car radios.

"Before a merger or take-over, information is vital," he explained. "We also check staff, but only some Americans want their political views as a specific item in the reports.

"There was a big U.S. soft drinks corporation that wanted to start up here but found that a London company was already marketing a soft drink under a similar name. They wanted to know more about it. We found the company in the West End. It had less than a dozen staff and a not very flourishing business. Two directors appeared to be financially embarrassed. An ideal setup for negotiations, but I don't know what has come of it.

"In another case, a South African company wanted to market wine here in a very unusually shaped bottle. They were warned that Henkel, a German firm in Wiesbaden, was already selling a sparkling wine here in a practically identical bottle. The question was, Had the Germans any copyright?

"There was nothing on paper. So I went to Wiesbaden and said I'd probably want to import a lot of their sparkling wine. Potential customers are always well received, and while we talked, I mentioned it was odd that nobody else used such bottles. 'But they do,' they told me, 'a French champagne is sold in an identical bottle.' That answered all our problems. My clients were free to use the bottle of their choice."

Some people may have reservations about it, but most business executives would probably agree with Colin Finlay that yes, these were straightforward commercial investigations. So was the one Irving Shumbord of New York had to conduct.

"Surveillance is expensive but that was my brief," he told me in his office suite on West Forty-third Street. "Watch two men and report everything they did, where they went, whom they met, and if possible, everything they talked about."

"What did you do?"

"We watched them. We even knew what the message was they received from the hotel receptionist."

"How did you find out?"

"They got the note, read the message, tore it up, and threw it in the wastepaper basket. My man picked up the pieces and put them together."

At a trade conference, the two men spoke to dozens of people. Shumbord listed them all—complete with description, names, and probable nationality. How? "The names we got from the lapel badges. Very convenient."

He also noted fragments of conversations. These became the subject of a brief exchange with the judge when the case went to court and the detective made a deposition as a witness. The judge asked if the investigators tried to overhear what the two men talked about:

ANSWER. "That is elementary. That is the standard practice, if it is at all possible."

QUESTION. "You try and overhear?"

ANSWER. "Yes. If you care to use the term eavesdropping, yes, sir."

Would techniques like these turn legitimate intelligence work into industrial espionage? The answer is disputable.

The Name of the Game

"Industrial espionage" is an unfortunate, vaguely generalized term that we all tend to use for want of a better one. It is supposed to differentiate between unseemly, underhand, and undoubtedly criminal methods and activities and the more ethical, acceptable, and presumably, more legitimate "intelligence."

The problem of ethics was summarized with commendable frankness by Peter Heims, editor of *The Investigator*, in the August 1972 issue of the journal: "No clear definition [of *industrial espionage*] can be made by the Association of British Investigators and each member must use his own conscience to decide."

The same is true of businessmen—and what can be more ambiguous than DIY ethics? Hans Niemann, a very experienced, Munich-based investigator commented when we met at an international conference in Brighton: "Financial interest is the most effective reducer of moral standards. The higher the stakes, the lower the ethics of industrial gambling."

So how far would ethics let businessmen and industrialists go? I asked this question of more than 120 people including professional spies, security men, and executives in various industries.

As far as funds allow them—this was the answer of the majority.

That view was shared by Barry Goodenow when we talked about some of the best-known American corporations: "And as far as money lets them go is pretty far," he told me. "A hundred thousand dollars a year is pin money to some of the guys who work for them.

"I know, for instance, the security chief of a company in the aviation business. [He named the firm.] He must have at present a slush fund, I mean a secret budget, of about a hundred grand a year. It's all covered up in some ordinary contract somewhere along the line for accounting purposes, and perhaps not even the corporation president knows exactly which item is the one. Top brass don't like to know these details. It's safer and more ethical not to know.

"But the slush money at the disposal of this particular guy is probably only for the day-to-day operations, to keep an eye on movement of key personnel and competitors' general activities, and to pay agents, regular retainers, and casual informers. When they prepare a big bid, particularly for an Uncle Sam contract, he gets special funds because success may be worth the difference between loss and profit, even survival of the company.

"Specifications for a new military aircraft are the same for all. Speed, landing speed and distance, fuel and armament capacity and the rest are given. That's the basis of the designs. So apart from some technical differences, the bidding is all about price—cutting profit margins and the various cost factors. They simply must know what the opposition is doing."

Several other people, like Vincent Carratu, are convinced that the availability of such secret slush money has become an international device, widely used in Sweden, France, Britain, Germany, and Italy, although understandably, its existence is everywhere vehemently denied.

Slush funds have an undeniable ethical significance, too, because they cannot be created and maintained without the approval of very senior executives—a fact that demolishes the usual excuses of not being informed about all the activities in their firms. Gentlemen don't read other gentlemen's letters? It is rather that they do not like to be seen doing it.

It is true that the old-boy network *within* a given country often defeats the spy, but internationally, the alliance is nonexistent, and it is not without precedent that a director will alert a victim of espionage *after* he has had a good look at the information offered for sale.

In order to protect the shine of their ethical armor, five-star generals of industry often disclaim responsibility for other ranks and indulge in sneering remarks about the low moral fiber of the younger management generation. They are supported by opinion polls and other studies, which have proved that younger executives are less averse to dubious methods of intelligence and outright espionage than their elders. This may be true in the sense that when an ambitious younger man is given an important task, he will leave no stone unturned to please and impress his superiors, and in fact, professional agents and private investigators claim that many assignments come to them from middle management—backed by company funds, of course.

Slush funds and direct financing of espionage apart, management must know the source and reliability of information. Intelligence is useful, sometimes vital, in decision making. The decision cannot be valid if it is based on data of doubtful accuracy. So when it is alleged that top men do not care about the "technicalities" of information gathering, it only means that they have delegated responsibility for the work to individual employees, a service department or an outside organization who, they know, can be trusted to come up with the goods one way or the other.

The manager who then receives from a reliable source some really valuable intelligence—meaning usually the unexpected in essence or details—must surely be credited with at least enough shrewdness and experience to have an inkling that information of such significance hardly ever arrives unsolicited in his mailbag. Or else he should not be a manager.

The recognition of this truth and the constant striving after face-saving formulas have created what a Hamburg director called "the unwritten German business code of ethical ostentations or ostentatious ethics."

Hans Niemann explained: "German companies like to do their own dirty work if possible because they know only too well that very, very, very few investigators who do espionage work can be trusted. Many detectives are not truly professionals in any sense; they do not observe any codes of professional conduct, may misuse information even for blackmailing or double-crossing the client by the sale of secrets to a third party. Besides, German executives don't like to appear unethical in front of others—especially those they cannot trust.

"This perhaps isn't only a German peculiarity. But one system certainly is. If our companies must turn to outsiders for help in getting confidential information for them, they insert a third party between themselves and the espionage agent. Because if the information goes first to a market-research firm or a lawyer, they can still despise spying and claim that in Germany it's not the done thing."

"Lawyers as a buffer are particularly useful to both sides—clients and investigators," added Manfred Kocks, head of Duisburg's Detektiv-Institut Kocks, which has several branches in the Ruhr area. "Take the case when a company asked me to investigate the affairs of a rival firm. I was told that the research, production, and sales managers had left their employer, my client, and started up together as competitors. The question was, What internal information had they taken to and utilized in their new business?

"My assistant who worked on it, had to find out the firm's turnover and all sorts of details about its production and marketing techniques. I felt it wasn't for me to decide whether the findings amounted to industrial espionage or my client's rightful defense. So I chose the only solution open to a decent investigator: I gave all our findings to a lawyer who was acceptable to my client and who could decide what would be right and legal to pass on to my client."

Unfortunately, such buck-passing exercises are no panacea because ethical codes and the law give us equally vague and feeble guidance in deciding what, in fact, should be regarded as industrial espionage.

For my research and the classification of cases I have come across, and for the work on this book, I have formed the following definition:

Industrial espionage is the search for and acquisition of confidential information about anybody's trade by lawful or unlawful means for the purpose of furthering or hindering a business enterprise.

The only exceptions would be genuine self-defense as in some justifiable homicide cases, and in service of the public interest like press inquiries and publication of rightful exposures.

Undoubtedly one could pick holes in this definition, too. What should be regarded confidential? Would the act of breaking somebody's confidence—a civil offense—become a crime if it was done for one of the above purposes? How far could one go in genuine self-defense? What are the situations when "lawful means" of obtaining confidential information become criminal because of the use this knowledge is put to?

It is immaterial whether this definition is foolproof or not. What matters is that industrial espionage must soon become a crime recognizable by any one of or by a combination of its methods and aims. For as long as we have no comforting Queensberry rules and no one is equipped with clearly marked belts below which one is not supposed to hit, we shall have to continue shadow-boxing, and each intelligence operator and security specialist will be free to write his own book of rules. Unfortunately the courts cannot do the same.

The Rule of the Game

Two private detectives were brought before an English court in 1971. The judge made some scathing remarks about the spying done by the defendants, and condemned industrial espionage as a crime. The papers reported that the two had been found guilty of industrial espionage. Technically, of course, the judge was wrong. Industrial espionage is not a crime. The men were, in fact, guilty of "conspiracy to obtain confidential information by corrupt and other unlawful means and offering a bribe."

It was not without a trace of despair that Peter Heims commented: "It just so happened that these offenses were committed during an act which could possibly be called industrial espionage. Needless to say, the sentence had to be commensurate with only the actual crime."

When the prosecution wants to bring *criminal* charges against a successful industrial spy who might have inflicted damages worth perhaps millions of dollars (subject only to *civil* action), lawyers have to pull various other, relatively minor offences out of the hat, and the spy is usually let off lightly with a sentence for trespass, break and entry, theft of a sheet of photostat copy paper, bribery and corruption, or conspiracy to commit an unlawful act.

Most of the laws that can be made relevant to cover some aspects of industrial espionage are much too old to bite. Their creators did not and could not foresee, let alone cater to, our current age of technology, the weapons at the disposal of the spy, and the accumulated values of modern trade secrets. The British Corruption Act of 1906, for instance, carries a maximum penalty of a £500 fine and/or two years in jail.

When bribing a single employee may put a firm out of business, destroy several hundred jobs, and cause considerable losses to a nation, this is clearly no deterrent.

The theft of a rickety boardroom table is punished more severely than that of all the invaluable boardroom secrets. Britain's revised Theft Act of 1968 referred to "intangible property" for the first time and that seemed to promise some protection for confidential information. It was doomed to remain a promise. It would be a waste of time even to put it to the test. Unlike thieves, according to the definition of the Act, industrial spies are never guilty of dishonest appropriation of property "with the intention of permanently depriving" the victim of it. Even if they steal a secret formula, it is unlikely that the owner would have no more than one copy in his possession—so he is not deprived of his secrets. To cause the loss of exclusiveness and future potential benefits of knowledge may be vastly damaging but still not criminal.

With that we are back to intrinsic values which—like the knowledge of an enticed scientist—are almost inestimable and unprotected. This anomalous situation creates, in turn, the dozens of crazy cases on record.

When an employee of Gramos Chemicals tried to sell the company's secret chemical formulae to a rival and was caught, he was charged only with stealing a few sheets of paper worth twopence and was fined £30.

Another "spy" knew that there was keen competition in synthetic resins but misjudged his potential buyer. He stole a logbook of formulas from Revertex, his former employers, and offered it to Vinyl Products. He was arrested when he was caught red-handed with the documents. Charge: theft of folder containing log sheets worth a can of baked beans. Fine: £100.

A third British amateur was sent to prison for three months

for the theft of three-pounds worth of code cards and correspondence. In law it was only incidental that these papers happened to be bearers of research secrets invaluable to the paint industry. Similar cases can be found in practically every country. A security agent told me about one with a twist in Germany:

"Two private detectives stole some documents concerning the construction industry. By the time they were caught, they had already cashed in on their loot; a competitor had bought the information from them but not the original papers! So there was no question of receiving. The two detectives were brought to court and fined five hundred and eight hundred Deutsch-Marks respectively (then about $149 and $238) for theft.

"Later, of course, the victim started civil action for damages, and in the interest of all concerned, it was settled out of court. In cases like this, nobody wants publicity."

When there is no actual theft involved, and none of the usual laws can be applied to a legal salvage operation because there has been no trespass, break-in, corruption, and so on, in other words, when a truly professional and modern act of espionage has been perpetrated, the victims have no real and immediately effective legal remedy.

A classic operation in this category was devised and carried out by Kubik alias Asquare alias Blockley at an early stage of his career.

An American cigarette manufacturer heard about the imminence of a rival's new European advertising campaign handled by a French agency. The timing was unusual; there was no chance to balance its potential effect by preparing and mounting a countercampaign quickly enough, so Kubik was assigned to delay the competitors. He found it a strange assignment—more sabotage than industrial espionage because the client was not particularly interested in the rival's secrets. But Kubik remained true to himself. His scheme bore the hallmark of his style.

He first revived his contact with the lonely, middle-aged secretary of the managing director of the French advertising agency. After a few lavish outings, for old times' sake, she was willing to help him. Yes, she would have access to the plans and drawings; yes, she could photocopy the main theme—but in this peculiar case, that was not enough. Kubik wanted her employers to know that the campaign plans had been stolen, but he was anxious not to expose this woman, a much too valuable contact with future potential.

During their dinners, Kubik picked up some useful but at first meaningless background information about the agency. She told him who went to bed with whom among the staff, who were the main clients of the agency, why the chief designer was negotiating a new job and with which firm, what chronic space problems the agency had in the old building where the managing director's first-floor office had to be halved to make room for files, stationery, and even spare typewriters, where the agency wanted to move if accommodations were available, who was backstabbing whom, who in television was receiving kickbacks from the agency for the inclusion of "indirect" advertising in programs, and what an insatiable appetite the managing director had for internal company gossip which would often enable him to hold the rein tight.

Kubik made his plan which had to serve his client and, at the same time, had to make the job really pay. (As far as I know, his client was keen to delay the competitor but not keen enough to pay more than five thousand dollars plus expenses to Kubik who considered this peanuts even in those days.)

After long consultations with a then-crooked lawyer—who

is now back on his feet, running a well-known reputable practice in Montreal, Canada—Kubik telephoned the managing director and offered him information about his chief designer. He got an appointment for the following day. He then asked the secretary to arrange a coincidence: the key drawing of the advertising campaign, showing the main theme, would be deposited on the director's desk during his appointment.

He offered the director his news about the designer free of charge, but let himself be persuaded to accept what he called a princely sum, the equivalent of about a hundred dollars, as a reward. At that point, a messenger entered and placed a drawing on top of the director's IN tray.

When the messenger left, Kubik pulled a small camera out of his pocket and quite brazenly took a photograph of the new design. He truly enjoyed the argument that followed. He claimed that the camera was his; the film was his; and the agency could not claim copyright because the undeveloped picture was not even a reproduction.

The furious director threatened to take the camera from him by force and summoned help on the telephone. Kubik was not exactly a novice to a scuffle nor afraid of one, but he always preferred the smoothest possible solution: he opened the window and dropped the camera to an assistant waiting in the street below.

Before he could be thrown after the camera, he offered the film for sale for twenty thousand dollars. The director was ready to pay him a thousand. Kubik then kindly explained the position as he saw it. He conveniently forgot to mention his collaborator in the agency, for he knew that the discovery of her existence and their association were the only risks he ran because a charge of corruption and conspiracy could land him in jail. He admitted that the director could get a quick court injunction restraining him from selling, publishing, or even reproducing his photograph, and might even sue him on the shaky ground of breach of confidence, but first it would have to be proved that the picture existed at all. The delay and unwanted premature publicity might, of course, displease the agency's client. And what about the director's pride? Why couldn't he have prevented his visitor from taking the photograph?

Hard bargaining continued for a week. Kubik developed the film and sent a print to the agency. Finally the director was happy to get the film for a mere two thousand dollars. It was cheap only because Kubik conceded that in the meantime he might have sold copies to a competitor. Which of course he had—three times.

Kubik's client was satisfied. Because of the uncertainty, the competitors decided to make several changes in their plans and alter the central theme of the campaign—causing at this crucial stage a full four-week delay.

The agency director was satisfied. That "stupid informer" had failed to realize the value of the photograph and the potential damage to the reputation of the agency.

Kubik, too, could well have been satisfied. He collected five thousand dollars plus expenses from client No. 1, two thousand from client No. 2, three thousand each from clients Nos. 3, 4, and 5 (for the exclusive piece of intelligence), and retained the valuable services of the agency secretary. Yet his final satisfaction had to wait for almost two years. That was when he went to the manufacturer whose campaign he had delayed, and told them about their rival's tactics and their favorite advertising agency's blunder. His services were then retained by his original victims.

Perhaps the careful planning makes this operation rather exceptional, but ad hoc photography of documents by visitors is not at all unique. An American corporation lawyer is right now knee-deep in litigation with a television company whose legitimately filmed report included a few unintentional shots "which may have a detrimental effect on company and national security." Some of these particular frames apparently found their way to a professional spy ring—probably via a laboratory technician. This lawyer believes that he could hold the TV company fully responsible, but his brief is to avoid any publicity, and this creates some unsurmountable difficulties because an influential union threatened to expose the whole affair if accusations were made against any of its members.

Apart from shame and the impotence of the law, the hazard of embarrassing publicity keeps many espionage victims away from the courts—a course that only leads to further strengthening of the spies' position. It is perhaps interesting to note what Michael Kempster, a barrister, pointed out to me, and what many companies fail to realize, that in Britain, for instance, civil cases concerning trade secrets can be held in camera. Only the action itself—A v. B, claim for damages—is then published in the court list without mention of the real subject.

On the other hand, Harvey C. Smith° firmly believes that open and vigorous action, regardless of the inadequacies of the law, helps to create legal precedents, encourages new legislation, and serves a warning to competitors: "By such aggressive action, certain [American] companies have become classified as unprofitable prospects for surveillance by the industrial spy."

The unsatisfactory legal situation is a global phenomenon with only a few exceptions. The state of Illinois was probably the first in the world to make the theft of trade secrets a criminal offense by removing such information from the undefended group of "intellectual property" and defining it

° Smith, *op. cit.*

as ordinary property. Now the theft of secrets is punishable by imprisonment for up to ten years whenever the value of the stolen property exceeds $150.

A law in Texas protects at least the oil prospectors' seismological data, which is regarded as being "in trust." Usually it is difficult to prove such thefts, but it has been done in some cases even if the thief, on one occasion, had already sunk an exploratory oil well with the guidance of the stolen information.

In France, the fashion industry has been singled out for some special legal protection against theft of secrets.

Switzerland has a rather peculiar "economic espionage" law that makes the theft of trade secrets a crime *if the thief is or is acting for an alien.* Presumably they recognize the national value of information which, if changing hands within the country, causes only a limited redistribution of wealth. It is in the name of this law that Swiss authorities have long been conducting intensive, though as yet fruitless, inquiries into the affairs of a highly specialized industrial espionage ring which obtains and sells Swiss banking secrets exclusively. Practically all other governments are, of course, potential customers of this gang, because they are anxious to trace tax evasion, tucked-away rewards of crime like Mafia reserves, and the thousands of dollar millions that have been smuggled out of their countries to be salted away illegally in secret-numbered bank accounts.

In most cases, however, the governments concerned adopt a crudely hypocritical attitude. "They never deal with this particular gang," my Swiss contact told me. "In some cases they haughtily turned down direct information offers—while immediately sending a negotiator to buy it in a totally unofficial capacity. The United States Treasury and the FBI have resident investigators in the country. But they all use slush funds that are earmarked, at least on paper, for tracking down certain criminals. If then their man 'misuses' the funds to buy the services of the spy ring and comes up with valuable banking information, it doesn't even need to be acknowledged. He's never questioned about his sources; everybody knows that the answers may be embarrassing."

The gang's activities and methods are clearly industrial espionage. Governments may condone this, but hate to admit their eagerness to get the facts whatever the price because the Swiss do not take kindly to tampering with the industrial secrets of their gold mines—the banks.

Although Switzerland now gives constantly increasing help to foreign police in tracking down criminal funds, and conducts delicate negotiations in Brussels over its future relationship with the Common Market, the country has no foreign-exchange regulations and does not regard simple tax evasion—as opposed to tax fraud involving forgery and so on—as a criminal offense. The revelation by the Swiss Credit Bank about Mrs. Clifford Irving's secret deposits from her husband's Howard Hughes biography fraud was a blow to sacrosanct bank secrecy and sent shock waves through the Swiss capitals of cash. But because the confidence was broken concerning a crime, the affair did not evoke a nationwide outrage. That sentiment was reserved for a British investigation, which ran parallel with the Irving affair.

The British Treasury has an Exchange Control Enforcement Branch to detect cases of currency-regulation evasion. Many of these cases concern money taken out of Britain or kept outside and banked in Switzerland in numbered and coded accounts. The object of the exercise is sometimes tax evasion, sometimes the accumulation of capital for foreign investment, sometimes only safeguard against the devaluation of the pound. None of these is regarded a crime in

Switzerland, so the Treasury investigators' routine efforts are viewed with understandable animosity. But in 1972 a nonroutine inquiry came to light—and hell broke loose.

A former detective-inspector, now a Treasury agent, obtained information about "vast sums of money," allegedly millions of pounds, which had been smuggled out of Britain and deposited in Swiss secret accounts. The Treasury did not deny that such information had been received, but insisted that its sources must remain confidential.

The Swiss, however, revealed it all. They treated it as a case of economic espionage. According to the Geneva police, two minor employees of a finance company sold the information to the Treasury agent. At one stage, the bribe was said to be £250,000, but eventually this sum was whittled down to "less than £1000," a more likely figure.

The Treasury admitted that it had a slush fund. A spokesman told the *Daily Telegraph*: "In the Treasury list there is a provision to make payments to informants, but I cannot confirm that payments have been made in this case."

As far as I know, £5000 is allocated to this annually, but the slush fund can be considerably inflated "if need be." The question is whether in this case such an extra was justified by the value of the information or the professionalism of the informers. I am inclined to believe that the information was worth far more than the "less than £1000," that the Treasury was prepared to pay a higher fee, but that the men were amateurs, and almost certainly the specialist ring I mentioned was never involved.

Swiss bankers were furious. "We expect such things from dictatorships, but not from you British," said one of them to *The Sunday Times* correspondent.

The two informers have been charged with economic espionage, serious offense against the Swiss penal code, which can be invoked whenever a Swiss firm complains that a foreign company—in this case, two Swiss citizens on behalf of a foreign government—has committed such a crime against its trade secrets.

The Treasury agent was warned against ever setting foot on Swiss soil because he could also be arrested and charged with economic espionage. There was no attempt made to disown the investigator or condemn his action. For there was further proof of British national interest in the case. From the Berne British Embassy, a first secretary was suddenly "reassigned" (transferred), and another was recalled prematurely. Both men were said to be involved with setting up the deal.

At the government level, Switzerland made an informal protest to Britain, but then let the case quietly drop. They already had enough problems with the United States government which was trying desperately to get at the American fortunes in Swiss banks—more than three hundred million dollars, according to the *World Currency Report*, excluding probably most of the Mafia money.

In 1970, Robert Morgenthau, the former United States Attorney for the Southern District of New York who had been fired by Nixon, criticized the administration for not closing the loophole to Swiss tax havens for Americans. As a veteran investigator of hidden-funds operations involving foreign banks, he found this the safest route in the entire field of tax evasion.

The old question is, Does the recognition of such problems entitle one country to conduct economic espionage against another, and, in this case, break its law? But there is a pressing new question, too: Is it a government's duty to support—even by economic or industrial espionage—the endeavors of individual companies that contribute to the national effort?

Israel had no qualms about this after the French embargo

on the sale of arms, including the Mirage 3 combat aircraft. Israeli agents discovered that Mirage engines were built for Swiss-assembled aircraft under licence in Winterthur. The head of the jet-engine plant there was willing to provide them with all the blueprints and specifications for the engine. He knew that a full set of more than 150,000 documents in some twenty packing crates was to be incinerated at the plant. He volunteered to do the burning, but substituted wastepaper, and gave all the prints to an agent who smuggled them out of the country via the nearby German frontier.

When the engineer was caught, he was charged with economic espionage as an alternate to a charge of treason because, it was argued, he did not betray exclusively Swiss military secrets. His defense was that he acted out of sympathy for Israel's fight for survival, that Israel already possessed such Mirage aircraft and could have obtained all this information by dismantling an engine, that all they had gained from his help was time, and that the two hundred thousand dollars he had been paid was only "risk money," a price not commensurate with the service. "If I had asked for ten million dollars, they would have given it to me," he said.

The state prosecutor demanded a seven-year prison sentence at hard labor because of the damage to Swiss military secrecy. But the Federal tribunal sentenced the engineer to only four and a half years' imprisonment. Some commentators interpreted this as the difference in gravity between economic and military espionage.

Most probably, the Swiss legal formula for the protection of trade secrets will have to be revised if the country wishes to enjoy a special relationship with the Common Market, because the special defense afforded to Swiss industry is, in effect, a discrimination against all competitors. Yet it would seem to be a backward step to bring Switzerland in line with all the other countries inside and outside the Common

Market where victims of economic espionage enjoy only the flimsy protection of civil law and need all the ingenuity of their legal advisers to present their cases in court and win appropriate compensation for damages.

Since the mid-1960's, much thought has been given to more effective legislation on both sides of the Atlantic. Unfortunately most of these efforts tried to kill two very different birds, espionage and invasion of privacy, with a single stone. This mistake usually introduced so many incompatible concepts that finally nothing was accomplished.

Another grave error in these half-hearted legislative attempts is that most people fail to recognize the true internationalism of the threat represented by industrial espionage. Alan Campbell, Q.C., a leading British authority on industrial law, strongly advocated away back in 1965 that the problem must be dealt with on an international level or else any national law would be rendered ineffectual. He recommended that an international convention should study the protection, retention, sharing, and theft of "know-how." In 1966, a resolution by the Council of Europe legal committee supported this view and called for national laws based on identical principles.

It appears, however, that even the Council of Europe is too low a level for finding a solution. Nothing can be achieved without the full participation of the United States and agreements with all advanced nonEuropean industries like those in Japan and Hong Kong. If legal experts, under the United Nations banner, drew up proposals to make industrial espionage a criminal offence everywhere, an international treaty could be worked out binding all signatories. This could also open the way to the extradition of offenders and eliminate the spies' present practice of emigration as a refuge from civil action.

The chief obstacle to concerted action are the governments themselves because in their tight schedules for various bills they constantly fail to give sufficient priority and time to the relevant proposals.

In Germany, much noise of approval greeted Dr. H. Riester's demand for imprisonment to punish industrial espionage. An official of Mercedes Benz, he warned the Federation of German Industries in 1966 that foreign spies "damage the interests not just of individual firms and the economy but also of the state." His estimate that losses through industrial espionage cost Germany "millions" might have shocked legislators. Yet to this day, only an old 1909 law against unfair competition, *Gesetz gegen den Unlauteren Wettbewerb*, gives industry any protection. This law and its numerous minor amendments deal mostly with bribery and illegal practices like the false description of goods. In its paragraph 17, it has however the probably unique feature of making the "betrayal of business secrets" a civil offense. A new bill for "economic crimes" has been drawn up, but despite its name, it will only assist civil, not criminal, cases. The proposed *Datenschutz Gesetz* aims to restrict disclosures of data from computers and other sources, and to introduce strict measures for the protection of privacy. In this respect, it would be more severe than the American Fair Credit Reporting Act and the Personal Information Bill.

Sweden has conducted extensive studies of German pre-war legislation with the intention of modeling a Swedish law on it, but the matter has still not advanced beyond the discussion stage.

Britain has also had her fair share of promising proposals that have come to nothing. After an international conference of lawyers in Stockholm, Justice—the British section of the International Commission of Jurists—began to examine the problem. In the same year, 1967, Alexander Lyon, Labour MP for York, introduced a bill to make industrial espionage a crime but only if it was the result of an invasion of privacy. The government declined to give it time for a second reading.

In 1968, Sir Edward Boyle presented another bill on industrial information. It soon collapsed under the weight of all-around criticism, even though it was about the best attempt at legislation to date. It would have made "misappropriation of industrial information" an offense, if without the owner's consent anybody "reads, copies, receives or records such information with any photographic and/or electronic device, or obtains such information from any computer, data bank, memory code, laser beam, satellite, or from any cable telephonic or television system." Also those who aided, abetted such misappropriation, or received, used, or sold such information would have been guilty.

As usual, one of the main objections to this was the restriction it might impose on genuine press inquiries in the public interest. If this hazard were not eliminated, the beneficial effects of any such law would at once be obliterated by stamping out an essential democratic right.

In 1969, the Law Commission recommended an urgent reexamination of the problem. In 1970, another Labour MP, Brian Walden, presented a Right of Privacy bill, based on a draft proposal by Justice. The emphasis was on privacy, but industrial espionage, too, would have been its target. And again it was the privacy aspect that defeated it, even though Britain was already *obliged* to introduce a law of privacy by being a signatory of the European Human Rights Convention. Other signatories like Sweden, France, and Germany, as well as Canada and the United States, already had such laws.

The debate, however, led to the appointment of the Younger Committee to advise the government on the question of privacy. The committee issued its report in 1972. Most of its forty recommendations were designed to curb the invasion of privacy and protect information in data banks, credit agencies, and so forth, but the majority of the committee rejected suggestions that a general legal right of privacy should be established by legislation.

The committee made no specific recommendations for legislation against industrial espionage, because it was felt that the general proposals would establish sufficient safeguards while maintaining the vital free flow and exchange of scientific and technical information. Paragraph 632, for instance, would make it a civil wrong to obtain information illegally.

Most probably, the committee experienced great difficulties with obtaining hard evidence about current industrial espionage practices. I suspect that this is why its members failed to suggest that it should be regarded as a crime. This failure is part of the whole vicious circle. As long as economic espionage is not a crime, the police will not take any interest in it; as long as the police do not investigate industrial espionage, there can be few well-documented court cases; as long as there are few cases, nobody will see the importance of really serious punishment; as long as there are no sentences that can act as an effective deterrent, few managers will want to make open complaints about aggressive acts against their firms. So it will remain difficult to obtain hard evidence as to the extent of what is going on.

Two of the Younger Committee's recommendations were, however, relevant to industrial espionage.

One was that private detectives should be licensed—as they are in most states in America, where nevertheless a recent Rand report has discovered "substantial dishonesty and poor business practices" in the security industry. The Younger Committee, like the German *Datenschutz Gesetz*, argued that licensing and supervision would improve the reputation of the profession by keeping totally unqualified and even criminal elements out of it. Stringent control would have given needed support to detectives' professional organizations, which at present can only deny membership to crooks but cannot stop them from setting up in business and cheating the public. It is therefore a mistake for the government to have rejected and shelved the idea. But at least in one respect, this proposal has implied a misunderstanding of the present situation. I believe that only very few private detectives dabble in industrial espionage, and their rewards are no more than crumbs from the professional agents' feast. These few would not be stopped by licensing. They would only operate more regularly under other covers like business consultancies.

The other of the two Younger recommendations concerned the notorious "bugs." It proposed that the use of various electronic and optical devices for surveillance should be made a criminal offence, punishable by fine and imprisonment. This deserves, of course, wholehearted approval because the present position is simply ludicrous. Pieces of legislation now in existence, which can be made more or less relevant by arduous process of interpretation, were created at a time when nobody could possibly foresee the technological revolution brought about by modern electronics and miniaturization.

The government's exclusive power to tap telephones in the interest of national security is based on a royal proclamation of 1663 that made it the crown's prerogative to intercept communications. Private phone-tappers and users of bugs can be prosecuted for contravention of the Wireless and Telegraphy Act, 1949, but this is so ineffectual that the police try to bring in other charges, like conspiracy, whenever possible.

A man who tapped a telephone to conduct industrial espionage, obtained information worth about fifty thousand pounds. His victim's business might have been ruined completely through the loss of trade secrets. The tapper was prosecuted under the 1949 Act and charged with tampering with post office equipment and stealing GPO electricity valued at twopence. He was fined thirty pounds.

To make tapping and bugging illegal sounds easy. It has been done by several countries, including Holland, where users of bugging devices can be jailed for up to six months with a fine of twenty-five hundred pounds (or five times that sum if the information is published), and Sweden, where the proposed punishment can be a maximum of two years in prison. Yet legislation is not all that simple. Should the man who uses a bug in genuine self-defense be deprived of this powerful weapon? A couple of crooked policemen can incriminate a man by false witness. Shouldn't the man be able to defend himself with the aid of a surreptitious tape recording?

In Germany, the courts accept tapes as evidence if the recording was the only means of self-defense, and particularly in blackmail cases, where the spoken words constitute the offense. It is illegal to listen in on or record speech without the speaker's permission, but sometimes wiretapping or bugging is acceptable if it can be proved that somebody had the right to know what was being said. Further complications are caused by the fact that the law varies from one part of the country to the other. In Munich, Bavaria, for instance, it is not illegal to own a bug (for study, research, and so on) but Section 298 of the penal code outlaws its use, and prosecution can be initiated on the victim's complaint.

State-to-state variations in the law have always been a cause of confusion and created peculiar problems for the prosecution in the United States. Vastly different laws for bugging and wiretapping used to be no exception to this rule. California, Illinois, and New York were the first to outlaw the use of bugs, but now there is a federal law that makes it an offense even to possess a surreptitious listening device.

Breaking this law can be punished by a maximum fine of ten thousand dollars, up to five-years imprisonment, plus the payment of appropriate damages. Yet even the interpretation of this law can differ from state to state. In California, for instance, a security specialist was warned not to demonstrate on a TV program the menace from electronic listening devices because he could be arrested in the studio for being in possession of bugs. The same man once conducted in an office a successful search for electronic bugs. The police, acting on a tip-off, arrived just after he discovered a tiny transmitter hidden in a picture frame. While he was removing the device, trying not to damage the frame, he was, in fact, guilty of the same offense as the spy who secreted the bug. He claimed, when we met in Los Angeles, that only his friendship with senior police officers helped him to get away without being charged.

Antibug legislation is a useful step toward better security for trade secrets, but it would be a serious error of judgment to regard it as the main weapon against industrial espionage. For it is an absolute fallacy that spies *depend* on bugging boardrooms and tapping telephones. They use these methods, but they are less dependent on them than many government agencies. And this is particularly so in America, the original land of the bug and the wiretapper's paradise.

Most Americans I have talked to seemed to favor antibug legislation. They do not like the idea that anybody with a good portable radio and five dollars cash can listen in on anyone else's conversation anywhere. But they equally dislike the blatant discrimination against the public in favor of the police and other government agencies.

Few people argue when police tap the lines of illegal bookies or plant a bug in the trailer serving as a Mafia headquarters. But when federal agents are forced to admit that they have "inadvertently" eavesdropped on people like

Martin Luther King and the former Cassius Clay, when testimony at congressional hearings indicates that in any United States city at any given moment police and others operate a minimum of a hundred snooping systems, when the Internal Revenue Service runs a secret school to train agents in bugging, wiretapping, and using the tools of burglary, one can sympathize with those who recall a sentence from the Fourth Amendment to the Constitution: "The right of the people to be secure in their persons, houses, papers, and effects, against unreasonable searches and seizures, shall not be violated. . . ."

I for one shall never envy those judges who have to decide from time to time where the "reasonable" ends and the "unreasonable" begins in a bugging, counterbugging, and defensive bug-preventive bugging affair.

6

From Here to Infinity

IT IS LESS than three quarters of an inch long, the size of a lump of sugar. Its plastic casing is so "surprisingly realistic" that saccharin users will not touch it.

The Little Thing is a bug. And not the latest, smallest, or most sophisticated type at that, although it weighs only five grams, has a microphone that picks up even whispers in a room and a transmitter with a range of up to a thousand feet.

Powered by a good-quality mini-battery, it will work for some eighty hours continuously. To pick up the transmission you need a very sensitive FM receiver with at least ten transistors, if you take the advice of BTC, later Translibex, of Rotterdam/Zurich; but it is "very effective for office eavesdropping," according to Guarda Security Services of London, the former Christopher Robert & Co. Although, unfortunately, it has no sugar content, it "may be placed into a cup of coffee without impairing its working efficiency" because it is "unconditionally waterproof," if you accept the guarantee of Security Systems International of Cambridge and London, registered in the Isle of Man.

Little things matter a great deal in any intelligence operation. This sweet Little Thing may be a lethal weapon in the hands of professionals and may attract their clients, but bugs—sometimes referred to in the trade as the Little Things—are not easy to use. That is why industrial spies seem to have a peculiar love-hate relationship with them.

First the agent must find out all he can about the place where the dear Little Thing is to perform its very own thing. Then he must gain preferably legitimate access to the hotel, office, conference, or board room; get the bug in; conceal it; test it; check to ensure that geographical circumstances, atmospheric conditions, interference from high voltage cables, and other factors like background noises will not reduce the range or clarity of the sensitive Little Thing. (In 1970 when the police tried to bug and tape a conversation with a pilot who was suspected of plotting to smuggle Pakistanis into Britain, they overlooked the fact that there was a church nearby. The toll of the bells of St. Mary's, Reading, came at the most crucial moment and ruined the evidence.)

The agent will also have to ascertain that the eighty-hour life and death of the damned Little Thing will include the vital few moments when the really important secrets are being mentioned and the decisions made. Then he can at last attend to arrangements for monitoring and recording. His final chore is to recover the corpse of the wretched Little Thing, not because it is so very expensive to lose—up to about $120—but because the subsequent discovery of the bug and leakage would initiate counteraction by the victim and reduce considerably the value of the information.

The whole operation thus becomes far more complicated, expensive, and arduous than the heroism and smooth efficiency of spy fiction. Not that those fantastic technical feats are beyond the reach of real-life agents. With a security specialist, who had worked on both aggressive and defensive assignments, we once scrutinized one of the episodes in *Mission Impossible*, the TV series. We reckoned that with expenses on dames, liquor, gadgets, and travel cut to the bare bones, such a job could be pulled off in real life for slightly less than half a million dollars.

"What do you think the profit would have to be to justify that sort of investment?" this specialist asked without expecting an answer. Unlike the "flat guys" of the screen, three-dimensional industrial spies prefer to do their jobs quickly, in anonymity, and without trying to become heroes in the process. No medals, please; the cash will be sufficient recognition of services rendered, thank you.

In some cases, however, bugs and other gadgets can be useful and, in a way, inevitable. A German operator, who claims to have scored even in Japan, perhaps the most spy-conscious non-Communist country, regards the use of electronic devices as "an ultimate resource, just one step away from admission of defeat."

The already mentioned bugging of a trailer, the meeting place of Mafia chieftains, was only one of many occasions when the FBI had to resort to electronic aids. In 1970, when some Mafiosi were on trial in Newark, New Jersey, it was disclosed that the FBI had listened in for four years on numerous suspects' private conversations. The selected transcripts from the tape recordings ran to twelve hundred pages. Although these "unsworn, hearsay documents" were not admitted as evidence, they gave an intriguing demonstration of contrasting methods.

One of the aims of this vast tapping operation was to find out who in government, finance, and business were in regular contact with the mobsters. Their phone calls promised to provide a useful chart of the network. The late Robert Kennedy was then serving as Attorney General, and his experience in combatting nationwide organized crime had already made him a fervent advocate of giving the FBI a free hand to bug and tap the confidential utterances of the underworld. A recording thus revealed that in 1964 the Mafia became interested in the Attorney General's own contacts. When Kennedy was attending the Democratic Convention at Atlantic City, they wanted a daily list of his telephone calls. The business investigation specialist who was hired for the job did not bother with electronic equipment; he befriended and possibly bribed a switchboard operator who agreed to pass on all the telephone numbers Kennedy called.

The moral of this and other similar incidents is not very pretty. It shows not only that it is cheaper, safer, simpler and more pleasant to make up to a secretary than to use bugs, but also that the bonds of loyalty and fear are stronger among the criminal than the law-enforcement fraternity: crooks seem to be able to buy the services of corrupt officials and police anywhere, any time, while available funds hardly ever go far the other way around.

In the early 1960's, however, when bug mania reached its peak in the United States, at least twenty-two large and numerous smaller companies concentrated on the production of electronic eavesdropping devices for the private user, including industry. *Business Week* estimated that industry spent up to four million dollars on bugs each year, and a sample survey revealed that in a single month of 1965, 250 miniature telephone transmitters were sold in Los Angeles. The popularity of bugging swept Europe at about the close of the decade when allegedly there were twenty thousand bugs owned by private citizens in Germany alone.

My own research and dozens of expert opinions have indicated that the current general role of the Little Thing is grossly overrated. The use of bugs and the menace they represent is far less widespread than some specialists, who cash in on debugging and selling defensive equipment, would have us believe. Nevertheless the hazard of private electronic eavesdropping is real, and from the review of several hundred buggings, including those I have already referred to, my impression is that in these days when professionals do resort to bugging, the result can be deadlier than ever.

One still comes across reports of truly private use, like the mother superior's bugging the sisters' cells in a Bavarian monastery, but today the typical cases are well-planned expert operations in which the planting of bugs is probably the only way to crack a firm's security network or catch a man off his guard.

Mr. J. E., a counterindustrial-espionage agent with military-intelligence training, who used to work for Management Investigations Services, had to deal with a case like that in Frankfurt. A slim, small, dapper figure, the type who would live on his nerves without ever showing it, he seemed to disappear in the roomy leather belly of a whale-sized armchair when we met at his club—the Army and Navy, of course.

He was not quite sure why the Frankfurt client, the head office of an internationally known firm, had chosen this particular London outfit. They might have heard about it as one of the few truly defensive specialists in the business. Or else they might have reasoned that British investigators were less likely to be in the pay of several German competitors simultaneously than a local organization.

"We made some preliminary inquiries with Major Matthews before the first meeting right here, probably in these same armchairs," he told me. Again and again he touched his glass to his lips, taking his Scotch and soda in tiny sips that were measured to see him through even a long discussion with apparently continuous drinking but without giving alcohol a chance to get the better of him.

"Three years before they came to us the firm had gone through a remarkable growth period. Then a major change of policy with a big sales and development campaign were planned but inexplicably everything went wrong. It slowly emerged that the plan had been leaked to at least one, possibly two competitors. That's why their operation had virtually collapsed. Their loss was tremendous—the missed opportunity and further growth potential were estimated to be in the region of a hundred and twenty million Deutschmarks. In fact, it took them three years to recover.

"They suspected that they had been the victim of some form of industrial espionage, but they felt they could do nothing about it, even though their troubles did not yet seem to be over. There were a couple of minor leakages followed by a more important one. They heard about them over the grapevine. They carried out a rather thorough check on the staff including directors, but found nothing. Finally a dummy plan was launched as a test. They went through the usual motions and put it on the agenda of their Friday board meetings, but nothing seemed to have leaked out this time.

"This was some eighteen months before we met. Since then they had had no security problems, but now they had to be sure about security. They were ready once again for a major international breakthrough.

"Part of the routine security checking I made was to try to discover how they had lost their main secrets three years earlier, how the minor leakages had occurred, and why, to the best of their knowledge, there were no more losses after that. If there were real professionals involved, they would conceivably keep their inside contacts dormant, in reserve and safety for another major assignment.

"The boardroom itself was one of my first batch of suspects. With the help of the firm's accountants and the bills on file, we listed all the outside contractors who had carried out any work there. A strange coincidence emerged: two different lots of builders had done two alteration jobs in the boardroom—the first about three years and the second about eighteen months earlier. Just when the leakages began and ended.

"The presence of a bug, however, seemed unlikely. Because of the given circumstances, any transmission would have to be received within the building complex itself. I had already checked that. Who could monitor it all and where?

"I gave a second thorough work-over to the boardroom with the bug detector. I got a few positive signals as I progressed inch by inch, and the reading seemed justified by normal features of the building and electrical installations— except at one spot which had already worried me during the first search.

"Now I had to be sure. The director, to whom I was always reporting personally, never in writing, gave me permission to open that wall. Within seconds of removing the fine textile that covered it, I saw a rather old-fashioned hearing aid in a small cavity. The wire led from it right into the wall toward an old chimney. When later I tested the aid, I found that the microphone might be old-fashioned but it would pick up any whisper in that room."

At this point, J. E. left me and that piece of wire hanging in midair, because he had to go and make sure that our wives, expected for dinner, would be allowed to enter an inferior little bar—not the club proper, of course—through a back door, once a servants' entrance, but now the only one that can be used by women. On his return he took another sip of his Scotch, ordered a third double for me . . . and we were back in Frankfurt.

"Oh, yes, the wire. I followed it up the chimney. At the floor above, I found it had been cut by some sharp instrument. I reckon it must have been cut accidentally by the second lot of builders who, I discovered, did some work on that floor, too. Continuing with the wire, I got to the roof where it ended in a neat coil. There was a mature layer of dirt and bird droppings all around, but a small oblong patch nearby was a little cleaner than the rest. It did not seem an unreasonable guess that some time ago a tape recorder stood there.

"All right, let's suppose the builders accidentally foiled the operation by cutting the wire. But because many of the Friday conferences in the boardroom continued well into the night, the recorder would have to be ready for long runs each time. How could anybody get to the roof regularly to change the tape and the batteries?

"The roof where I now stood belonged to the oldest part of the firm's premises. When they had a taller office block built, it adjoined this roof at its second-floor level, and there was a door from one of the new offices to the roof. When I saw that, I thought I'd catch the spy. But to my great disappointment I found out that the woman who used to occupy the room with the door to the roof in the suspected period had resigned some sixteen months earlier—soon after the work was carried out by the second lot of builders and the leakages stopped.

"I talked to several of her former colleagues and the pattern of a thoroughly professional job became apparent. The woman had been with the firm for some fifteen years. She had lost her husband during the war and lived with her sister who seemed to have inherited all her remaining affection. About four years before our investigation, this sister contracted some mysterious illness, and my suspect began to spend all her savings on specialists in a vain effort to find a cure.

"It is likely that some intelligence outfit, looking for inside contacts, discovered her at this stage. She needed money, and they bought her. Then the bugging was tailor-made to suit her circumstances. She was known to be lonely because her sister was now being moved from one expensive sanatorium to another, so none of her colleagues was surprised when suddenly she became a devoted bird lover.

"She spent most of her lunchtime watching the birds on the roof, and one day she arrived at the office with a large, lavish contraption to serve as a birdhouse. She placed it carefully on the roof, and from then on, she went out to feed the birds religiously even in violent snowstorms—but only on Fridays. The day of the weekly board meetings, of course."

E. J.'s was a performance of great precision; he took the last sip of his whisky almost as the reward for this extraordinary amount of continuous talking. When asked about the outcome of the investigation, he reverted to his more characteristic military staccato.

"Nope, no more trouble. Did a full survey—some tightening here and there for security—quarterly electronic sweep for bugs—limited staff access to records and photocopying—that's all. Oh, yes, taught them the need-to-know principle. Very useful. And recommended the cashiering, I mean sacking, of two secretaries. Sad, but had to be done."

The birds' benefactor was never traced. It was established that her sister had died before her resignation and she herself probably emigrated. It was a further proof of professionalism that those who paid her did not blackmail her into staying on and did not try to devise a new wave of operations; as the game went on for a long time, the risk of discovery increased in geometrical progression. They knew that once a bug was found, the tables would be turned.

This is what happened when a vice-president, in charge of a vast American mutual fund's investments, heard that some people in his circle had their offices debugged. Purely as a status symbol, he invited a Washington specialist to carry out an electronic sweep for bugs in his office. He was absolutely astonished when a bug was indeed found in an expensive electric clock—a present from an old school friend—which had stood on his desk for more than two years. The "friend" must have made a fortune taking advantage of inside knowledge of the vice-president's most confidential daily buying and selling activities. After all, the fund operated with multimillion stakes, and every move could influence the stock market.

The vice-president's understandable fury was quelled only by the bug hunter's most professional advice to pay the man back in kind.

Every day for three months the vice-president pretended to make several telephone calls instructing his imaginary brokers to carry out certain moves that were the opposite of his actual sales and purchases, now conducted from another office. These fake operations were as elaborately conceived as the real ones to sound convincing. He would pretend to warn the broker at length to proceed with extreme caution when buying thousands of a certain stock so that the price should not shoot up too soon, when in fact he was selling and knew that the price was bound to go down. Hoping that his "mistakes" were copied by his listener, he would complain to the broker about his own losses.

The "friend" swallowed the bait, and perhaps even the line and the rod with it. He was ruined in a single month. The game was kept going for another two months only to make sure that anybody else who might have been involved with the bugging would suffer the same fate.

For every successful bugging, there must be scores of botched-up attempts. Apart from the lack of expertise, this must be due to the notorious overvaluation of certain devices through the exaggerated claims made both by dealers selling the equipment and users selling their electronic services.

Most regular users find that they can really rely only on

bugs specially built for them by their own trusted craftsmen, who can also adapt a standard design to suit a particular job. Harold Lipset, who demonstrated the various devices to a Senate committee and who was described in Samuel Dash's book, *Eavesdroppers*, as "the busiest electrical eavesdropper in San Francisco," once took me to an inconspicuous little workshop. A safe distance away from his headquarters, it was here that all his gadgets, including a lavish detector and surveillance van, were produced, and where allegedly, the first bug in a cocktail olive, with the stick acting as the aerial, was tested successfully.

Tom Ponzi, the greatest Italian electronic showman, who always seems to have a vast armory of listening devices for client-attracting publicity, also has his own technicians for the more refined jobs, like the tracking down of an illicit distillery in Naples and obtaining the evidence against copycats who manufactured counterfeit Chanel perfume.

The bug peddlers' claims about the optimum radius for "clear reception with an inexpensive radio set" are always suspect. But concerning the most controversial and probably most dangerous bug, some telecommunications specialists question the feasibility and very existence of what is known as the infinity transmitter.

This vicious device consists of two parts: the bug itself and a whistle or harmonica to activate it. The bug, the transmitter, can be fitted into the mouthpiece of an ordinary telephone. Experienced agents claim it takes them only twenty seconds to replace the original microphone with the gadget designed not to interfere with the ordinary use of the set. From then on, whenever the spy wants to hear anything spoken or whispered in the room where the phone is, he dials the number, and just as the connection is being made, he blows the whistle. Its high-pitched tone apparently prevents the telephone from ringing and transforms the receiver, lying in its cradle, into a live bug that transmits every sound over the open line.

While the telephone is serving as a bug, other callers of this number get the ordinary busy signal. If the victim tries to use his phone, he cannot get a line. The exercise can be repeated indefinitely because the bug does not need a battery.

The performance of "the infinity" was demonstrated to me in circumstances I alone chose. A friend of mine in Chicago agreed to let his own telephone be "doctored" in my presence. I then drove with two specialists out of town, and at the prearranged time of 9:30 P.M. on Monday, October 14, 1968, we called the number. At the same time, my friend listened for thirty seconds for any unusual noise from his set (he heard none), and then started a sequence of sounds listed by and known to only the two of us. And I could hear it all. Frank Sinatra sang; my friend talked about bridge near the telephone, read a few lines from a magazine in a whisper, ran the water in the kitchen with the door open, and switched on for a moment the television set.

There was no doubt about it, the infinity transmitter worked.

Although it is claimed that this bug can be activated from anywhere on earth in the same way, experts have told me that international calls would encounter various difficulties, such as differences in voltage. Others explained that because of various devices in the telephone system, such as the relay trip, "the principle on which the 'infinity' system is supposed to be based" is simply not valid. I am not qualified to argue the technical capabilities or sheer impossibility of the infinity. But I must confess that my own skepticism toward this frightful five hundred dollar gadget was shattered in Chicago.

The Bug Peddlers and the Stereo Bra

Russian security and intelligence services have always been among the first and foremost bugging practitioners. Many of their exploits are widely known. The much publicized detection of a remote-controlled miniature microphone-transmitter in the beak of the eagle emblem on the wall of the U.S. ambassador's room in Moscow was followed by a long series of startling discoveries by various embassies in Communist capitals. Electronic and physical searches revealed bugs in carpet nails, radiators, table legs, and even in the heels of shoes just returned to an American diplomat after repair by a Moscow cobbler.

More recently when Bonn sent a new advanced encoding and decoding machine to its Moscow embassy, a porter seemed to have made an error at the airport, and the crate containing the diplomatic consignment was mislaid. It was missing for only an hour and a half—not the most serious blunder by any freight-service standard. Nevertheless Ambassador Allardt grew a little suspicious, not so much from nature as by experience. A quick examination proved him painfully right. In the ninety minutes, while the crate was missing, a powerful bug with an almost two-mile range had been planted in the machine. Because of the machine itself, the device was immune to electronic and metal detectors, and could be discovered only by visual inspection. As usual, for the sake of diplomatic peace and courtesy, the incident was played down by Bonn, even though the bug would have picked up all coded embassy messages and, as a bonus of utmost importance, given away the current German coding system.

I have also heard lately about the mass production of the most advanced Russian listening devices—for export. Instead of foreign currency, it seems to earn them friends. Nasser was among the first heads of states to receive a cupboardful of gleaming bugs for his personal use. Egyptian generals and higher officials ready to further submission and Russian influence got mahogany boxes of electronic tricks. In Latin America and Africa, Russian diplomats are quick to exploit the natural curiosity of emerging dictators who feel safer if they know what their best friends are thinking and saying about them, and if gadgets of unquestionable loyalty whisper a steady stream of information about plots being hatched against them. Although Soviet diplomacy failed to woo General Amin of Uganda, the great man did not hesitate to accept a selection of "telltale miniatures for any occasion."

Much of all this has been known to the newspaper reader—let alone the espionage trade itself—so it was amusing and rather surprising when a few years ago a New York manufacturer sent his illustrated brochure and offered his five hundred dollar luxury wares for eavesdropping to *Komsomolskaya Pravda*, the mass-circulation daily of the Young Communist League. It was suggested that bugs would help to check the loyalty of the staff. The Russian paper answered the offer with haughty consternation. An editorial explained that in the Soviet Union, everybody was trusted and nobody was ever spied on. It did not fail to notice the stamp, one of the series depicting the Statue of Liberty with the motto In God we trust, on the envelope. The opportunity was too good to miss. It appears, the paper concluded, American trustfulness was restricted to God excluding "those near to you."

Yet was it really surprising that this firm had such absolute self-confidence and unlimited faith in the American "we can teach you a trick or two even in your own national game" sales technique?

Bug peddlers belong to a strange breed. They all seem to share a childish and, in a way, quite innocent fascination with their toys. They love to show them off despite the increasing legal risk involved, and when I met several of them, I frequently had the impression that they were the first to be taken in by their own exaggerations and flowery advertising copy. Many of those who invent, improve, and manufacture bugging devices live in an odd electronic dream world, unaware of or unconcerned with the damage they may inflict. I suspect that much of their cynicism stems from ignorance. Few of the makers have become really rich, and these exceptions made money on branching out into arms dealing or joining the ranks of successful industrial spies and other users of their products.

They all show symptoms of a desperate craving for respectability, which seems to be to them like heroin to the addict. They like to talk about "the simple pleasures of listening," and to brand even their most blatantly aggressive wares as "weapons of self-defense." In common with private investigators, they maintain their personal armory of gadgets as "collectors' items" used for "study, defensive work and demonstrations," although undoubtedly most dealers are willing to carry out actual bugging assignments.

A few years ago numerous American private detectives advertised openly their readiness for any surreptitious bugging and wiretapping jobs, and offered detailed technical advice in books and articles for the do-it-yourself "sound enthusiasts." Now that legislation has swept bugging under the carpet in more ways than one, investigators in the Manhattan telephone directory may claim to use only scientific methods, recordings, modern technical aids, and electronic equipment. That is why Americans have begun to copy a method developed and tested successfully in Britain, Germany, France, and other European countries. The dealer or investigator in dire need of advertising has to do no more than to make sure that he gets caught committing a most trivial electronic offense with negligible consequences. Public outrage, the judge's scathing comments, and the press will then give them all the publicity they want.

To safeguard themselves against prosecution, dealers claim that they send their illustrated leaflets and sell their products only to "bona fide users," although they fail to state who would *not* be regarded as one.

Another standard formula is to stamp the word "restricted" on certain pages in the brochures. W. J. S. Electronics of Las Vegas, Nevada, marked some bug descriptions as "Sold to Law Enforcement Only," while other units were "sold for use subject to pertinent regulations." The latter included a stethoscopelike instrument, the "contact amplifier," to detect sound vibrations in "door panels, thin walls and partitions"—from the outside, of course.

The already mentioned B. T. C. catalogue included this "health warning": "The use or importation [of this device] may be subject to laws, tariffs and/or government regulations and is therefore not to be used in an illegal manner." Christopher Robert & Co.—operating lately under Guarda Security Services and also National Investigation Bureau—advised potential customers that its CR V.O.R. Mini T.X. Mark III "radio microphone," a mighty bug, "when used in the U.K. is classified by the G.P.O. regulations as an unlicensed transmitter," but gave no such warning about its SUB MINI T.X. Type A, a miniature room transmitter with internal microphone. The Whithers brothers, who still sell their old wares under the new company names, were themselves convicted of bugging, tapping, and commercial espionage.

B. R. Fox of Holmes Protection Service, New York, represented at the time by Leonard Wadsworth & Co. in London, marked its sales literature "very confidential" to safeguard "the value of security and intelligence devices." The description of some equipment ended with this note: "Since these devices are of a legally controversial nature, it is recommended that, before using, local counsel be consulted to make certain there is no conflict with existing laws and/or court decisions."

By the time I met the B. R. Fox sales manager in New York (oddly enough on the thirty-eighth floor of Faberge Inc., a cosmetics company building) on February 3, 1970, it became a not too gentle understatement to describe the legal situation as "controversial." He told me that because of the law introduced in 1968 the firm had had to dismantle $65,000 worth of equipment which could no longer be offered for sale even to the police. For the same reason he would be unable to show me, give me, or send me by mail any device or catalogue. He then, of course, proceeded to present me with a selection of technical bulletins, some of them dated December 1969, with a price list effective from July 16, 1969.

Bernard Spindel, who was the mastermind behind B. R. Fox operations, established himself as one of the three wise men of American wiretapping in the 1960's—the other two being the much-publicized John Broady and Charles Gris. Spindel was known as a most original bugging wizard. He wrote a book and demonstrated his method for *Life* magazine. When I visited his company, he was in jail where, I believe, he died in 1972.

Great wiretappers and great magazines may die, and the birth of severe legislation may create the widespread fallacy that bugging and tapping have become obsolete and practically extinct in the United States, but I can only agree with those who are convinced that electronic devices are alive and well and living in the top drawers/walls/telephones/pockets of many American executives. As Californian agent Harold Lipset told the Association of Criminal Defense Lawyers in a lecture at Monterey, in 1972, "Eavesdropping is taking place on a much larger scale in industry than it is normally believed to happen."

The key to this is that the bugging trade has gone international. If you approach the dealers, many of them will tell you that their goods are "for export only"—a rather curious state of affairs since no country encourages the import of bugs any more than it does local production. They may also claim that "law enforcement agencies" are their main customers, and you will be expected to understand from an additional wink or a vague gesture of the hand that even national intelligence services are snapping up their wares. If so, the government departments would have to stop making their own "electronic aids" and start dumping their stocks fast to keep their consumption on level with private production.

Although American products still reach Europe, and some American specialists have moved to Europe to manufacture bugs, most of the American market is supplied from Britain. Some companies like, for example, Guarda ask no questions; show the color of your money, and goods will be supplied from stock on the spot or within twelve hours. Others, like Security Systems International which prides itself on its products being "absolutely resistant to tropical conditions," will emphasize that locally they sell only to recognized agencies but that sales for export are unrestricted. Yes, outside Britain, they will deliver absolutely anywhere; just specify your requirements and name the airport where you want it sent. (Their catalogue is in French and English.)

The "export only" method saves the dealers from local embarrassment, while "delivery from a foreign source" is the current subterfuge employed by agencies that accept local orders.

The "import" of bugs is usually carried out, I understand, in one of two ways. The main American, Italian, and German dealers—located in San Francisco, New York, and Chicago; Milan and Naples; Hamburg, Krefeld, Mannheim, and Blaichach, a village in the Bavarian Alps—trading under a legitimate company name or from a private address only pretend to fulfill orders from abroad. They have the invoices and other printed forms of foreign partners, pack these with the goods, and use a local delivery service.

This system is facilitated by the fact that many items in the bug peddlers' catalogues differ only in name; manufactured by a few mass producers, even the illustrations in the sales literature are frequently the same. Dealers change their addresses more regularly than their underwear; firms disappear like rabbits from a magician's hat but only to reappear, perhaps, under another name. New firm—old management with well-tried goods, brochures, and pictures. Export-import business as usual until further notoriety is achieved, and the dealer steps out of yet another worn name and address dirtied beyond the might of the dry cleaners.

The second method may involve some actual smuggling, because the postal authorities do not welcome consignments of bugs anywhere. In Europe, transportation across frontiers is easy. Customs officials are likely to stop only their own countrymen returning from abroad. A British tourist's car is hardly ever scrutinized at the borders of the Continent, and this is how France mostly receives "electronic equipment for surreptitious surveillance."

Rotterdam appears to be a major distribution center. Goods with a European destination are said to leave Holland in foreign visitors' cars particularly during holidays, like Easter, when a tremendous influx of tourists prevents all but the most cursory checks. In a single April weekend at Elten, during the bulb season of 1970, a German car with Düsseldorf registration crossed from Germany to Holland and back eighteen times. On each eastward trip, it was practically covered by huge colorful garlands, giving support to the seasonal Dutch joke that every local driver buys a small garland, every tourist buys a large one, and every German visitor buys two of the largest size. I heard that every time the car left Holland, it was fully laden with electronic gear and almost every tulip bulb was bugged.

Britain and the United States were considered difficult from the smugglers' point of view—but only until a roundabout way could be established. Allegedly bugs and other goods now travel in boxes marked "radio spares" routed via Canada to the United States and via Ireland to Britain.

Ireland has always been known as the Achilles heel of British customs. It is child's play to smuggle anything from Ireland across the border to the north. The ease with which this can be done is demonstrated daily with weapons and explosives. This has also been a favored route for porno films and magazines from Denmark. Once the contraband goods are in Northern Ireland, the smugglers can use the internal postal service which is not subject to customs inspection.

The Irish radio-assembly industry is a particularly good cover for the import of bugs. According to one of my sources, a Dublin warehouse is now reserved exclusively for the storage of bugs in transit. If a legitimate sender, like a radio factory or electrical wholesaler, posts the goods direct to Britain, it is most unlikely that anybody can be caught. "What can we do?" an exasperated British customs officer exclaimed. "If it says 'radio spares,' I can perhaps count the number of bits in a parcel, but one printed circuit looks just the same as another. Only an expert can tell what's what."

On the night of April 17, 1972, I was taken to a peculiar assembly plant—two rooms with stores behind them—in Düsseldorf. It was in a large, impressive villa in a wealth-oozing district which was, I guess, in or near the *Zoo-viertel*, because we passed Brahmsplatz on the way not long before we reached our destination.

The place looked like a souvenir shop for tasteless customers. There were some crates of hideous oil paintings, ashtrays, and ghastly flower vases, a few dozen gilded leather boxes big enough to house a boxing promoter's best cigars, hundreds of fountain pens, table lighters, watches, electric clocks, wall and desk calendars, note pads, table lamps and, unexpectedly, a selection of onyx and alabaster knickknacks and marble statues that might have claimed a place even in luxuriously furnished homes and offices.

Four girls and a manager worked there through the night—fixing a bug in every item. I was told that it was a safety precaution to have only short intensive production runs for two or three nights, disperse the goods, and leave behind no traces of the work, until once again reserves began to run down. In a corner there were a couple of sewing machines for finishing work on "brassieres that will listen" and transmit "any whisper exchanged between wearer and friend." (A more advanced design is "the stereo bra," copied from a CIA device that was declassified after an agent goofed. With a separate microphone in each cup, a girl seated in a bar can simultaneously transmit conversations from both her left and her right.)

The firm that keeps this workshop busy is said to be the biggest of its kind in Europe. It has offices in several cities, uses a Swiss accommodation address for incoming orders and correspondence, can also supply a very wide choice of firearms and other weapons in sufficient quantities to outfit a small army, navy, and air force, and runs a unique "verification bureau" in Paris for the sole purpose of checking the credentials of new, would-be customers. If you are not crooked enough to be trusted, a cool letter will answer your inquiries about bugs and explain that you must have mistaken them for somebody else. Is that perhaps what dealers mean when they say that only bona fide customers will be served?

Under increasing legal pressure in most countries, this firm was among the first to learn, I believe, from the experience of the "radio spares for export" trade, and introduce the latest, most expedient, and inspired innovation—the sale of do-it-yourself kits.

Admittedly, detailed instructions for the simple assembly of bugs in four or five easy steps are issued with the spares, but no actual bug is sold, and the dealer cannot be accused of helping snoopers or encouraging industrial spies. After all, it is "beyond his control" what the customer will do with all that junk. The Düsseldorf firm now plans to market a de luxe kit in America. It will contain enough to make two good-quality bugs of different sizes and function, and a compact unit for telephone tapping. Each will have no more than three components and only a screwdriver will be needed to put them together. The kit is already available for five hundred Deutsch-Marks (about $210) in Hamburg.

In Britain, Mulhall Electronics was the first to jump on the bandwagon. The company base is in Ardglass, County Down, Northern Ireland, with a London forwarding address, a London agent, and an appetite for recruiting subagents everywhere. "Specialists in design and manufacture of miniature electronic devices and surveillance equipment," their catalogue for 1972 declared that "electronic equipment can be constructed to your submitted specification or ideas" for which special quotation would be given as required.

The Mulhall list includes, for instance, the "Ranger H.Q. Radio Microphone," claimed to be "the latest in high quality" wares with a range of a hundred yards, internal aerial, and batteries. Shaped like a torch it may be too bulky—eight by one and a half inches—to serve as a hidden bug, but perhaps it is intended for use as a walkie-talkie. The finished product is so cheap at fifteen pounds that the construction kit allows only 10 percent for the customer's own work. The "TX MK 1 Miniature Transmitter" with microphone is, however, so tiny that it was obviously designed for easy concealment and bugging. It costs only twelve pounds, but the D-I-Y man can save a further 20 percent by buying it in kit form: "Step-by-step instructions help even those with limited knowledge to successfully construct this kit in a short time. Soldering iron, cutters, screwdriver, and pliers being all the equipment required. A service is available for construction difficulties."

Another item in the same price range is the TX MK 3, an "ultra sensitive" telephone transmitter, which according to the sales talk, can be monitored from a quarter of a mile away. Priced at twenty-five pounds, it "fits easily inside the telephone" and conveniently gets all the power it needs from the telephone itself for ever and ever. From the one-sentence instruction and simple diagram it appears we can take the makers' word for it: a one-minute operation is all that is required. (Not available in kit form.)

To the careful observer, a device called Ranger Personnel, a "tone transmitter" for security systems, is most interesting. The description tells us that its specifications are similar to Ranger Super, a VHF transmitter. Presumably it can be used with a microphone, too, when "this equipment can be worn inside a jacket and the aerial clipped around the waist or over the shoulder." Yet another transmitter, one is tempted to say, but its picture looks very familiar. There is a label on the gadget with the name of an old American acquaintance: Stoelting, a Chicago company, "founded in the year of 1886 for the purpose of manufacturing laboratory apparatus for educational institutions."

A couple of years ago I called the telephone number given in Stoelting's own catalogue for 1965 and was told that their "surveillance equipment," including the "Tele-tap," described as "the new line monitor for professionals, nondetectable, inconspicuous, effective . . . for use by law enforcement agencies, and ethical commercial or industrial security organisations" was no longer available.

Customers must have been sorry to hear that because the installation of Tele-tap was alleged to be particularly quick and easy "anywhere along the line to be tapped"—as illustrated by diagrams—and the price, $95, was most reasonable. It could be operated in conjunction with Stoelting's FM transmitter, Catalogue No. 17302, which would then enable the tapper to overhear the intercepted conversation in safety a couple of miles away or, with the aid of a voice-activated tape recorder, maintain unattended automatic monitoring. In 1965, the transmitter cost $325.

Fortunately, however, all is not yet lost. Loyal customers may still have hopes. In the Mulhall catalogue, only the word Stoelting is legible, but the layout of the same old label is unmistakable. The security tone-transmitter costs only twenty-two pounds—about fifty-two dollars, which is bound to turn the gadget into an undoubtedly successful currency earner to the doubtful delight of the United States Treasury Department. And, who knows, the dear old Tele-tap may also reappear one day from under the counter of a European bug peddler.

"Gives You the Creeps, Man"

When you read some of the catalogues, bugging and wiretapping emerge as an innocent pastime, an aid to the hard of hearing, a professional hobby, or a way to amuse children for hours on end.

A bug built into a hat is said to be "ideal for taking notes at conferences"—by the ill-mannered, I suppose.

A ball-point pen is recommended as being "specially handy for plant inventory." The bug is activated by removing the cap from the tip and placing it on the other end of the pen. The pen sold by SSI is reckoned to be "the real sensation"; it is a bug all right, but it will actually write, too! The user can leave it on the table, and it will continue the work—transmission, not writing—in his absence. If he trusts the people around the table, that is, for the gadget costs $155. It "opens untold opportunities during conferences, negotiations, talks, etc.," and it must be suitable for marathon sessions of the United Nations with its seventy-hours working life.

The Parabolic Sound Collector Transmitter is allegedly capable of picking up faint sounds a hundred feet away or twice as far over water. It is described as "practical, instructional and entertaining for young and old." When used "indoors or outdoors" for anything "from baby sitting to bird watching," it "opens up the fascinating world of sound around you." Complete with tripod legs and earpiece, it costs around fifty pounds, which is not very cheap if you consider that it is practically useless for the industrial spy; even the least security-conscious executive cannot fail to notice the large, cumbersome shiny disk directed at his open-air board meeting in the park or through an open window. A riflelike, handier, more serious and less conspicuous directional "tele-microphone"—also "ideal for birdwatchers . . . or field recording"—will cost five times more.

The microphone in a watch connected to a tiny transmitter in the pocket is made to appeal to the joker with a twisted sense of humor. The dealer reckons that it will be the source of "a barrel of fun. . . ." It is expected to be "a useful home or office device . . . great for party fun, kids' games," and to keep in touch "with playroom, bedroom or sickroom."

Further amusement and titillation await you—particularly if you are a robber, arsonist, or spy—if you purchase a "Listen-In" device that can be tuned "to the exciting events while they're happening on highband police or fire department radio." It will also enable you to get your kicks from "ambulance, taxicab, civil defence or business" communications.

There is plenty for the telephone-tapping enthusiast, too. Apart from a variety of taps, telephone transmitters that are guaranteed not to make any give-away switch-on clicks on the line or interfere with normal use of the tapped set in any way, he can buy tone generators, search probes, neon ringer indicators, and a flashlight, the tapper's best friend, that will actually keep giving light while providing "talking voltage for communication over a pair of telephone wires" and so eliminating the "need for walkie-talkies when tracing pairs in buildings." And that is not all. The hilarity-galore catalogues can help him to become the proud owner of wire-tracing, line-identifying, cable-locating technical aids. And if his whim and heart's desire carry him away to dangerous heights where all the beauty of human sound may travel, $250 will put him on the magic carpet of a "Pole Climber's Kit, designed for ultimate in safety with all belts made of nylon which will not rot, supplied complete with gaffs, spikes, etc."

Should the police or some other killjoy physically object to the true audio enthusiast's activities, the determined bugger can protect himself with chemical Mace or CS gas pistols also obtainable from his friendly neighborhood bug dealer. A "shockrod" offered by some brochures may prove, however, an attractive alternative. No bigger than a pocket umbrella, this handy toy is a give-away for fifty dollars. It weighs only a pound and gives a nasty electric shock "penetrating even the heaviest of clothing." Although the BTC catalogue warns customers that the "shockrod should only be used in self-defense," it is not specified whether giving a shock to a zealous policeman would count as such or not.

These dictionaries of euphemisms and all their lightheartedness may be dangerously misleading. For even if the general use of bugs is often exaggerated, if the range and clarity of transmission will seldom live up to the lavish praises showered upon them by the sellers, and if only experts can fit and conceal the gadgets fast in the right spot with noises and interference properly filtered out, the mere easy availability of electronic equipment represents a serious risk to business and industry. For the prices are not at all exorbitant and the more expensive bugs can often be hired by the day, although the deposit is high because of the loss risk.

Lapel badge, cufflink, earring, tie-pin microphones cost up to $35 each, depending on size and quality. The latest mini-miniature one, no bigger than a match head, comes for under $90. The price of basic transmitters varies with range and size, but you can get a reasonably good one to fit into a cigarette pack—and leave room for a few real cigarettes to allay suspicion—for about $165. Another one is offered as a virtual giveaway for $55, and the makers claim that all its components have been "proved and tried in astronautics," that its microphone will pick up whispered words from eight meters away even if the gadget is hidden in a drawer, and that its transmission range of "truly astonishing fidelity" is approximately a thousand meters.

Bugs already built into household and boardroom objects are also priced according to the quality of the casing. A presentable Butane table lighter—lay it on its side and it's off; stand it up and the program continues—costs $155. Or there is an ashtray that can be "received on every VHF radio set." Part of the price—$120—pays for the good quality porcelain and "pleasing appearance," but it is definitely not for ashtray fiddlers because a turn and it's on, another turn and it's off the air.

It is, however, interesting to note that for the truly professional eavesdropper, there are cigarette-pack size and smaller bugs with various technical refinements from a thousand dollars upwards.

A stethoscope to listen to asthmatic breathing through walls and closed windows is available for about a hundred dollars. Microphones with or without a transmitter built into a nail, which can actually be hammered into a wall from the outside, are more expensive; and the price begins to rise steeply with the tiny dart model because it can be aimed and fired with accuracy from a fair distance through an open window, thus eliminating the need of access to a room and the hazard of planting a device.

Better-quality bugs no longer use batteries. They can be connected to ordinary electric power outlets and so their usefulness is not limited by battery life. Some come inside ordinary table or wall sockets which retain their normal function. It takes time to replace the original socket, but once this bug is in the right position, it is hard to detect. "The efficiency will amaze you"—for a mere $145.

And do not despair if access to the target room is very limited, if there is no time to change the socket, or no chance to keep returning—excuse me, sir, I must replace the old batteries. Four hundred and fifty dollars will buy you a shockproof bug and an equally shockproof remote-control unit to fit into your shirt pocket. (Shirt and pocket are extra.) The system ensures maximum utilization—no battery is wasted on irrelevant chitchat—and makes detection almost impossible.

Beyond these now standard techniques, equipment for truly frightening 1984-style operations is already in experimental use. Wiretappers just cannot wait for the widespread introduction of the video phone. They already have a method to tap sound and picture alike, and when ultimately, a room can be bugged for both, our current interpretation of the words "privacy" and "secret" will become meaningless.

Micro-miniaturization combined with long-life-span atomic-powered batteries created a new range of tiny "drop-transmitters," as bugs are sometimes referred to in political espionage. If one of these is dropped and pressed "accidentally" in between the wall and the edge of the fitted carpet, it is likely to escape even the most meticulous cleaner's attention. I have heard about a popular Savile Row tailor who earned himself the lasting gratitude of Britain's Security Service, the former MI5, when he agreed to sew a special set of shiny buttons, supplied by a counterespionage agent, on a new blazer for a foreign diplomat. Only a slight difference in weight indicated to the tailor which of the buttons contained the bug.

It is not beyond the electronic wizards to secure information "right from the horse's mouth." A cooperative dentist may easily plant a bug in an unsuspecting patient's tooth, but an American technician very earnestly advised me against dentures which "may be submerged in a glass of deafening water on a bedside table during some crucial pillow-talk."

The same model, designed to transmit electronic signals,

can be inserted in an ordinary aspirin or vitamin pill to be swallowed by any regular user of such tablets. It turns the victim into an electronic beacon that can be tailed by an inexpensive receiver without the pursuer ever showing himself. Allegedly some experiments have been carried out to receive speech transmissions from swallowed aspirin bugs by utilizing the vibration of the bone structure, but I have never been able to obtain any authoritative confirmation of this.

The most menacing, revolutionary technique of eavesdropping will need no microphones or concealed transmitters. The basic idea was to aim a beam of light or infra-red rays at a window and pick up the reflection with the help of a photocell. The "mirrored" pattern would vary with the vibration of the glass caused by sounds inside the room. These fluctuations could then be deciphered and re-converted into sounds.

Theory has now been turned into a practical proposition as a result of experiments with the laser beam, which can be aimed at the window or through the window at a map or picture on the wall inside a room. It will pick up speech-caused vibrations and transmit them to the eavesdropper. Price is not the main obstacle to its widespread use. In 1970, I was told that a complete laser listening unit would cost "well in excess of a thousand pounds"; in 1972, however specialists reckoned that the initial investment would be "under a thou." Governments already have and sometimes operate such laser equipment. Private dealers plan to buy or manufacture a few units with the idea of letting industrial spies hire them for particular assignments.

The remaining snag is the size of all the hardware. In most of the usual circumstances, industrial spies would find it somewhat impracticable to hide and operate a truckload of electronic gear next to the dagger under the cloak. It is now expected that a lighter and more compact version will soon be marketed both for legitimate and illegitimate industrial purposes. Incidentally, eager safebreakers also await the arrival of a portable laser unit that can cut metal fast and in silence, and against which safemakers have not yet produced a satisfactory defense.

The future of bugging is in the hands of those scientists and strategists who control military research. Not that the Pentagon, for instance, with an annual research budget of eight thousand million dollars, is particularly anxious to help the Kubiks and Landaus of private espionage or to discover a soft-drink manufacturer's advertising plans, but it is inevitable that numerous specialists, totally unconnected with the vast projects of technological warfare or concepts like the electronic battlefield, should eventually enjoy the usual fringe benefits of military endeavor.

Bug peddlers have therefore become avid readers of all publications dealing with the various *sensors* introduced by the Americans in the Vietnam war. The sensors, carefully camouflaged as pebbles or even animal droppings, anything to blend in with a particular terrain, pick up and relay heat, scent, vision, or sound. They can be monitored by devices aboard low-flying aircraft.

Thermal sensors that reveal the presence of an unseen intruder and "sniffers" that detect chemicals in the body wastes may one day be useful to the defense of industrial plants.

The *Peeping Tommies*, sensors too tiny to be known as Peeping Toms, may become the replacement for the already available and ever cheaper infrared viewers and light intensifiers for clear vision and photography in the darkest night.

(It is perhaps not untypical of the differences between aggressive and defensive forces that I have known two and heard about another two German full-time industrial spies

who have used infrared viewers, instead of ordinary flash-
lights, for searching offices in darkness ever since the late
1960's while the German police did not even consider
purchasing such equipment. Fred Bath, technical consultant
of HQN Ltd. and Infrarot Technik, told me that in 1970 the
police examined and tested some viewers. Twenty night-vi-
sion instruments were ordered in due course, but the order
was soon canceled. No funds were available because other
investments enjoyed priority. As a result, in 1972, at the time
of the Munich Olympics and during the airport gun battle,
only spotlights were used, and these were, of course, shot out
by the Arab kidnappers. German police marksmen had no
night-viewing facilities, which, being invisible and so invul-
nerable in the darkness, would have helped to prevent the
massacre of innocent athletes. In the tradition of putting up
traffic lights after several accidents at a dangerous junction,
the police suddenly found money for infrared devices—after
Munich. In 1973, negotiations were still "pending." Perhaps
they must wait for another shoot-out.)

For the professional industrial spy, the *audio-sensors* may
be the most significant. In Vietnam, these gadgets proved
themselves sensitive enough to pick up sounds that were
hardly discernible by the human ear. They detected and
transmitted speech that was not at all audible to observers in
the jungle. The sensors can be dropped from helicopters by a
miniature parachute which—thanks to the assistance of
Playtex Corporation of girdle fame—ensures safe passage all
the way down but destroys itself on the ground, thus
protecting the sensor from premature discovery.

By suitable application of this device, industrial spies will
one day be able to achieve "saturation bugging" of a plant.
They will drop scores of sensors during visits to every
department and workshop or from the air into backyards and
on test tracks of, say, a car factory. All it needs is the stake to

be big enough. And there are cases like that today. Security consultant R. B. Matthews of Management Investigations Services has told me about one. It caused an estimated damage of £8,250,000, and apparently the foreseeable profits justified the investment of several years of planning and all-out effort by an international organization, the risk of at least two known murders, the corruption and intimidation of numerous executives in several countries, the tapping of dozens of telephones, and the bugging of offices and private homes. Had the audio-sensor been commercially available, a comparatively small, extra capital outlay for saturation bugging would have been no obstacle to a determined bunch of professionals.

"Determination" and "professionalism" are, in fact, the key words to be considered by the defenders of business secrets when the hazard of bugging is evaluated. In the light of the reviewed cases, techniques, and equipment, I am ready to accept several security specialists' gloomy warning that against totally ruthless professionals, the total demolition of a building is the only total defense. If a particular management finds this suggestion not quite endearing or practicable, perhaps other, cheaper, and less radical solutions can be chosen, keeping always in mind that only extreme measures can truly counter a good spy's planning, timing, resources, ingenuity, and dogged determination.

Within the framework of general security—control of access to buildings and documents, the application of the must-know principle, and the surveillance of staff, which will be dealt with elsewhere—the most positive line of defense against electronic eavesdropping is the creation of a constantly bug-conscious attitude by *all* employees.

Learning from diplomats, many Japanese, American, and European executives are taking special precautions when confidential matters must be discussed in "enemy country."

Several French companies now teach their top brass how to find drawing pins—*punaise,* the French word for it, is also espionage jargon for bugs—in hotel rooms.

Certain defensive techniques are well known—and dangerously overrated. In 1970, when German Foreign Minister Scheel visited Poland to negotiate a pact, his counterintelligence agents spotted and neutralized nine bugs in window frames and furniture in the office and telegram room placed at his disposal. He then restricted all confidential exchanges among his staff because there was no guarantee that every bug had been discovered. Urgent thoughts had to be written down and passed around on a memo pad. Businessmen who also use this method often forget that the notes must be burned and the ashes flushed down the drain, or, even better, the whole pad should be totally destroyed in a portable shredding machine.

So-called security experts sometimes advise clients to turn on the radio or TV set loud or to run the shower at full blast to spoil the eavesdropper's effort. What they forget is that some microphones, like the one that can pick up a whisper through a pillow in bed, are several times more sensitive than the human ear, and even the devices of poorer quality can "hear" at least as much as participants of the conversation; if there is more noise around, they must raise their voices to hear one another. But this method will, indeed, cut out the amateur who places his bug in radio or TV sets.

Talking in muted tones and, particularly, whispering and turning constantly when talking are also recommended, but it must be remembered that a professional will use at least four bugs for a fair-size room to cover the changing directions of speech.

In the course of long negotiations, it is good tactics to change hotels frequently and quite unexpectedly because the possibility of bugging increases considerably with the length of stay in one place. The moves also reduce a spy's chances for finding the maid or room-service waiter ready to accept a bribe. When Australian press-magnate Rupert Murdoch negotiated his spectacular take-over bid for the *News of the World*, his first firm foothold on which to build an empire in Britain, he was said to have changed hotels almost every day.

Firms which use conference rooms in hotels for important meetings have recently discovered that, according to legal advice, special antispy precautions are open to them. All they have to do is to draw up a contract with the hotel to guarantee general security including bug-free premises. The hotel can be held responsible for certain leakages and intrusions.

Understandable worries about spies and bugs led to the most peculiar arrangements when a major merger negotiation was conducted between two giants of the British beer industry. Two Rolls-Royce loads of directors were driven separately by roundabout routes to a selected point on the Yorkshire moors. The drivers were then asked to withdraw to a safe distance, so that the final discussions could only be overheard by the wind. There was no suitable hiding place for any directional microphones within several hundred yards.

Executives who cannot bring themselves to demolishing their offices or conducting their business from the moors, using carrier pigeons instead of telephones, must learn to live with the bugging and phone-tapping hazard. They are not entirely defenseless, either.

Double-glazing or heavy curtains drawn across the windows can filter out laser listening devices. Like the United States State Department, some major supranational concerns have completely windowless conference rooms. For confidential discussions requiring maximum security, portable rooms are now available. Walls, floor, and ceiling, made of a material that will not conduct sound vibrations, electricity, or radio signals, can be latched together in a few moments creating a temporary spyproof enclosure within any office.

To discover telephone taps, perhaps several miles away, can be a very complicated job even for suitably equipped specialists. But "scrambler" sets, now removed from the "Governments only" list, are available for purchase by private firms at about $185 each or for rent at about $70 a year. These work on a lower frequency than the ones used by heads of state and security services, but the principle is the same: the scrambler minces the speech signals into a meaningless jumbled code of sounds understandable only to the unscrambler that must be used at the far end of the line. This, however, is no defense against a bug hidden in the room where the phone is used. (Some executives who already use desk-top scrambler units install a small neon sign near the telephone to upset bug transmissions.) The new portable scrambler set can be used anywhere, even on public telephones. This may become as natural a part of the traveling executive's luggage as the toothbrush.

For the time being, private firms will have no access to the latest kind of telephone network that cannot be tapped at all. Britain's Signals Research and Development Establishment has based the new system on "fiber optics"; wires are replaced by glass fiber strands along which a light beam carries the conversation, not necessarily in a straight line, but as yet over only relatively short distances.

Pessimists—or the really security-conscious?—who never quite believe themselves to be bug-free, may install antibugging devices in their offices. With an audible signal, these can scramble all sounds including, unfortunately, the speaker's own voice, so that it also turns most of the conversation in the room into unintelligible noise. Which is one way to stop bugs.

A more advanced antibug device generates noise over the

wide range of frequencies favored by eavesdroppers, and this interference garbles all transmissions from planted or carried bugs. Allegedly a German desk-top console gives complete cover; it jams bug transmissions and warns the user if his telephone is tapped.

Bug peddlers usually like to cash in on both aggression and defense. Their lists include two kinds of bug detectors. One is an ordinary metal detector, similar to those used by archeologists and military mine-sweeping units. Depending on sensitivity, the price may be up to $700.

The "squealer" is a more professional piece of portable equipment for bug detection. It may or may not actually squeal when, in the course of sweeping through various frequency bands, it picks up and locks onto a radio signal. As the user approaches the hidden bug, the reception of the signal grows stronger, and so the exact location of the transmitter can be found. The price ranges from about $115 to $700, but to carry out a proper sweep is not as easy as dealers would like us to believe. Amateur security officers, like managing directors who want to do even this job themselves, encounter many snags.

Passive bugs can be found only by using metal detectors, but the signals may be misleading. I know a German executive who ran up builders' bills for DM11,000—some $3200—by detecting metal in several parts of his Essen offices, having the walls opened, finding no bug, and having the damage repaired.

Active bugs can defy the squealer if they have been properly planted by a professional in the right location where misleading background noises confuse the detector; if the bugs are designed to emit very weak signals which can be picked up by the spies' super quality receiver but are beyond the sensitivity of the standard detector; and also if the spies use a great variation of frequencies. Only a few years ago, frequencies below 30 megacycles and above 500 megacycles were hardly ever employed for bugging. More recently, both these limits have disappeared. With each aggressive step in both directions, the defense needs new equipment, and the cost begins to soar beyond acceptable levels.

For all these reasons, the amateur spy catcher is ill-advised to rely on D-I-Y security and attractively cheap equipment. The job is best left to professionals—but to choose the right debugging expert is not easy. Many bug peddlers and spies themselves offer this service, and doublecross has always been the bread and butter of this game. Although you often need a thief to catch a thief, there is no guarantee that he will *want* to find all bugs, that he will not plant a bug for his own purposes while discovering others, and that he will not misuse the information and access to offices he inevitably gains when he carries out an assignment.

Debugging can be specially done occasionally, for example, before an important conference or after building work has been done in a boardroom, but usually it is part of an annual contract for a general security program. Such contract fees vary a great deal because the program must be tailor-made to suit all circumstances and reckon with specific factors like the location of premises and the likelihood of attack.

In London, bug "fumigation" of an office with four telephones costs about seventy-five dollars, but follow-up inspections are cheaper. An annual contract for electronic sweeps, advice, emergency visits, and test raids at irregular intervals, may cost an average factory three thousand dollars. A day's external monitoring to detect transmission from bugs on any frequency throughout a crucial meeting costs sixty-five dollars per day. In Paris, the charges may be up to 20 percent more for the same services, because of the difference in general price levels. Thus to keep a boardroom and three or four key offices reasonably bugfree may cost about seventeen dollars a week.

Prices are similar in Germany. The Italians do a great deal of security work all over the Continent because their prices can be very competitive, but clients must ensure that they find and contract the few who can be relied on not to sell them down the drain.

In the United States, a single visit to search just a few offices may cost a thousand dollars. The fee is reduced by contract work.

A great advantage of professional security consultants is that it pays them to stock the right equipment for hire for special occasions, whereas it would be uneconomical for most commercial organizations to invest, for instance, in a twelve hundred dollars degaussing unit, which can prevent any secret tape recording from leaving an important conference.

In the same way as ships can be encircled by a current-carrying conductor to neutralize the magnetic belt around the hull and give protection against magnetic mines, the degaussing unit creates a demagnetizing barrier at a door and ruins any concealed tape or wire recording that passes through it. This in itself may prevent the sale of industrial information, because the buyer is very often, and not without good reason, suspicious of the seller's true intentions, and the tape may well be the proof that clinches the deal. For although trusted top secretaries and even board members have sometimes sold their companies' secrets, others have offered dummy secrets for sale with the chairman's full backing to mislead competitors. To fake convincingly the complete recording of a board meeting would be just as difficult as to get every member's cooperation in the deception.

Despite all these available services and electronic paraphernalia, security-conscious executives are rightly worried when they sit in their bug-swept windowless offices, talking on their scrambler-protected telephones with antibugs hissing and neons buzzing, radios blaring and hot showers sizzling. They never fail to emphasize that a fraction of soaring bugging costs is better spent if you dine and wine a talkative executive or sleep with the chairman's secretary, or with the chairman, for that matter. They also repeat their credo, "Beware of the Secretary With Expensive Tastes," ad nauseam—and yet not frequently enough. People can still leave offices carrying secrets not only on paper, in the form of original documents or photostatic copies, but also on tape because palm-size pocket recorders just walk in when the bug detector has left.

Miniature recorders, that can tape five hours on a single cartridge, cost from $750 upward. It seems likely that models marketed on both sides of the Atlantic come from the same source.

The answer is an American device, also sold in Britain and soon to be available in Europe, which is specifically a tape-recorder probe. Its price tag, $600, is probably bigger than the gadget itself. It fits into a jacket pocket and has a sensor that can be worn on the wrist under the watch strap. No matter how silently a recorder works, the sensor can detect the running motor—but only if it is brought into close proximity, no more than two feet but preferably nearer, to its quarry.

An American vice-president, lately in charge of his company's security, told me with a shudder: "The school I went to gave warning that the meticulously sculptured teeth that smile at you, the waist you embrace, the thigh you gently squeeze, the button you hastily undo, and the bra you so diligently caress, may well conceal a mini mike, and you may find yourself trying to sleep with a proper radio-transmitting station.

"What am I supposed to do? Promote celibacy in the company? Or advise all staff to touch a girl only with a metal detector and cuddle her with a bug detector—but only after giving her the once-over with the tape-recorder detector?

"Gives you the creeps, man. . . ."

7

Sex and the Single Spy

ONE OF THE FEW PRIVATE eyes with tear-resistant mascara subjected me to an embarrassingly long and perniciously impersonal gaze. I suddenly knew what it must feel like to be a nude painting on public view prior to sale by auction. The good quality of the mascara was clearly wasted on her—those immobile eyes would never experience the tingling sensation when that precious liquid begins to overflow and run to ruin the makeup.

In Zurich, behind the sleepy old guild houses and near the bottom-heavy Romanesque Grossmünster, we were sitting in a lively first-floor bar, where the white piano was built into the counter to support perching patrons and their drinks, and to give a touch of Hollywood to the upstairs in contrast to the girlie joint downstairs. During the unnerving period of silence between us, submerged in the clinks and rhubarb of gaiety all around, I had a chance to wonder why we were there at all.

By that time I had known Vera Fielding for about six years. Plump as an ice bucket—with no more warmth than that—aged anything between thirty-five and fifty years—depending on the good will or malice of the onlooker—her manners, gestures, and exquisitely chic clothes were as

French as only an Englishwoman's can be after twenty years of residence in Rheims, Cannes, and Paris. She had trained herself to speak English with a French accent "because it was good for business."

I knew she used to run a small cabaret agency, assembling groups of girl dancers for the Far and Middle East. That was when we first met, and she kindly arranged a couple of introductions which were most useful to my research in the Far East. A few years later I had heard that she had set herself up as a private eye with a rather exclusive clientele. Perhaps she was helped by her widespread contacts, including those at the lower end of the social scale from her former unsavory business.

It had been odd to see her again here in Zurich, only the previous night, at a party attended mostly by financiers and industrialists. There were three snippets of conversation I could recall.

First a man, who had no idea that we had met before, introduced me to "this most remarkable lady" whom, he said, I wanted to meet. It was, of course, plain party chatter. I had not even known she would be there. Yet she was not at all surprised, and it soon emerged she knew I was "interested in business intelligence." How did she know? "One hears about things."

Later I was talking to a banker about the IOS when Vera Fielding suddenly reappeared from nowhere and asked me quite casually: "Is that why you wanted to meet me?"

"No. I told you. I'm pleased to see you, but—"

She walked away in midsentence.

As I was leaving the party, she buttonholed me. "All right, *mon cher*, I'll meet you tomorrow."

Now, as we sat propped up by that white piano in the bar, my companion finally broke the silence. "So you know my husband."

"Your husband? I didn't even know that you were married."

"You were talking to him last night."

"Was I?"

"Come off it. You went out of your way to meet him, *n'est-ce pas?*"

I was at a loss. I had no idea who her husband could be. If she was determined not to believe me, it would be pointless to argue.

After another long pause, she gave me the lead I was hoping for. "Look, let's make a deal. I'll try to help you, and you leave him out of this."

"Your husband?"

"Of course."

She told me that her husband was "just a very ordinary accountant." They lived in a style that he could never afford on his income. They often traveled together, but he was totally unconnected with her business and, in fact, had no idea what her profession was. Yes, this might well be the secret she was trying to protect.

Although I was no threat to her in any way, she must have decided that I was because I knew her past and could discover her current work. I suspected that she had become the victim of her own way of thinking, because she knew only too well that any fragment of information could be power— and that power could be used in many ways. Blackmail, for instance, was never far from her thoughts. I knew I could never change her views about the world, so I chose to accept the deal and promise to "leave him out of it." This was easy. I had no intention to track down an accountant who lived off his wife. The hard part of the bargain was to get her to say whatever she was ready to reveal and to ask some questions without giving away how little I knew about her. What was her exact line of business anyway?

"How did you get into *this* racket?"

The question proved to be correct in one respect. Hers was a racket all right, though she strongly denied that she was a high-grade call-girl madam.

It all began for her with a request from an American-controlled, electrical household-appliance company.

"They wanted me to get a few girls together and put on a show at their annual sales convention," she said. "You know the sort of things they do. Pack the reps into a hotel; give them a good time and a hearty pep talk; cheer them up; let them see the winners of sales competitions receive their prizes, the gold watch and a diploma, a pen with the inscription of the chairman's signature, a weekend in Le Touquet or Jamaica depending on the generosity of the firm, anything to let the lads know what a great and successful family they belong to. At first, European companies just laughed at the Yanks. Now they begin to copy them. The effect is unbelievable. Some of these hard old reps just sit there with tears in their eyes. Out in the cold, on the road, pushing their shoe polish and fancy goods, they're nothing. Here, they're VIP's. Directors talk to them; girls belly-dance or strip for them, only for them; the general public is not admitted. What a treat!"

Her first such show was a big success, and firms from all over Europe began to ask her to put together "conference specials" for them. The girls were sometimes invited to stay on after the show for a meal and the general booze-up, but Vera Fielding did not like that.

"They were taking advantage of the girls. They had company for nothing. It's none of my business to safeguard the artistes' virginity—and I certainly get no commission for their sex life—but providing company is an entirely different matter. So we came to a new arrangement. There was a fee for the show, and if the client wanted hostesses to chat up the boys afterward, that was extra. Business was good, and I was even asked to send some 'genuine French cancan strippers' to a few American conventions, but the big break came when a stranger made me an absolutely crazy proposition. It was so crazy that I became suspicious. Nobody is that crazy. But there was no catch. Not for me.

"He wanted me to continue with my artistes, but whenever hostesses were required, I should send out *his* girls. Instead of my usual commission, I could collect the full fee for each girl because he would pay them himself, separately.

"I accepted, but I'm nobody's fool. By keeping my ears to the ground, I found out within six months what his business was. The girls picked up a lot of confidential company chitchat during the fun and games after the conferences, and they reported it all through him to a man called Kubik." She looked at me sharply from the corner of her eye. "You know him?"

"Sounds familiar. I'd like to meet him one day."

"That makes two of us."

We left it at that.

How she muscled in on the main business she refused to say. But in she was. And soon she sold out her original business because she found something much more profitable. It is what could be described as a "middle-aged escort agency" for special clients chosen by Kubik and some others.

"You see, *mon cher,* there're lots of men who have never taken out a really pretty girl," she explained. "They're afraid of the dolly-bird. Will she be too much for him? What will she want from him? What if he is seen with a girl like that? The escort I can provide is pleasant to look at but no beauty. Even if she were found in a hotel room with him, nobody would seriously scream adultery. On the other hand, she's good company. Easy to talk to. Usually well versed in the business the man is in."

"Do you ask about his occupation in advance?"

"Sometimes I'm told what his job is. Sometimes I have to find out a bit of his background. That's what the private-eye setup is for. You know something? I have two professional detectives working for me full time."

She was rather coy about the duties of her escorts. Report pillowtalk? Sort of. Ask specific questions? Sometimes. Stick to the once only good time or start more lasting affairs?

"It depends. Show me the man who doesn't want to have a good time away from home especially when he feels safe about the partner. An affair is more difficult. You see, none of the women who work for me are single. Sex is a dangerous thing for a single agent. These all have their families and love their husbands. They do the job without ever falling in love. Professionals, you might say; but don't forget, in most cases, it's only tea and sympathy. They're not even asked to sleep with the client. And many of the husbands are also agents working for one outfit or another—although this must be checked regularly because they can easily join the opposition."

She never used three words: *spy, espionage, enemy.* I recognized this as a hallmark of her professionalism.

As we talked about "female operatives," she reeled off some strong views of experience.

"The Mata Haris of modern political intelligence are more likely to be male than female because of the blackmail potential of homosexuality. Whatever we'd like to believe about our grown-up attitudes, the adolescent prejudice of society still compels the gay to keep his sad secret. You see? Even I called it sad. As if there weren't enough disastrously sad ordinary marriages.

"People also have a false picture of the Mata Haris of economic intelligence. The real ones are usually much plainer than those cavorting with Messrs. Bond, Palmer, and Napoleon Solo.

"Sure, some agents employ a glamour puss or two for publicity or some proper blackmail setup. Sometimes they succeed, too. I know a girl who was asked to pose as a Lesbian for a particular assignment. It was part of a long-term plan to trap an Italian research scientist whose private life and background were fully investigated, and who was found to be suffering from some sexual inadequacy complex. She got herself a job where he worked, and at the first good opportunity, pretending to be drunk, she bared her soul and confessed her 'secret' to him.

"This frankness led to a friendship with endless talks about their sexual problems, and eventually, she came to represent a tremendous challenge to him: Could he turn her into a heterosexual? The old story. The ultimate glory for the Walter Mitty in all men. Which Italian doesn't secretly dream about having such fantastic sexual skill that he could make a prostitute fall in love with him, with him alone, the best she ever met?

"Well, I can tell you, this scientist was on to a good thing—he was bound to succeed. The girl became his mistress, but there were 'problems' with her 'Lesbian past.' Money problems, of course. He was so hooked on her that she could get anything she wanted out of him. He had no money, not enough to 'help her'—but he had access to information that was worth a lot.

"It took almost a year, but the operation was a complete success except for one little hitch. The usual one. She fell in love with him. Soon the flow of information was down to a trickle, and then she persuaded him to change his job. The girl was, of course, dealt with, but the scheme was wrecked."

"What do you mean she was dealt with? How?"

Vera Fielding ignored the question and declared with a sigh, "No, single agents are no good. Too vulnerable. Especially the women. Pity, really, for they can be very efficient and reliable. In this game, it's only a matter of money to turn an agent double and treble and turn him yet again. Girls can often be more trustworthy. The difference is that men are usually loyal to a firm or organization, while women are loyal to a man, a husband, or a boss, if he's a good boss, and that's a much stronger bond. What do you know about Kubik?"

The question came so suddenly, without any pause or warning, that I almost began to tell her about New York, the auction in Bangkok, Mory's death in San Francisco, and everything else I knew or suspected, perhaps all in one breath without a chance for having second thoughts about what to say and what to leave out. Lighting a cigarette—what a blessed device to gain time!—I mumbled something about her position which ought to enable her to find out as much as she liked about him.

She followed it up regardless with more questions—and not very subtle ones at that. Had I heard that Kubik was regarded as the biggest bastard in the business? Was it true that he was involved in the offshore investments' battle? Did he sell out on all sides? Was he a police informer in several countries at a very high level?

It was a most odd and nonprofessional performance indeed, and I told her so in so many words. There was not much to choose between the two of them, and I cannot say I had much admiration for their lines of business, but if anything, my sympathy went to Kubik. At least he relied on his bent ingenuity, whereas she lived on straight and unadulterated sexploitation. I could not care less if she was a menace to Kubik or others in the industrial intelligence game, but her particular trade and some of her remarks were so repugnant that I wondered if I should try and send a word of warning to Kubik.

She dropped the subject as suddenly as she had brought it up, and continued her tirade in praise of older spies.

"Most people who may be targets because of their knowledge and important position are in the middle-age group," she explained. "Employers tend to regard them more and more trustworthy as their years of service accumulate, but in fact, they're an increasing liability mostly because of frustration. So are the 'born spinsters.' But the agent who goes for such a target must be matched correctly to avoid arousing suspicion and to make the 'love play' look natural.

"A couple of years ago there was such a perfect match made in France. During the protracted Franco-Algerian oil negotiations, Rachid Tabti, an Algerian agent, sought out a thirty-eight-year-old woman in the French Foreign Ministry. She was the secretary of the director of economic affairs—a perfect choice. I never met her, but I'm sure that this long-serving mademoiselle was extremely loyal to her boss— until Tabti promised to marry her. She then copied confidential memoranda for him and his helper, a chap called Boumaza, and information on French policy and plans for tactical moves began to flow to Algeria.

"The trio were among the unlucky few to be caught. The men were sent to jail [Tabti for ten, Boumaza for seven years], but she got away with a suspended five-year sentence. Because their offense was concerned with oil, they were charged with economic espionage, but surely the sentences would have been ten times shorter if that was not regarded, in fact, as political espionage against the state. Anyway whoever planned the operation must have been a professional. Probably one of the old school of Dr. Nkrumah's administration. We have a lot to learn from the politicals. Do you know my Bible?"

"Depends what you call your Bible."

"The documents released in Ghana after Nkrumah got his marching orders."

She was particularly full of admiration for one of these papers, used in the training courses for intelligence and subversive agents, that which gave detailed directives for seducing and exploiting officials. The courses, code-named False Flag, were run by Russian and Chinese specialists under the aegis of the Bureau of African Affairs.

Eventually I saw this document, and although some of the language it used was amusing, the seriousness of the exercise seemed beyond doubt. One training example referred to "a lady secretary" who might be twenty-five years old and work in an African embassy.

"Because she is not very beautiful she has never enjoyed the love of men and though she is anxious to get a husband she does not get even a boy friend to live with. . . . In such a situation" an agent must be "put in her way to win her love."

The directives then specified the right agent. "Such an informant must not be too handsome, must be within the agehood of the woman, must have certain good qualities which will attract the woman and make her feel that the love being proposed is real and lasting, leading to marriage which will be a permanent one. When such a woman is won by the officer or the informant recruiter, she is gradually made to understand that it is necessary to lead a good and happy life and therefore will it not be necessary if she brings some of the secrets of her office to someone who is willing to offer a fat sum of money for such secrets?"

The woman "who is won" would then be left to chew it over and make her own decision about the usefulness of betrayal in maintaining their house and future family.

The document emphasized: "The most decisive point here is the officer himself does not fall in love with the woman, but that someone else is allowed to do it." Was she then supposed to take a husband and a lover at the same time? Wouldn't such a sudden windfall make her suspicious?

Disregarding the ambiguity of this "most decisive point," Vera Fielding quoted long passages from the document, and added that it should be made compulsory reading for every student of the subject.

With a gentle touch of irony, I thanked her profoundly for her most enlightening lecture. She reacted with a rather unexpected question: "Oh, how did you know?"

We were back in square one—she talking in riddles, I at a complete loss.

"Know what?"

"That I'm a lecturer now."

I just about managed to resist the remark that the existence of an academy of whoring was news to me. Where else could she be a lecturer?

Congratulating her heartily, I asked what her subject was.

"Security, of course."

"Where do you teach?"

"In America. I've just bought a home in California. My fourth. I have to be there for four weeks twice a year, plus I have to go frequently on other business, so it's worth it. Anyway, the school paid for half of it. It's cheaper than my hotel bills."

"What school is it?"

"Very reputable and quite well known. Training executives for management is its bread and butter. Security is part of the ordinary curriculum, but there's a—let's say, more specialized service, sort of postgraduate course. I think we'd better leave it at that."

Could I get in touch with them? No. Can't she say more

about the school? No. How do students enroll if its where-abouts are secret? No dice. Could she put me in touch with a former student? No dice.

I suggested we have another drink somewhere. She accepted. Then I thought we ought to have a meal. She smiled and agreed. We chatted about mutual acquaintances, hotels, holidays, the fate of the Dalai Lama, and her experience in learning French without tears while I was just waiting for the right moment for more meaningful questions —and she knew it. It was when I asked her about the success of her marriage that she chose to answer the question I didn't ask.

"Yes, *mon cher*, perhaps you could meet someone . . . How about a school teacher?"

"Could you arrange it?"

"I can try."

"Sex Is Optional"

It was one of those don't-call-us-we'll-call-you affairs. In the months of waiting I made some inquiries and met a stone wall. People either did not know about the school or refused to discuss it. Vera Fielding told me some impressive facts about the schoolteacher when we met again in London. An American security adviser did not "rule out the possibility of some government interest in the course."

I was in Washington when I finally received the call from the schoolteacher.

"I'll be in New York tomorrow. Want to come over and meet me there?" It was a gently undulating, educated drawl. Yet the question sounded like a command. Answer was not expected or waited for. "Shall we say 11 A.M. in the United Nations delegates' lounge? It's one of the only two places in New York where you get a decent Italian espresso."

As good a reason as any for a choice. She rang off. She only forgot to ask me if I could get in there at all.

I arrived early. At 10:58 I ordered two espressos. She appreciated that when she joined me a few seconds after 11. "Schoolteacher" had hardly ever been a more ill-fitting description than when it was applied to her.

Just under thirty years of age, she was the live cliché of the all-American dream, the long-legged, blonde, suburban household beauty with the eternal college-girl smile. True to style, she crooned "Hi," the way other women might whisper "I'll be yours"—but you couldn't cajole a single word she did not want to say out of her. When she opened her lips and all those pearly teeth joined in a sparkle, one expected to hear a Doris Day song, but she was more likely to reel off Dow Jones averages for the last thirty years or so with effortless fluency.

"Shall we call me Isabel? Let's—unless you dislike the sound of it."

Her record was quite remarkable. She was an economist by trade, studied psychology in her spare time, completed a crash course in computer programming, another in basic electronics, and by the look of it, a third in beauty care. For two years she studied in Milan where she picked up fluent Italian, learned to love espresso coffee, and made her first contacts with "some industrial security people."

In her first job with an American market-research company, she was assigned to economic intelligence work. "It was strictly routine and very boring," she told me. "Had to read a lot, and my languages were useful. Yes, I speak French and Spanish, too. Speak? Well, not quite, but it's useful.

"I suppose I could have spent my entire working life reading company publications and the trade press, but I could see from the start that there was something fishy about my employers. That's what fascinated me. So I did a little homework and came up with quite interesting results. I discovered that we commanded a strange respect, perhaps fear, though we were not very highly thought of in the trade. Also that we had about a hundred people on the payroll who never came into the office. There would have been no room for them either. They all worked full-time for other companies in most of the major industrial countries and only did part-time work for us. What exactly they did, I could only guess. When I started to ask questions about them, I was told that it was not very healthy to be too bright and inquisitive. But then an assignment came up, and I was the only one on hand to do it, so I got it."

"What sort of assignment?"

She sidestepped the question by asking for a drink. By the time I returned from the hand-to-hand fighting in the trenches around the bar, she had conveniently forgotten the question. "Now where were we? Oh, yes, I was told it was not very healthy to be too bright and inquisitive. Anyway you were interested in the school, not me."

I was ready to widen my field of interest there and then, but she was determined to steer the course of the interview. So I asked how I could become a student of hers.

"You can't. The courses at the ordinary business school range from six months to three years, and these are open to anyone. But I have nothing to do with that. There's only a financial connection between this legit school and our more specialized courses which have never been advertised or openly acknowledged. Applications come only through rec-ommendation by people we know, and each applicant must agree to being checked out completely *before* acceptance."

"What sort of checking out is that?"

"Pretty full. Yes, pretty full." She smiled, and I noticed a rather vicious tightness at the corners of her mouth. The pleasure she derived from being in control of the situation was unmistakable.

"Do you enjoy being in the know?"

"Doesn't everybody? Isn't that what life is all about?"

I was not there to pick holes in her philosophy. So I asked how long she had been at the school.

"From the start—er—it's coming up to four years. My god! The longest job I ever had."

She told me that the "special course" for business postgraduates was devised to fill a gap. "The Russians teach economic intelligence work as a matter of routine to every spy they enlist. One hears that in Japan ten thousand potential agents are trained each year. In the West, most business schools forget about teaching security, or like some American colleges, they give only very superficial, perfunctory guidance. True, California, New York, Michigan, and some other universities can give you a degree in industrial security, but that's concerned mainly with plant security, protection from pilferage, and things like credit checking.

"You can't train people in large numbers. Their knowledge of practical intelligence work loses its value if it's free to everybody. Our success thrives on the exclusiveness and confidential nature of the courses. So we have only a very few places in the two or three standard three-month courses, and our output is usually no more than, say, sixteen people a year—perhaps fifty-five in all since we started."

Most students were Americans, many with some sort of government security service behind them. There were a few applications for places from Europe, but only two Germans and a Swedish director of a supranational company were accepted. They never had any approaches from England.

"We have to be careful," Isabel said, "for what people learn from us can be used as effectively in defensive as in aggressive operations. We have no control over that." She smiled again. Secretly I apologized to all American college girls for any comparison I had first made. "After all, defense requires aggressive moves. Through our exclusivism, if you like, we practice what we preach about the 'must-know' principle—publish only what the public must know; each employee should be told what he must know to perform his duties, and the less known to outsiders about executives' functions and private lives the better."

"Why the secrecy about private lives if an executive is honest with nothing to hide?"

She sat very upright now, in an almost unnatural posture; the pupils of her eyes widened as if trying to overflow their allocated circle; and her gaze went right through me, the swirling crowd, the wall, and the East River beyond, perhaps to bore into the Midtown Tunnel. When at last she answered me, her voice hit a negative crescendo—reduced to a whisper but reaching a climax in emphasis—and the words poured out in an almost unintelligible, intimate purr. Unintentionally my question must have touched an open nerve end.

"My father was a preacher. He led an open life. And he was trampled on. By everybody. And I told my first boyfriend that I loved him. Just like that. So he laughed. And he told his friends that I was easy. I was a known quantity. But not the second time. My second boyfriend did not laugh. I made him forget how to." Gathering speed all the time, she was in top gear now. "They called me a teaser. But I wasn't. I just wanted to understand boys. So I asked questions. And I'd kiss them only for something really intimate about themselves. And nobody ever laughed at me ever again. They couldn't afford to. Because I *knew*—I knew it all. And it made me strong. Because information is power. It's muscle. The more you know the stronger you are. You just sit back and let your muscles ripple—and one word will make people jump. You

can crush them—men, companies, corporations, countries—
for a tiny scrap of info can be the trigger that controls the
gun that can be pressed against anybody's temple—or stuck
into their groins. . . ."

She closed her eyes and relaxed shivering. It was an almost
total collapse with only an instinctive reflex making her
fingers hold her glass in midair. If any sensation or mere
thought of power had ever given anyone an orgasm, this was
it.

When she opened her eyes a few seconds after this most
peculiar spectacle, the college-girl smile was back with a
touch of the arrogance of the leading drum majorette first
time on parade. "Any questions?"

I cleared my throat.

"What? Yes—er—would it be possible to visit the school?"

"Sorry, the answer is negative."

"Where is it? Even if you name the town, I can't conduct
door-to-door inquiries. Right?"

"Affirmative. We have two centers. Here in New York and
in California."

"I was told it's in San Francisco."

"Who told you? . . . Won't you tell me?"

"I'm afraid I have to take a *negative attitude* to that."

She laughed. "Bad habit, I know, to say affirmative when I
mean yes. Sorry."

"Is my information correct?"

"I'd say affirmative, but I mean almost. Let's say it's near
Sausalito. Nothing much to look at, apart from the world's
largest collection of electronic devices. But these are only
teaching aids. We're not selling them. Just like to keep up
with new developments."

"What do you teach?"

"Oh, shall we say 'extracurricular' subjects? No, that's not
very helpful, is it? Well look, we first teach sort of physical

security, safe office procedures and the like, including the use of electronic gadgets and their disadvantages. When they got the idea, we show them how to break the best security. We do exercises. Only to warn them about the dangers, of course. . . . You don't quite believe that, do you? OK, they learn how to plan and carry out aggressive operations. It's up to them what they use it for."

"Which explains the secrecy. None of your students would like to advertise his interest in what the public call industrial espionage. Is that it?"

"That's where you're wrong. Silence is a matter of principle. The power that comes from every scrap of info knows no exceptions. If, for instance, our course and its whereabouts were widely known, somebody could trace back who our students were. That in itself would be a risk. We've had top executives as well as fairly influential politicians who also need intelligence methods in their squabbles. And I doubt if the dumbest of their wives would be pleased to hear that the curriculum includes certain aspects of sex and the dangers of pillow talk."

"What do you tell them—to take deaf lovers?"

"Not a bad idea if they must have a girl friend at all. But seriously, we outline the usual principles especially in the selection of staff. The very glamorous secretary is less of a security hazard than the plain girl who struggles against the growing fear of remaining a spinster, and things like that. It's amazing how little people will think about it if their attention is not directed specifically toward the problem."

I suggested they ought to give Vera Fielding's "Bible" to each student.

"So she told you about it," she laughed. "I gave it to her originally, and it's quite funny how obsessed she became with it. But you're quite right—we do distribute copies; they're part of the file each student receives."

"Is that the subject Vera lectures on?"

"Affirmative. And she's very good, you know. Personally I think that her lectures are one of the most vital parts of the course. I wish somebody warned me at the start of my career about her basic principles."

"Why do you say that?"

"Experience."

"You don't look particularly plain or spinsterish to be singled out for easy seduction."

She mulled over the thought, then nodded. "OK, listen."

She talked about that first important assignment that eventually shaped her career in the intelligence trade. "My target was a particular piece of info from the British aviation industry. Don't ask me what sort of information or what part of the industry."

All she would say was that her "inquiry" concerned "some variations on a revolutionary new idea" that was not unknown in countries of great experience in aviation—presumably, the United States—but it involved a tremendous race in "economic feasibility studies." The firm that employed Isabel wanted to know about British experiments that had failed and also how immediate the plans for a multimillion investment were.

"When I got my briefing, I thought we were in a terrible rush. Which only showed what an amateur I was. A team of five people had already been working on this target for more than a year when I was to join them. They had already been to several countries, had resident agents in Japan and France, and spotted a potential gap—for me."

Apparently the team tried to get the necessary information out of a "research establishment," but the security arrangements were too good. Only three, possibly four, people knew all the details. To obtain each bit separately and then to try and put it all together would have been too difficult and, even worse, too risky.

The target was attacked from several sides. A great deal of money "was invested in a key secretary," but it did not pay off. Through a subcontractor, an agent penetrated the premises several times posing as a typewriter mechanic. He picked up a few fragments of conversations in the offices, pinched several memos and miles and miles of carbon ribbon.

The latter has become a particular hazard to firms using electric typewriters of the "golf-ball" design. The letters of such a typewriter are on a small globe that punches ink off the plastic film onto the paper. The machine prints with great clarity, but the ribbon can be used only once. Once it is thrown away, it can be read as easily as the letter or document which was typed with it. I have now heard of several firms that have failed to destroy such "waste material" and lost valuable secrets through this minor negligence.

It was, in fact, a crucial few-yard section of such a ribbon, recovered from a wastepaper basket by the "mechanic," that gave the much-awaited lead to Isabel's team. For it told them that the highly confidential documents of the target project were looked after by a forty-eight-year-old man who was classified as a "personal assistant" but was actually no more than a glorified ideal clerk.

"Without that strip of typing, we wouldn't have paid any attention to him in a hundred years," Isabel said. "But then, of course, the hounds were let loose on him. One of the people we used was a British private detective, and he was very good. He seemed to have the killer instinct you need for fox hunting. It makes me sick."

"Work like that?"

"Oh, no, fox hunting. The poor animal hasn't got a chance. And don't talk to me about the poor Indians and the Viet-Cong because they can fight back."

It appears, however, that not much of a chance was given to her quarry either. He was found to be a single, quiet man, reasonably well paid, satisfied with his work, without any strong desire to climb higher up the ladder. He lived alone in the suburbs and hardly ever left the house in the evenings.

Every Saturday morning he did his shopping, returned home to have an early lunch, had a shower, caught a train to London, and, as Isabel put it, "a short ride on the subway took him to the only fun and luxury in his life"—a regular date with a call girl, in her flat at 3:30 sharp. If he was early, he would walk up and down the Mayfair street for a few minutes.

"We first thought about trying something through the girl," Isabel told me, "but it seemed unlikely that he would ever tell her anything we needed. My colleague talked to her, and two five-pound notes helped to break down her professional secrecy. But she could only tell us that he was very quiet, undemanding, with no perversions, and never tried to chat to her about anything.

"He was chosen as our main target—and that's where I came in. Through a perfectly legit staff agency, anxious to do us a favor, we heard that the target outfit had an opening for a "female to make coffee, no experience required." I was hired as a temporary help for a week or two, but stayed on for six weeks because they liked me.

"Within the first three days, practically every single and married man in the office tried to date me. Our man was the only exception. He was kind and polite to me, but showed no interest. So I had to take the initiative.

"I invited him to a party in my apartment—a place with some listening devices, specially set up for me by my chiefs. Rather reluctantly he came along—only to be surprised, quite shocked, really, that nobody else from the firm was there. The other guests, three couples, left soon after midnight, and I persuaded him to stay for another drink.

"OK, I admit, I was very, very keen to get results. The assignment was a test for me. So I slept with him that night. He was sweet, and I pretended to be in love with him. I said I couldn't stand young guys. Poor soul. He went mad about me."

They spent every evening together, and he canceled his next appointment with the call girl. She spoke about an evening course she went to, and told him she had to write an essay on the handling and presentation of information. She was particularly interested in the format of summing up research reports. "It would be fantastic," Isabel said, "if somebody like you, a man of great knowledge and experience, could help me in some way. . . ." He sadly confessed that writing such summaries was not among his duties, but volunteered to look through the only set of reports in his safe and come back with a few useful hints.

"It seemed it was only a matter of time to get him to show me the full report we were after as an example of how these things were done," Isabel recalled. "He fully believed me when I said that I wouldn't understand the contents of such reports anyway. And this was not a lie. The details would have been meaningless to me. But I had already completed a short course in handling a miniature camera at high speed.

"We knew he wouldn't leave anything with me overnight. But we had two plans. My colleagues could photograph the documents while we were in the bedroom. Or else I could ply him with drinks fortified by a few fast-acting knockout drops. It would surely give him the most unforgettable hangover in his life."

The team was only one vital step away from complete success, and negotiations began with potential customers.

The call girl revealed that her "Saturday 3:30 regular" had canceled the dates for good. He sent her a fifty-pound check as a parting present. Considering that she collected a hundred pounds from the agents, she could be well satisfied —although most probably, it would have infuriated her if she had found out that his client's new girl, Isabel, expected to receive a minimum of ten thousand dollars as a bonus for the job.

"Which was peanuts for a valuable operation like that," Isabel told me. "In my dreams I had already spent that money several times, when our original planning mistake hit back. We knew everything about him—we knew hardly anything about the girl I was supposed to be in his eyes.

"I shall never forget that Friday evening. It was one of those cold clear nights, and we had dinner in a fine and expensive Indian restaurant near Piccadilly Circus. My apartment was very near, and we decided to walk there. I mentioned my essay, and he sort of half promised to bring along the set of documents from which the final report had been put together. That was it. I was so happy that I stopped and kissed him in the street.

"Back at my place, he was very quiet. Then shyly, with apologies for his 'daring and absurd' idea, he asked me if I'd marry him. Hastily I said yes.

"Now I know—I should have said, 'I don't know,' or 'Let's wait,' or 'I must think this over,' or I could have laughed in his face. That's what he expected. My yes surprised and shocked him. He stared at himself in my full-length mirror, and he knew that something was wrong. He was wrong for me. I was too young, too beautiful.

"He sat there in silence for two hours. I spoke to him, but he never answered. He loved a bourbon or two at night, but now he wouldn't have any. At last he began to talk in a whisper. It was really pitiful. He said he accepted that perhaps I had plans. Perhaps I wanted to stay in England or had my eyes on another job in the company, and I needed his help. Perhaps I was young and naïve and greatly impressed by an older man and his important position. But he knew that he wasn't good enough for me for life. And he realized that this must be clear to me, too.

"So why had I said yes? What was I after? And why did I work in a low-paid job if I could afford this apartment? It was too late to argue. The real art is to know when one is beaten.

"I never saw him again. Three days later, my job booking was canceled. The same day the Mayfair girl reported that he had renewed his Saturday 'booking.' We never got those papers.

"But the final blow came a month later when we heard that he had been forced to retire. What apparently happened was that the security men at his office had been watching both of us. They spotted the basic mistake: Why would a girl like me fall for a guy like him? We'd have been in an awful mess if he had ever tried to remove those papers from the safe and bring them to my apartment."

An analysis of her own case history is now among the exam papers at the school, where sex is a far from extracurricular subject. Isabel and her colleagues are convinced that theoretical knowledge of principles and techniques is not enough. Practice and actual experience are vital. Students must take part in mock operations—and it is recommended that sex exercises should be no exception. Although, according to Isabel, "actual sex is an optional extra," most students "conscientiously opt for it."

The basic exercise is very simple. An experienced and glamorous female agent is assigned to the student, and the pair spend two full days and nights—an imitation "dirty weekend"—together. At the beginning, and at least twice again later on, he is expected to frisk her, without ever giving grounds for indecent assault charges, and to find any hidden bugs on her.

They can stay indoors, drink, and dance, go for walks within the grounds of the school, and use the swimming pool day or night. He is expected to make up to her and prepare a full report of what she said in the two days. The girls are trained to drop certain hints and information at the most unexpected moments, and he must spot and remember them. At the same time, he is supposed to give nothing away about himself, which is not easy because the girls are good drinking partners and conversationalists.

At the end, the entire two days are analyzed by the student himself and lecturers. For this task they use the two-days nonstop recording made on videotape by carefully concealed equipment.

"You should see the red faces at these sessions. You just wouldn't believe how innocent many of those terribly masculine and sexy-voiced American big shots can be," commented Isabel with the most innocently tinkling giggle. "It's a pity that films must be destroyed because"—she stopped and looked toward the door; a half dozen Asian delegates were about to leave the lounge—"I must have a word with one of those guys." She promised not to be long.

I waited for an hour in vain before giving her credit for the half-finished sentence and all. It was a smooth way to go—leaving me no chance to follow her out without making it blatantly obvious.

A Bird in the Bush

I am shortly to reside in Kalgoorlie.
Any firms desirous of acquiring an
attractive intelligent young woman

to act on their behalf in this area,
ring——[telephone number]

This small ad appeared in the "Partnerships, Agencies" column of the *Sydney Morning Herald* on May 23, 1970. I know one man who intended to follow it up. If he did, and if a mutually satisfactory arrangement was worked out, she could look forward to profits she had never contemplated in her wildest dreams. Where? In what's-its-name? Kalgoorlie?

Those who have never burned their fingers by playing the stock market will be forgiven for not knowing that Kalgoorlie is in Australia. It serves as a major outpost of about the weirdest business intelligence operation I ever came across.

Some people claim that Perth in western Australia is the end of the world. Others dispute that it is in the middle of nowhere. Whoever is right, Kalgoorlie is three hundred miles farther on.

On the parched, cracked land, with its few twisted, crooked, shadeless trees, subjected to the occasional puff of a breeze that would be piped through hair dryers in a colder climate, Kalgoorlie was decaying slowly into the ghost town of an old, long-dead gold rush. But then, in the late 1960's, another 150 miles farther into nowhere, something happened at Mount Windarra, which can be approached by air, hitching a lift from the unstable pilot of a rickety flying machine, or by the "road," if one is prepared to end up with a sandbag for a lung.

Nickel was found at Mount Windarra—a mountainful of it.

Early samples indicated the presence of at least thirty million tons of high-grade ore. It came at the right time, too. With global nickel famine and constantly soaring industrial demand, with dwindling resources and disputes holding up production in nickel-richest Canada, prices hit an all-time high. The setting was perfect for a new Klondike.

Rough conditions and the heat, niggling details about the true quality of the ore, and the hairsplitters' questions about the cost and practicalities of lifting the earthen lid off the Golden Mile, would not deter the dreamers, geologists, would-be geologists, self-made geologists, true adventurers, and get-rich-quick enthusiasts—anybody who could afford a few colored pegs and the seventy-pounds fee to stake out a claim. And those who could not afford to stake out a second claim, a third, and a tenth, but were prepared to dig six-inch trenches from peg to peg with the inevitable waterbag and, preferably, a rifle slung over their shoulders, those found that backers galore were falling over themselves to help. The whole world seemed to scramble for a share in the action.

Poseidon became the first name to be whispered in awe everywhere. The company's holding straddled all the length of the precious Windarra ridge. Hundreds and hundreds raced through the red dust to find a spoonful of desert still free near this largest piece of the cake. If a claim could only half snuggle up to the ridge, the Midas touch of the Poseidon boundary guaranteed a fortune overnight.

The initial explosive news about Poseidon—nickel sulfides had been struck—blew global interest in its stock sky-high. The price doubled in a single day. But that was only the beginning. Three months later, in early 1970, every pound of timely investment was worth about three hundred times more, and rising.

Everybody wanted to buy, buy, buy. But who would sell? The answer was to get into the elevator on the ground floor or even at basement level. But which elevator? Which will rise fast to the top floor and above, through the roof? The VIP's could only guess, and with the roles reversed, they had to hold out the begging bowl sheepishly to the elevator man into whose palm they would normally drop the odd nickel with routine nonchalance.

The elevators were everywhere in the region stretching north from Kalgoorlie. News from the elevator men in the know was weighed in carats. A quiet yes would mark the births of a few more paper millionaires. Mount Windarra and Poseidon's promising hole in the ground were valued at three hundred million pounds.

No wonder that when I got there, in February 1970, strangers were unwelcome, and nosey strangers were dealt with very curtly indeed. In "downtown Kaly," the standard friendly advice—"mine your own business"—sounded much more like a threat than a piece of local witticism. Nobody cared if you studied the claim slips pinned to a board outside the out-of-place Victorian building or if you sipped your beer quietly at the long bar or on the wild-west-style verandah of the Palace where the locals—from a hundred-mile radius—came to burn their money. But ask a few questions, and conversation within earshot was as good as dead. Only the eyes, sharply staring eyes all around, did the talking. Not the place for shrewd intelligence agents and gossip-picking industrial playboys. It would take a couple of generations to camouflage such an operator well enough to blend in with the local roughies, the genuine fortune hunters, and the traders who follow them from boomtown to boomland.

In the sparsely populated outback that could hardly support struggling sheepmen, aborigines, banded anteaters, a few kangaroos, and the odd wild goat and emu, the Keep Out signs surrounding the plots were meant to be observed. And the men, who punctured the earth here and there with their diamond drills, were ready to give weight to the warnings. Probably they never stopped to think about it, but three components had been totted up to elevate these men to the rank of the just about best-paid work force in the world.

Although at the time, there was a tremendous influx of transient population, and the millionaire density was higher there than in Florida, available labor for hire remained extremely scarce, and would-be employers had to offer very competitive wages. Rough working conditions, a scorching climate, long hours starting at daybreak six days a week, and the loneliness month after month, with only a few beers or a spot of gambling to alleviate boredom, also had to be compensated for. But the third part of the fat pay packets was hush money to tie the tongues and make the eyes outstare the inquisitive stranger in *High Noon* fashion.

A neat lump sum could, of course, buy the occasional word, but it would have been much too costly to finance a regular flow of information from at least one man from every plot and every gang, when a pair of hands to shift an oildrum now and then or pour endless cups of tea was valued at fifty pounds a week plus extras including free food and shelter, and when a man with any claim to skill, enough to permit him to touch the drill or drive the truck, would command a weekly pay of anything from a hundred pounds upward.

But there was one place where all the lonely, the thirsty, and the amorous congregated, and where those parchment-dry, chord-tight, cash-sealed lips could naturally be expected to melt into smiles and word shapes. Its name was Hay Street.

A wide thoroughfare of Kalgoorlie, Hay Street was like an old jaw with the denture out; more gaps than houses and a few trees for the Saturday drunk to lean or pee on. In one group, Hay Street sported a string of brothels that in peculiarity would beat hands-down the old tit shelves of Hong Kong, the cages of Bombay, and the window-shopping of Amsterdam prostitution.

A few of the girls looked like relics of the gold-rush days, but most of them were shapely newcomers, young campfol-lowers of the boom, ready to make hay while the nickel shined. And they behaved like ladies. It was expected of them. Not only because of local prudery, but also because the sober among the men, back from the hills for a short spell, came to buy pretentious companionship as much as crude sex. So no swear words, if you please, and none of them micro skirts and navel-deep splits as if she did not know how to make needle meet thread.

The ladies sat in waiting silently under ever so gay colored lightbulbs on the wooden verandahs that ran the length of the bungalows. Each girl had her own door like the Dayak families in their communal longhouses in Borneo. Very efficiently the doors led directly to the individual cell-simple cubicles only a step away from their seats as if designed by experts of time-and-motion study.

It was not without good reason that some people referred to the "houses" as the surface gold mines of the region: all the girls could earn more here in a couple of months than in a year elsewhere, and there were a few who could look forward to real riches and retirement with the social upgrading of having private means. Those few understood that news mattered more than facts, that the nickel boom was a trade in hopes, and that hearsay could make dreams come true or ruin multimillionaires.

The other requirements were not particularly demanding: long ears and a good memory, the knack of listening and making the taciturn chat, and a marked lack of sophistication never to outclass the clients. All that and a contact in Sydney—and they could mine their own business.

A big, beefy, red-faced man, known as The Brigadier, who thoroughly rinsed his throat with pink gin every time he lifted his glass—and that was not a memorably rare occurrence—introduced me to one of these girls of privilege in the basement bar of Sydney's luxurious Wentworth Hotel.

An Italian by birth, now calling herself "Jean . . . 'cause it's easier for the fellas," she pressed trousers in a laundry before the boom. In pre-Kalgoorlie days she felt really rich when she could afford to buy herself a dilapidated second-hand car. A friend photographed her at the wheel, and she ordered a dozen prints; she kept one and sent the rest to relatives all over Italy. Now she treated herself to a "leettle holy day" in Sydney, and in four days, she spent several thousand dollars "on a leettle zis and zat."

By then she owned an expensive apartment, a "unit" in fashionable Double Bay, and she had installed her mother in another unit nearby. Most of her money was shrewdly invested for her in the "nickel bizeniss."

In her laundry days, she made an odd buck or two on casual prostitution, and it was her employer's wife who caught her once with the boss in the back room and suggested that her prospect of making a fortune would be better among prospectors in western Australia than with her husband in Sydney.

Jean was already firmly established on a Hay Street verandah when this "kind gentleman," our gin-gargling companion, came along with an easy proposition to cut her into the "nickel bizeniss."

She did not need to expose herself to the sun or learn anything about prospecting. When I asked her what she knew about nickel, she informed me that it was "ze bit zat glitters" on her latest car.

All she had to do was to give clients time to show off, complain, or indulge in homely gossip. They loved her for it. She listened to stories, spotted long faces, and watched who was spending more than usual. Between two gulps The Brigadier explained:

"Her field reports are invaluable. All we get is a clue but who needs more? She might report, 'Joe so-and-so has a lot more money than ever before.' So? Is somebody backing him? Why? Or 'Bill what-ever-his-name boasts he's on to something big.' Fine, we'll keep an eye on the company he works for."

How does she report her news?

"A piece of cake. A friend we call the news collector parks his car some fifty yards up the road, and they use a walkie-talkie. It wouldn't look right and proper if he visited all our girls every day. He's a married man, and it's no good to expose anyone to blackmail.

"That's all there's to it. But I'll tell you something for nothing. A bird in the bush is worth two in the hand, so to speak."

There was, of course, a great deal more to it. It took me a year of maneuvering and a chain of introductions from seven people in four countries before I got anywhere near this worldwide, multimillion business venture and the man who runs but does not control it in Australia.

Our first peripatetic meeting took me on a long gin-to-gin walk in Sydney. We were then met by his chauffeur-driven car, and as agreed beforehand, I was deposited on a deserted stretch of road where they left me stranded. Waiting for the cab they promised to send for me, I discovered I was near the Castlecove golf course where, in fact, our second and much friendlier meeting took place.

The Brigadier was convinced that I was about to set up a rival outfit but did not seem to mind that: "There's room here for you, me and anybody else. Your credentials are OK; you're welcome to look around. Anyway we don't do anything illegal, so my legal boys tell me. You don't get titled people to invest in a shady deal, do you?"

He explained that he ran a "thoroughly professional stock-market operation which depended on inside information. You see, this is the biggest quarry in the world. We've got a thousand million tons of iron ore in the Northwest. There's bauxite near Darwin, gold, platinum, uranium—you name it, we've got it. Some of this is for real. The rest is for business. That's what people don't understand.

"When I was in London the other day, brokers asked me about ore bodies, pay zones, assays, sampling techniques, and whatnot. Because they tried to learn about it from books. But in real, a *big find* means usually no more than a couple of hopeful geologists in the bush, a dirty diamond drill, and a six- or nine-inch hole in the ground. A *big disaster* may mean little more than a first piece of gossip from the lab where samples are looked at. True, not true—Who cares? Information is as good as money in the bank, if you have it in advance. It doesn't matter *what* you know—but *when* you know it."

Hay Street girls and their pillow-talk reports were a vital source of news, but not the only one. The organization had retainers in practically all, big and small, mining companies. Some girls, who must be considerably more sophisticated than Jean, worked in Sydney and Melbourne. They went to all the important cocktail parties, socialized with stock-exchange people, knew "how to bribe a man here and there," and understood business as well as men. One of these girls had the added advantage of two years of geology, but all could be counted on to remember stacks of facts and figures. They all had a good laugh at Jean who once, in the bar of the Palace, overheard the words "molybdenum found at Tamworth." Although she never attempted to understand that mysterious remark or find out where Tamworth was, she was desperate to get it right. She kept asking, "Molly who? Vat did you say?" so many times that finally, some twenty people chanted for her like a football crowd: "Molyb denum found-at Tamworth, molyb denum found-at Tamworth. . . ."

These various sources were backed up by a large, perfectly legitimate intelligence group.

"Tip-offs are the basic clue we need," my contact lectured me with understandable pride, "and although we know that the real goodies, like the nickel, come from the bush, we cannot bring up the artillery and commit large sums of money without some checking. We study pointers and the market trends like any good businessman."

He called my attention to a "pointer," an advertisement, which appeared in *The Australian* on March 2, 1970. Newmetal Mines Ltd. claimed to be "going through an exciting growth period" and was looking for an additional "keen young geologist" because it had "promising prospects in the Cloncurry region." To industrial spies this was a straight come-on to look at the company, the region, and the applicants who might be interested in picking up two salaries—one tax-free in cash.

The same paper, on the same day, carried an interesting article about Eastmet Minerals. It employed an "unusually high ratio (of geologists) for most new employers," but because the company program had not yet reached the drilling stage, its "share market prospects are very dependent on reports issued by its next-door neighbor, Tasminex, and rumors from the west suggest that these reports are more likely to be initially disappointing than encouraging."

"Well, what about Tasminex?" I tried to ask as casually as I could, while ordering yet another large pink gin, but he flatly refused to discuss the subject.

This was the company hailed as the "new Poseidon" only some thirty-five days earlier, when after rumors of a new nickel strike, Battling Bill Singline, ex-bullock-driver chairman of Tasminex NL (for No Liability), announced their nickel sulfides could be better in grade and more in quantity than Poseidon's deposits. The stock rocketed from under three to over forty pounds and at least three new multimillionaires were made in thirty minutes. By the end of January, directors advised investors to be cautious until the final lab reports came out, and the press regarded Tasminex as one of the "speculative hopefuls."

Two days after my unanswered question came the crash, which matched the initial miracle in spectacularity. Stock prices met their Hiroshima, and my contact's remarks like "gloomy prospects from the lab? . . . we sell before the crowd" began to make sense. Hadn't he mentioned the possibility of "a big upheaval"?

In a subsequent telephone conversation I inquired about Tasminex for the second time. "Had I known about the news in time, I'd have certainly saved myself and those I'm protecting a lot of money," I was told. I would have sworn that the receiver was definitely oozing gin under my nose. "After all, we're in business not only for ourselves but also to provide a protection service to subscribers against unexpected market fluctuations. So it would have been our duty to know about such things in advance."

Whether he did know it or not, I could never find out. He not only refused to admit it, but also warned me against jumping to conclusions: "You see, it may happen, after all, that one day, in the years to come, they will find good nickel down there."

Was this a pointer to a fantastic recovery to cash in on yet again?

"All I'm saying is that one day, nickel may actually be mined out there on those Tasminex plots. But that's irrelevant at the moment. Haven't you heard the current Australian joke about the tin of sardines in postwar Britain?

"That old tin was sold for a few bob, then resold for a pound, then for two pounds, and so on. The chappie who bought it for fifty quid wanted to make a meal of it, but found the sardines were stale. He complained to the man who sold it to him but was rebuffed. Those sardines were not for eating; they were only for trading.

"It's the same over here. At this stage, nobody should care what really is in those holes. While everybody sees a bright future in them, they all want to buy, and prices go up. When the faith is gone, shares are not worth the paper they are printed on."

The Tasminex debacle itself was an excellent demonstration of this point. At the dawn of March 1970, when there were persistent rumors that the pending report of the company could be "very disappointing," the stock prices dropped dramatically. At the Sydney Stock Exchange, amid unbelievable screaming, shouting, booing, groaning, cheers, and catcalls, shirt-sleeved professional operators and visitors —the regular gamblers and occasional punters dressed in anything down to T-shirts—were ready once again to break through the sound barrier of stock dealings. Standing there, one could feel why sweatshirts were the most suitable attire for the floor. Not that supersonic business was a novelty to them: in 1969 two thousand million shares changed hands.

At 9:20 on the morning of Black Tuesday, the third day of March, it was announced that the Tasminex report would be out by the afternoon. From seventy-five dollars, the stock was already down to twelve. Those with hopes against hopes began to buy. The price went up to sixteen.

At 1:35 P.M., the long-awaited report was released in Sydney. From one second to another, the price came tumbling down to seven dollars. But in Melbourne, the stock was still fetching twice as much!

Apparently a mistake had been made. Instead of releasing the report at exactly the same moment at both exchanges as usual, the text was Telexed to Melbourne only *after* the Sydney announcement. In all, there was a seventeen-minutes delay. During it, some people bought shares above the Sydney prices. The sellers, who had guessed or known what was to come, were laughing. In this case, a quick telephone call from Sydney to Melbourne was enough to slash some people's losses drastically.

In retrospect, one can see the pattern of "not just pure gambling"—those who had a strong instinct or timely information took the right elevator at the right moment and got out at the right floor with disturbing regularity. Yet the "well-informed" often excluded the boards and principal shareholders of the affected companies.

Quite out of the blue, my Australian contact turned up in London in May 1970. He showed me the strange advertisement by the girl who was to reside in Kalgoorlie and asked me how my "plans" were progressing. He returned twice in 1971, and we met again in the bar of the Mayfair Hotel in 1972. It was a most curious encounter.

He spoke contemptuously about market rigging by brokers but did not fail to point out the profits that could be made on it with "some inside information." He recalled the Poseidon collapse with undisguised glee, the Minsec and the Leopold Minerals affairs, the new lease of life for Poseidon—"It's all very different; it's actual digging now"—and the ups and downs of platinum discoveries.

I wondered what he was getting at. But he was not yet ready.

"You remember the Nabarlek [aboriginal word for small kangaroo] uranium discovery? Japan was most interested because of the nuclear-power program for the end of the century. A Japanese client of mine wanted to invest heavily. I had some doubts, and I told him about them. This must have leaked to the Japanese Nuclear Power Agency, which came out with some skeptical comments.

"But what happens? Five days later they all change their minds, my angry client cancels his subscription, and I'm told off by my superiors. Everybody wants to buy a slice; the Australian government decides to limit the possible foreign holdings because of the rush, and nobody cares about my warnings.

"I understood then how Sorge and other Russian agents must have felt when their reports about the imminence of a German attack were ignored by Stalin.

"Since then, of course, I've received some outright apologies. Because in August 1971, the Nabarlek deposits were downgraded overnight. Bit of difference to have fifty-five thousand or something like eight thousand tons of reserves.

"All this wouldn't happen, of course, if one had some insurance, so to speak."

"What insurance? Against bad news and false information or against client incredulity?"

"Something like that."

He then, gradually, outlined his ideas. By the time he finished, the barman of the hotel must have been busy ordering some fresh supplies of gin and bottles of Angostura bitters to tint it all pink.

The plan was simple. We two should go into some unofficial partnership. He was still firmly convinced that I belonged to a rival outfit which, apparently, he had welcomed from the start only because it would give us both the opportunity to double-cross our bosses and clients. Presumably he could then use me—double-crossing his partner in double cross—for his own purposes.

Yes, I could see the fine possibilities for further zigzagging with the mineral vehicles of information-trafficking. I was sorry to disappoint him with the news that I had nothing to contribute to this promising operation, and that he would have to carry on single-handed with his own double cross. Which only convinced him that I had already deceived him in some way.

Since then he has kept away from me. But as far as I know, the operation continues in several parts of the world, including Fiji, South Africa, the Middle East, and the regions of offshore oil and natural gas explorations.

The basic essential elements of the intelligence effort will never change—if informers, retainers, and forlorn little prostitutes in the bush may grow too old or rich to continue, they can always be replaced by a new, equally willing generation of agents. But this human armory of the espionage war is increasingly supported by the new weapons developed originally to aid the modern prospector.

Aerial photography is one of the techniques used by both sides. Intelligence agents, working for investors or rival companies, would frequently fly over drilling rigs or mining sites and photograph every detail. Sometimes pictures of an unusual amount of activity in a remote area may indicate what is happening.

In America, I have seen the grainy photograph of an ordinary automobile license plate. It was from the enlargement of a speck in the original, showing a sleek black limousine. What was a car like that doing on the site near the oil rig? The license plate was soon traced to the user of the car—the president of the oil company. Well, if it was worth his while to make the journey, it would certainly merit an investment in the company. The agent, whose camera captured that car from the air, framed the blowup of the license plate—he made twenty thousand dollars by the sale of that single shot and by buying a few shares of stock himself.

A Canadian company is using a magnificent invention to detect minerals on Fiji. It records very low-frequency radio signals from a United States Navy submarine communications station. The signals travel through large sections of the ground, and their pattern is affected by minerals. When the recording is analyzed, the presence of various deposits down to a thousand feet in depth is shown. I believe that this has already attracted some most unwanted attention to the Toronto research corporation which has developed the system.

The camera that was first used on the Apollo 9 space flight photographed the moon from forty miles away. By a complex system of four lenses and filters, it recorded color images on a black and white film which were "read" with the aid of a computerized viewer. The result contradicted scientists about the composition of certain moon rocks—and the camera was later proved to be right.

In South Africa, this camera was further developed for exploration reconnaissance. The new model can spot ore deposits in the earth, pollution in the air, and fish feeding grounds under water from practically any height. Spectral Africa, the newly formed company to market this technique, realized that there was a serious misuse potential in their aerial prospecting equipment. The firm's articles of association include, therefore, specific regulations against the use of the camera for spying on competitors' exploration sites.

A far cry from the Italian girl's "nickel bizeniss"? Not quite. For it appears that a bird in the bush—aided by modern technology and access to some computer time anywhere on earth—will remain worth more than any number of birds, security apparatus, and hush money in the hand.

8

Computer Crackers

Espionage work is at its best when the theft of secrets is virtually undetectable until it is too late to do anything about it, and when it has a built-in fail-safe element to ensure that if, by pure chance, the loss of information is discovered, nothing more sinister than ordinary human error will be held responsible.

A typical example is the case that cost one of the largest American oil companies "something in the region of a million bucks" and possibly more. They still do not quite know how it all happened, and the company is not particularly proud of it. The security official who told me about it did so on a strictly nonattributable basis.

"After several years of research, we had enough seismic information to draw up geophysical maps and mark out the areas where we would drill," he said. "A top-level meeting was called; the decision was made, and the land men were instructed to start leasing property. Zero hour was set at 7 A.M. the following Monday when they'd all swing into action at the same time. They must buy anonymously and fast, or else the prices start rocketing when it becomes known that a major company is interested in the area. For unlike in Europe and Africa, American mineral rights belong to the landowner, not the state, and the lease only gives us the right to bore holes in the ground. If oil is found, we have to pay royalty on it.

"Anyway. The landmen went out and found that much of the land had already been leased, although only since the previous Friday, to somebody else. The guy was too small to mount a full operation by himself, and probably no decent major company would have gone in with him against us, so he was ready to let us in—at a price. We had no choice but to pay up.

"That doesn't mean we didn't try to discover what happened. Because to beat us to the land, he must have had our own inside information all right, no question about that. But how did he get it?

"In the final stage we needed three copies of the map. The blueprints were prepared, as usual, by one of a number of trusted outside contractors who would be under obligation to make three copies and no more. What if the guy who bought up the leases had a contact there and had a fourth copy made for himself? Possible, but rather a long shot. He would have to know where exactly the copies were to be printed and then bribe someone in a rush. On the other hand, there might have been a genuine human error. Perhaps a copy didn't come out well enough, and an inexperienced employee threw it away instead of destroying it or returning it to us to be put through the shredding machine. But that's another long shot. The guy would have to find the extra copy in the dustbin by chance—unless he knew which dustbin to watch.

"Now there was another possibility. See what you make of this.

"From the records we discovered that on the very day of the top-level, decision-making conference, the guy had visited our company HQ with some genuine inquiries. He wanted to see someone who was at the meeting, and he was asked to wait in a room with a secretary. OK, I grilled her myself. Did the guy try to look at some papers? No. Did he ask many questions? No. Did he leave her at all? No. He sat there for more than an hour, didn't he go to the john? No. No, no, no. She insisted he didn't do anything suspicious; he was quiet, friendly, and patient, and he wanted to pay for the cup of coffee she got for him. Ah! So *she* left the room. He was alone. What could he do? What could he look at?

"A quick check answered all the questions. It was as simple as hieroglyphics after the discovery of the Rosetta Stone. Only two of the blueprints were used at the conference. The third was to be filed away in the safe by this secretary. She couldn't remember if she had already filed it before the visitor came. I'd say she hadn't. It must have been on her desk all the time, and he photographed it or just copied out some information while she was getting his coffee.

"Another genuine human error? Was the guy a real opportunist who couldn't resist the temptation—or was it all planned? Was she in it with him from the start? Or was somebody higher up preparing the opportunity for them?

"Anyway. We more or less had to leave it at that."

What did he himself think?

"Well, if you ask me, and there's nobody else in the room, well . . . let's put it this way. I don't think it was just one of those things. You know what I mean, not just a mistake. The guy wouldn't have enough time to make the most of it. But if it was all planned in advance, if he knew what areas our geologists were interested in, and especially if our seismic data input was monitored on the way to the computer. . . . Anyway that's pure speculation. Not my line at all. Particularly if it involves computer-tapping—near enough the perfect crime."

Oil exploration has always been a spy-riddled business.

Because of the involvement of national interests, the CIA, for instance, played an important, regular part in oil politics. Nigeria and the Middle East provided numerous examples— and in return, it was by no means accidental that successful CIA agents switched to business and rose to some of the highest posts in the oil hierarchy.

Competitors, in their purely commercial struggle, had to use their own agents who breakfasted on blackmail and dined on bribes—the bread and butter of their trade. Part-time headhunting was one of their specialities, and the *Harvard Business Review* reported a brief revealing dialogue between a bank executive and an oil-company representative, who was asking for a loan. At some point, the bank raised the question why the oil company did not hire a geologist. "Why should we?" began the answer that must have made the question sound awfully naïve: "We have five geologists from five different competitors, and all of them only cost us five hundred dollars a month on a part-time payroll. Any one of them would cost ten times as much if we had him full-time." The moonlighting geologists were ready to offer their skill as well as their inside knowledge about their employers, but should they ever change their minds, a little blackmail could always buy back their unconditional goodwill.

Agents, however, have begun to shed their old-fashioned cloak and dagger. Much of the romance has gone out with the discarded garments, for hardly anything can be less romantic than the new creature of the computer age—the digital agent.

His main asset is that he speaks the digit language of computers. As for being a "secret agent," his espionage work is about as spectacular as a weekend car wash in suburbia, and to the layman his "revelations" are as shattering as a telephone number.

And yet he belongs to the new elite of criminals, much

greater a menace than the determined train robber, the shrewd con man, the clever forger, or the skilled safecracker, because he is able to ruin a company at one fell swoop or do irreparable damage to an entire trade or nation.

An elementary target for the digital agent is the research itself, concerning the new design and application of computers. The importance of the "hardware" can be gauged by just one fact: IBM, with an American stranglehold on world sales of computers, had a turnover of $8,425 million in 1971—greater than the gross national product of Finland or Portugal.

Items of "software," the know-how of computer usage, may easily carry seven-figure price tags. To write a program, the system that tells the computer how to calculate anything from weekly payrolls to aircraft load distribution and flight paths, may take much ingenuity and numerous man-years—it is impracticable to talk about man-hours—and the result is a highly salable commodity.

Security men still talk with a shudder about the "inside job" that hit BOAC in 1968. After years of research that cost about three million pounds, the airline invested forty-three million in Boadicea, a most advanced computer system. Its star performance was the ticket-reservation program through which any BOAC booking clerk anywhere in the world could get up-to-the-minute information on all vacant seats on any aircraft. The program had to enable the machine to understand questions and answer them in plain English on a television screen, "talk" simultaneously to several hundred offices in busy periods, register cancelations, accept last-minute bookings for, say, the last three empty seats on Flight X from Hong Kong to London, erase obsolete data, update its memory accordingly, and so, only a second later, tell New Delhi that "I'm afraid your passengers to Rome will have to take Flight Z because those three seats on Flight X have already been occupied"—or something less polite to that effect. This most sophisticated system outside America gave BOAC a probable world lead of about three years.

As soon as the program was completed, it was offered privately, at a cut rate, to a rival airline. Officials still refuse to talk about it, but it is generally understood that the competitor reported the offer to BOAC and assisted in tracing at least some of the culprits. It emerged that several documents had been stolen and copied. After the pirates were forced to return the documents and "certain assurances were obtained," a member of the staff was dismissed; the resignations of three others were "accepted"; and the corporation decided to forego any legal action.

Was the theft worth it? The price demanded from the rivals has never been disclosed. But it was unlikely to consist of fewer than six figures. Since then, BOAC Boadicea software sales to Qantas, Aer Lingus, KLM, South Africa, and American Express have totaled more than two million pounds.

The huge investments in hard- and software are now inevitable. Not only because the results are tremendous administrative savings, but also because many key factors of twentieth-century life would soon be in utter confusion and jeopardy, if not at a virtual standstill, without computers— which can do no more than people but they do it faster and better. They beat us hands down at the memory game. A machine can retain a vast amount of information that, in a printed form, would fill forty or fifty thousand unabridged dictionaries, and it has instant recall on demand.

Such ever-increasing quantities of data and know-how stored in computers are, of course, even more valuable than the program, and this concentration of modern wealth is tempting the new professional computer cracker in the same way as large quantities of cash and valuables kept in inadequate safes used to invite specialization in safecracking.

"Disaster is on the punch cards if I may say so," commented Philip L. Schiedermayer, when we met in the San Francisco Press Club. His Profitect Inc. of Professional Protection Consultants is greatly concerned with computer defense from both embezzlement and espionage. "At first it was hard enough to get the damned machines working at all without having to bother about security. Now we can no longer have the luxury of oversight."

The first serious warnings came from the very occasional capture of a few knowledgeable and ingenious "key-punch crooks." Several of them pocketed anything from fifty thousand dollars upward by slight fraudulent changes in the computer program which thus began to authorize payments to dummy wholesalers for deliveries of only one kind of goods—invoices.

Others instructed the computer to direct large consignments of various products to temporary accommodation addresses. All the crooks had to do was to pick up the loot and sell it in bulk at cut prices—sometimes in competition with the manufacturers.

"Insiders" found numerous ways to make money by pressing the right key on the machine. One increased his own authorized bank overdraft limit from $200 to $200,000 by the simple addition of three digits in the program. A New Jersey National Bank employee "transferred" $128,000 from thirty-three accounts to the savings of an accomplice. Eventually he wanted to erase the withdrawal data from the victims' bank statements, so that nobody would complain and the bank's money would just be inexplicably missing. He was caught only by the bank's unexpected change to another computer system.

A programmer, whose name began with the letter Z, discovered that his own account was the last on the alphabetical list of his bank's clients. He decided to effect a minor alteration in the program. The girl who operated the card machine punched up the transaction for him without any question. As she was not expected to understand a word of what she was doing, she could have no idea that from then on, every day, the computer would automatically round off every client's balance to the nearest ten cents, tot up the "surplus" and add it "to the last entry on the list of accounts." Nobody missed the odd cent—maximum $2.70 in a thirty-day month—and Mr. Z. resigned from his computer job—although he kept his account with the bank.

He was well on his way to his first million when, unknown to him, a Pole opened an account. The new customer's name began with Zy—and so it duly went to the bottom of the list. When he found he was getting rich a little too fast, he followed the trend and cursed the computer for everything. He was probably afraid that one day, the bank would demand the return of the accumulating thousands of dollars.

The most stylish fraud was based on a simple observation. A sharp-eyed Washingtonian noticed that the deposit slips on the desks for clients had no computer code numbers in the Riggs National Bank. People who came in without their personal deposit slips to put cash or checks into their accounts filled in a blank form, leaving it to the clerks to sort it all out and code it for the computer. Mr. Hawkeye pocketed all the blanks in sight and replaced them with neat sheaves of forged ones—which were already electronically coded in his favor. He could sit back and wait; every client using a "blank" slip thus paid the money right into Hawkeye's account opened under a false name. He had the good sense to call a halt after only three days. By then he could withdraw a hundred thousand dollars. Bank and police are still considering where to start looking for him.

It is difficult to choose, but my favorite computer crook is the Frenchwoman who has been sought by police forces in three countries for four years—in vain.

She worked for banks and finance companies as a computer programmer in all these countries, and opened a "spare" bank account under a pseudonym in each. Before she left each current job, she planted a time bomb by inserting a private program in the computer: the machine should kindly note in its "diary" that the bank must pay a certain sum into her dummy account on a given future date, in six, twelve, or eighteen months. Until that date, nobody would see this "standing order" in the brain. After execution, the machine should equally kindly forget this most embarrassing evidence by rewriting (copying) its full program with the omission of this work-well-done item. (Computers must be able to do this rewrite job if they are not to be maddened by overloading.) The coinciding advance dates for transfer and erasure gave this bright trickster a chance to change her jobs without any hurry, rig a second and third computer, resign yet again, prepare herself for payday, and disappear—with half a million dollars—into the blue yonder.

Another wave of warnings—that computers must be better controlled and protected—came with the much too real menace to *privacy*. Today, there is hardly anyone about whom huge amounts of personal details are not stored in government, bank, business, tax office, medical, or if relevant, police department computers. Many of these facts—like name, address, general interest, and financial bracket—are on mailing lists that are expensive commodities and that change hands freely in an open market.

The severe intrusion of privacy and the frequently unrestricted accessibility of mammoth data banks are much publicized subjects of ceaseless, impassioned debates everywhere, and undoubtedly, some form of legal protection must soon be given to all the information on tap. In the argument about the numerous practical difficulties, a massive problem still enjoys, however, the luxury of oversight—even though it is protruding more and more prominently from under the carpet where we have swept it. Laws can restrain only the essentially law-abiding citizen, and at their best, laws may authorize the dishing out of severe sentences to criminals. But how severe can the sentence be for the theft of intangible property? And what if nothing is actually stolen? Not even the proverbial sheet of paper with the sketch of the Great New Invention? Which takes us back to the theft of invaluable know-how—and some ridiculous "punishment" for tampering with telephone lines and pinching a flash of electricity, which the thief used when the computer printed out the stolen information on *his* paper in *his* office.

"Thief? Who, sir? Me, sir? I ain't no thief, sir, never stole no information, honest—"

It is true. The information remains there, in the computer where it belongs, and the rightful owner is not deprived of using his property.

With the two great menaces, fraud and loss of privacy, looming viciously over the computer, the espionage issue is still shrouded in mystery. It seems somehow too remote, involving bribery and corrupt scientific experts from fiction land.

Only three years ago, I wrote about computer espionage as "the crime of the future"—and I did not mean today, this early part of the future, I must admit. Yet computer spying is already here to stay, and those, too, are wrong who believe that the style of my sample thief's self-defense is a self-contradiction, because "surely, only learned men can prey on the computer." For the attack against the computer is sometimes a large-scale operation in which a dumb "girl in the bush" supplies the first clue—for example, the usual length of code words—and when a highly qualified systems analyst finds it impossible to smuggle out a note from the computer room, he will ask a cleaner to do it for him.

Philip Schiedermayer told me: "Only a tiny fraction of any nation is spying for foreign countries. Perhaps there aren't enough national secrets going round for all those spies. Industry, on the other hand, has far more enemies, and the proportion of potential spies is much higher. People still argue that the introduction of the computer and sophisticated defenses cut out the petty criminal and the opportunist. That may well be. But the computer's secrets are a worthy prize, and that increases the danger from big organizations which have the resources to play for high stakes."

Initially, like any intelligence operator, the digital agent needs as much basic information as possible about his target. This is a more complicated task in theory than in practice. A twenty-one-year-old engineering graduate who wanted to con a computer, visited Pacific Telephone and Telegraph's offices twice, posing first as a journalist and then as a potential customer. What he discovered was not much, but enough for him to place huge commercial orders for telephone equipment by punching out the right bleep tones on the ordinary touchphone in his home. He sold these products, and by the time they caught him, his dummy firm had run up unpaid bills to the tune of a million dollars. He got away with a forty-day jail sentence—to live happily as a security consultant ever after.

Similar methods are also open to the spy, but usually he finds it no problem to bribe an insider or go into partnership with another.

The security adviser of an international oil company said: "There's a great demand for skilled computer personnel. Pay is not very high, and so they don't stay long enough to grow loyal to the firm. A few months, then a better offer from elsewhere, and off they go. Usually a programmer is not supposed to have access to other records, but you never know. In fact, you hardly know anything about them, yet they handle confidential information that used to be seen only by a company's most trusted executives."

Computer security specialist Guy Parker was once quoted as saying: "The real danger is bribing operators with twenty-five pounds or so to print out information that looks worthless to them, but could be worth a million to a competitor. . . . Industrial espionage is all too easy with computers, and it is definitely growing fast."

Many large computers are housed in all-glass cages, so that the operators are always in sight, and guards circulate among the machines. Yet most of the "audience" have no idea what the operator is and is not supposed to do in the course of his duties.

A. S. Cormack, chairman of the Computer Society's Technical Board and director of the largest British computer "software" firm, told me: "Executives in industry tend to think in terms of physical security—padlocks, special passes, safes—when they try to deal with computer protection. That is because they fail to realize that it doesn't require tremendous expertise to extract information from computer files. It is, in fact, a relatively simple task if system security is not built into the software itself." (This is partly why IBM experts reckon that undetected United States losses amount to $20,000 million a year.)

Is then computer cracking the perfect crime? The answer is a vague maybe. For the battle between the attack and the defense is similar to that fought in rocket technology: the invention of the ballistic missile is countered by the ABM—the antiballistic missile—which is eliminated by the anti-anti-ballistic missile only to come up against the AAABM. . . .

Frequent checks can reduce the time it takes to discover

unauthorized interference and withdrawals. "Computer au-dits" can monitor the uses of the machine. A computer can be programmed to warn security men if there is an unusual amount of general activity going on or much more than average use is made of certain sections of its memory. In the same way as a telephone bill that falls well below or rises high above a subscriber's average will be thrown out for old-fashioned totting up by clerks, the computer can be programmed to clamp down on too numerous erroneous attempts at extracting some secrets out of its brain.

Is computer crime undetectable because the action of committing a crime is invisible and because the evidence in the program can be automatically destroyed by the machine itself? Maybe. But then there are many other avenues open to the defense. It is possible to instruct the "brain" to make a copy of every single line of printout, and dispatch this copy direct to a vault to which only the chosen few will have access. If the work of checking becomes too much, a second computer can do the job. Then at least the victim knows that he has been robbed or that his secrets are no longer exclusive to him. It can be done—at a price.

The aggressor could retaliate with the computer bug, a little-talked-about device which is said to be an aimed sensor of electrical fields. It can pick up and transmit electronic signals from inside the working computer, and thus read, in effect, the tape itself without requiring a telltale printout. Yet this need not compel the defense to throw in the electronic towel. Some computers already contain decoy programs to confuse the opposition and slow down his progress through the maze of signals. If the attacker is not alert and swallows the bait, he may lose out on, say, building a factory to use a hopelessly unworkable decoy process.

Listening to several security specialists and two men who, I believed, could be classified as active digital agents, I was reminded of a throw-away remark by Terry-Ann, my thirsty-for-cocks'-blood guide to Bangkok: "I call it the Kubik Principle No. 1. Intelligence work is a matter of relative costs. What's worth what to whom? How much investment is justified in protecting/obtaining a piece of information? The advantage must always be on the side of the agent. Those who pick another man's natural or electronic brain may have to spend more on the operation than the defense—but they don't have the initial cost of learning, research, and experiment to create knowledge and put it into that brain."

Cash Makes Money

The difference in values is most predominant in computer sharing—an inevitable necessity of modern life, the fiercest computer-espionage battlefield, the best opportunity for the true computer cracker, and the greatest headache to the security man.

Computer time-sharing has been thought of, and numerous companies to provide such service have been set up, because many firms find it uneconomical to install their own computers since they could never find enough work for the machine to justify the considerable capital outlay.

The system has two main built-in hazards. One is that the central computer must be operated from perhaps hundreds of miles away. Each sharer has his own terminal, which is connected to the center by ordinary telephone lines. To tap these lines is no more difficult than to listen in on any conversation, and it is no greater a crime either.

Sometimes a radio link is used between computer and terminal. It is no offense to tune in on any radio transmission. Many British subscribers to a particular time-sharing system, for instance, have no idea that when they press a few keys asking a question from or feeding something to the computer, the signals from their terminals are flashed via satellite to Phoenix, Arizona, where it is still nighttime, and the company's American center has spare capacity for London. (Not using a nearer computer causes only one second delay in the communications.)

Although both input and output travel along the telephone lines in data character form, this gives no security against the tapper, who can record it and translate it at his leisure with the aid of terminal equipment that he can freely purchase anywhere.

The oil company that lost its confidential seismic data was suspected of being a victim of such line tapping. Agents, who knew the company's current exploration area, probably intercepted exchanges between geologists and the computer.

The search of the seabed for building materials is conducted with sometimes ludicrous secrecy because of the international cutthroat competition brought about by dwindling resources and the increasing difficulty in obtaining permission to open up more ugly scars in the ground. Protectors of the environment fight hard against every new gravel, sand, and stone quarry, and recently a legal wrangle over some land for research had to be heard in camera to protect the secrecy of plans and avoid early arousal of local protests.

A German company which is in the race for the seabed failed to keep its most valuable secret—the sea area it was exploring. An unauthorized leak led to the monitoring of its ship terminal to shore computer radio link, and their data was sold to a competitor who thus saved the entire large initial research cost of spotting resources at considerable depth under water.

Eavesdropping on financial transactions is one of the oldest forms of industrial espionage, and within that, wiretapping is practically as old as the telegraph and the telephone.

In California, a law had to be introduced against the interception of telegraph messages in 1862. Two years later, a proper industrial espionage organization was prosecuted under this act. Masterminded by an ex-stockbroker, the conspirators tapped the news coming from the East coast about stock dealings, and sold the information to regular subscribers.

Thanks to early telecommunications, it became only a matter of cash to make money safely on racing. "Past-posters" was the name given to the nineteenth-century racketeers who paid several moonlighting telegraph company operators and linesmen lavishly to monitor race results telegraphed to various towns. While the message was being taken down in the local telegraph office and a runner reached the bookmaker, they had time to place bets on horses already past the post.

Today the past-posters' grandchildren concentrate on the stock market—and computers offer them information in a handy concentration. It has been estimated that if someone traced the daily pattern of the buying and selling operations by a dozen leading stockbrokers' clients, the entire market could be influenced and exploited. The continuous tapping and monitoring of all those telephone lines would only invite the detection and quick collapse of the operation; but the existence of outside terminals solves the problem, and it does not make much difference whether the machines belong to subscribers of a time-sharing system or to the investment analyst whose company owns and has exclusive access to a computer.

Once a terminal user has gained authorized entry into certain limited and well-defined cells of an electronic brain, a security question arises: How to prevent him from exploring other cells of the brain farther afield? This is the second built-in hazard of the terminal, and it has been recognized as such from the start.

Computer-sharing companies that may hold the portfolios of dozens of stockbrokers, finance and insurance companies, must make sure "who the computer is willing to talk to." Terminals are therefore connected to the computer through direct lines which are thought to be hard to trace. Each morning a light comes up on the terminal, and the computer has a brief chat with the operator. The machine asks for the password of the day or week, and accepts transactions only after checking if that password has really been allotted to that terminal. From then on, the computer is ready to talk but will give only that information which is preceded by the password or a certain bleep tone on the tape.

It is therefore rightly claimed that it would be cheaper and easier to buy the daily printout of all operations from an insider than to crack the computer. But, according to specialists like A. S. Cormack, it is a gross exaggeration to assert that any terminal can be 100 percent foolproof—and even the United States government's own advanced system is no exception.

A terminal protection study has recently been conducted by IBM. The results, tailored to suit top security government requirements, looked most promising. The Pentagon was provided with an experimental terminal to IBM's central computer which was protected from Bleeping Toms by a new method using a series of passwords, codes, and electronic locks. Twenty-four hours later, the Pentagon came back with a full printout of IBM's own, most confidential, seven-year plan—only to demonstrate that all those locks had been picked.

Returning the compliment, IBM could recall that some strictly science-motivated students at the Massachusetts

Institute of Technology had once tapped the computers that handled the most highly classified data of the Strategic Air Command—and they did that *without* having any legitimate access to terminals!

The weakness of the system is recognized and admitted by the manufacturers themselves. The problem is that anything a man can do another one can undo—and one computer's ingenuity can always be matched by another's.

Codes and passwords are just so many variations on a theme, and the number of possible variations is—although sometimes enormous—always limited. Any given two letters of the alphabet can form only four versions. For example:

> AA
> AB
> BA
> BB

Any given three letters, say A, B, and C, produce twenty-seven variants:

AAA	ABA	ACA	ABC	BBC
BBB	AAB	AAC	ACB	BCB
CCC	BAA	CAA	BAC	CBB
	ABB	ACC	BCA	CCB
	BAB	CAC	CAB	CBC
	BBA	CCA	CBA	BCC

If among these, one looked for a password, not a code, it would be easy to spot "cab" as the only likely one.

Once the code can use *any* three or more letters, perhaps in combination with numbers, we run into astronomical figures—yet the range is still limited to all the calculable variations of a code format in which, say, four letters are followed by five figures and three more letters. These variations may run into thousands of millions that could all be assembled by a regiment in numerous man-years—or in a few computer-days by a machine that can do one or two in every one thousandth of a second, twenty-four hours a day.

Perfectly true, it takes a computer to beat a computer, but it can be done, and has been done not only by MIT and the Pentagon but also by embezzlers and spies. Confidential data was extracted from a Louisville computer, and in Cincinnati, an agent obtained road-planning information with the help of a second computer.

A similar technique was used in the now notorious Californian case when a Palo Alto computer spied on and robbed its larger brother in Oakland. The thief belonged to and was "instigated" by an electronics engineer who used a special code and account number to obtain confidential information worth twenty-five thousand dollars to his firm. The victim computer was used by time-sharing subscribers who could make ordinary telephone calls to the center, give their code number, and talk directly to the machine. The robbery went on unnoticed until the security program in the victim's brain realized what was happening and began to yell blue murder. The owners called in the Oakland fraud squad, which in turn, obtained the first search warrant "for electronic impulses" in the suspect's memory.

Although many terminals are authorized to "read only" to avoid accidental erasure of important data, the input-blocking code locks can be broken, and then even these can be used freely, like others, to submit data for storage. New data and new programs cannot be distinguished by the computer, and this creates the danger of sabotage—vital information can be wiped off or falsified by competitors, staff with a grudge, or political organizations. A civilian employee who was sacked by the United States Army made a tiny private alteration in the program of the computer; as a result, when his name was crossed out from the payroll, the computer committed suicide by erasing its entire memory bank.

Against the potentially inestimable damage by sabotage, many companies have back-up tapes. Unfortunately these copies are frequently kept next to the original. Others are stored in virtual industrial fortresses, well away from the premises, where precious computer tapes and microfilms are nursed in an extremely low magnetic field with perfect air-conditioning at constantly monitored humidity level.

I once visited such a Shangri-la for tapes. It was at Neston, near Bath, a hundred feet below the rolling Wiltshire hills, where the walls of a former stone quarry, steel doors, combination locks, guards, a variety of alarm systems, secret arrangements with all the police forces in the area, and the quietness of the village—any strangers would be spotted within minutes—provided security from theft, fire, and sabotage. Inside this British industrial Fort Knox, small, individual steel lockers held tapes that were the chief assets "of leading companies in numerous countries," and microfilms, each containing an average of 43,200 engineering drawings.

Perhaps it is needless to say that the underground vault is nuclear bombproof—which should fill the heart with the delirious joy of knowing that whatever happens to us all, the pick of computer tapes will remain there to greet agents from another planet of higher intelligence. Unless, of course, the human element interferes, and a tape or two disappears in transit to or from the vault. For whatever security experts can and computer-cracking experts are willing to do, the greatest danger comes from the organization that searches for the weakest link in the chain—the lowest-paid man in any operation.

To protect secrets against these dangers, the British Computer Society has now published a "Code of Good Practice." Keeping in mind that in Britain alone, three hundred thousand terminals are expected to be in use by 1980 and five times more by A.D. 2000, they have made a series of recommendations for security. One of these calls for "a personnel security check into the background of staff working in confidential areas."

Background checking? In Europe? Among civilians? Breaking the privacy of one man to protect the computerized privacy of another? How will that coexist with the usual European sneers at American security precautions?

9

Seek, and We Shall Find

ON A WET FRIDAY MORNING in September 1972, a French executive was late, for the first time, to his office. When he arrived at last, he picked up a few personal belongings from his desk, said good-bye to no one, handed in his resignation for "personal reasons," and refused to give any further explanation for his premature decision. He was fifty-three years old, married, had been with the company for fourteen years; his chances of becoming a director were good, and at the time he was earning the equivalent of about twelve thousand dollars. Sadly they let him leave right away. Puzzled colleagues discussed his inexplicable retirement throughout the weekend.

On Monday morning, the German press carried an item of business news that occupied no more than nine lines in any of the papers. At 7:50 A.M., the head of the French company received a telephone call from his baffled chief German representative, who kept losing his voice in excitement as he read over the news item and asked for an explanation. The cause of his shock was that their German rival had just come out with a new product—practically identical with their own great trump that had been prepared for three years with

cloak-and-dagger secrecy and which was to go into production in four-weeks time. The launching date would have
followed a month later.

The French also had a most original marketing plan.
Strangely enough, it would soon transpire, the German rival
conducted an almost identical campaign.

In all, the news item announcing the German move
signaled to the French company an estimated loss of almost a
quarter of a million dollars in exports. It also meant that more
than three hundred Frenchmen would lose their jobs within
six months.

At ten o'clock that Monday morning, Tony Shepherd,
European director of the American Burns Security Services,
received a call from Paris. He was to investigate what
happened—and it was he who asked me not to identify
details and participants in the following account of the case.

"When we got there, the first thing we did was to compile
a list of executives who had access to all the plans. The one
who had so suddenly resigned on Friday appeared on this list.
It didn't need a Sherlock Holmes to notice the 'coincidence.'
Three days later, we already had all the circumstantial
evidence we needed.

The man had traveled several times to Germany—always
over weekends. Each time he took a briefcase with him—and
returned without it. The documents librarian recalled that
this executive had once lost a few papers—it had been
regarded as just one of those things. We were able to identify
a man who visited this Frenchman in his German hotel
during each trip; he was an executive of the rivals, but there
was nothing to indicate that his colleagues or superiors knew
anything about his dealings. We also suspected, although our
client did not very much like to discuss the subject, that a
few years earlier, this German firm had good reasons to
believe that the French had stolen something from them. So

apart from profit, revenge could have been a second motive.

"And we made one more discovery. A week before his resignation, our suspect repaid several hefty debts *in cash,* including more than four thousand pounds at two casinos.

"We never got further than that, but I knew we had a strong case. Our client decided, however, not to make accusations or start legal action. They said 'because, for the sake of security, no patent had been taken out.' I think they had other reasons, too. But that had nothing to do with me."

Not a pretty story, you might say. The worst part of it is that it all could have been avoided. Could have been, if anybody knew about this man's circumstances in time.

He had a bedridden wife who had been 60 percent paralyzed for seven years. He was supporting his troublesome grown-up son. He had a mistress whom he wanted to marry eventually, and with whom he had set up a second home. His good salary was not good enough to run two households, two cars, two wives. Apparently that was why he began gambling. He ran up mounting debts, sold one of the cars, sold some stock he had, and then sold whatever else he could lay his hands on—his firm's plans.

"It is more or less irrelevant whether he was approached or went to the rival firm," said Tony Shepherd. "What matters is that his employer knew nothing about his problems. It would have been easy enough to help him out. He was a good man; worth it. Or else he could have been transferred to a job where he would be no security risk. Or they could have fired him. As it happened, they didn't even know about his wife's illness."

All over the world, people are increasingly concerned about safeguards for their privacy, but perhaps nowhere more than in Britain. In fact, utmost social and individual tolerance combined with ferociously intolerant insistence on privacy are probably the greatest charms and internationally most alluring qualities of life here. I would not venture to call it an absolute majority, but there must be millions and millions of Britons who would not hesitate to put up with the disease of irritating inefficiencies and security blunders if the loss of privacy was the bitter pill to cure it. Those of us who are not directly responsible for the country's economic secrets and other assets may call ourselves lucky; it is not for us to carry out thorough—ruthless?—checking of staff and to scrutinize their background, a cornerstone of industrial self-defense.

The case for privacy has frequently been argued on both logical and emotional levels. Unfortunately encounters with commercial spies are a painful reminder that there is also a strong case for certain curtailments of our cherished privacy.

The usual question is this, Would the protection of jobs and potential earnings justify the regardless exposure of *all* key employees' private affairs? If yes, where would you draw the line to separate key employees from the crowd with the right to privacy? Would you subject a secretary to security checks—or would you fire her boss if he failed to deny her access to confidential information?

There is no oil exploration in the Manchester area, but its sites suitable for development can be as bloody battlefields as any patch of desert in a sheikhdom. In a recent war there, a rather plain secretary with an eye "for the beautiful things in life" might have been responsible for the slaying of an army.

She worked for a medium-sized company that marketed a widely used consumer product in the Midlands and the North. The firm was threatened by an American take-over bid and the board was determined to fight it off. They knew they could convince their bankers and shareholders if their current expansion strategy succeeded. They needed several new sites and their scouts worked with great secrecy.

Eventually twenty properties were chosen, and from these, a preliminary list of seven was drawn up by the board.

The secretary, whom I shall call Mabel, was known as "an odd bird" among the staff. Her dreams were rather limited, but they were dreams all right. She relished the thought of a week's holiday in Majorca instead of Bournemouth, and eagerly anticipated the day when she would buy three pairs of tights at the same time although she needed only one. She had just married a young clerk, who she was convinced, had a great future, although at the time he could offer her only his poverty to share. They rented a furnished flatlet—two tiny rooms with communal bath and kitchen—and saved so desperately for the deposit on a house that sometimes she would sell her luncheon vouchers at half price to a colleague.

Nothing so far to single her out for a security check with all the inevitable delving and probing and prying. But there was something that might have caught the eye of a security man. While her dedication to savings remained undiminished, she turned up one day in an Italian-import double-knit three-piece pants suit which, according to the consensus of opinion in the office, "must have cost a fortune." A week later she was carrying a sixty pound handbag. Whenever she acquired one of these "beautiful things in life," she told everybody that it was yet another present from her husband. (Her husband believed that these were gifts from her aunt in Canada.)

Were these a cause for concern? An investigation might have discovered that she had a generous lover. No harm done—except to the husband—none of her employer's business. Or that she indeed had a rich aunt. Or that her husband did have moments of extravagance. Or that actually there was cause for concern.

The wealthy director of a smaller but upcoming rival firm—quite unconnected with the Americans pursuing the take-over bid—had befriended Mabel and made up to her several times over a few friendly glasses of sparkling wine. He sympathized with her problems and gave her some presents "out of the sheer goodness of his heart," she would claim one day.

Perhaps it was true—up to a point. Perhaps he merely enjoyed the company of a young girl. ("Me with him? Don't be daft! Could be my granddad. No, he's perfectly respectable. A real gentleman.")

In fact, he picked up some useful information from her about her firm. Although she denies it to this day, he probably heard from her about the expansion plan, too. He wanted to see the list, with one of the two usual plans in mind. He could buy some of the selected seven most likely properties in the name of a front man and then sell them to the company at a rather excessive profit. Or he could slow down the expansion by simply alerting the owners—mostly small shopkeepers and pensioners including a ninety-year-old widow—to the fact that their cheap little holdings were very valuable to his competitors.

If only he could see the list—

He mentioned to Mabel the fast-rising property prices. That frightened her. Their savings toward a deposit accumulated much too slowly.

Would she like to earn a little extra?

Of course, but how?

By doing some photocopying.

Easy enough—she had the machine in her office. She was willing. What was to be copied?

Well, the papers to be copied were—er—in her employer's safe.

She hesitated, and he made a mistake.

An operator of C.S.S., the security service that was asked to investigate the case and produce evidence, told me: "The chap was a real green amateur. Fifty or a hundred pounds would have persuaded the girl to overcome her scruples. For that sort of money she would have committed a minor indiscretion—well, sort of doing him a good turn. But the fool offered her five grand!

"The thought of that much money terrified her. In her world, it would have been the price of a family massacre. So she discussed it with her husband, and he insisted on contacting her employer at once.

"With her cooperation, we caught the man red-handed, but the company didn't take him to court. The spy got away with a fright. After all, it's an unsavory business to buy cheap from poor pensioners by keeping them in the dark, and it would come out in court. Silence was in the best interest of everybody, as usual."

And Mabel? The managing director himself shook hands with her. She was commended for her loyalty. She was praised at a Christmas dinner for the staff, and everybody knew that in some mysterious way she had saved the firm from a take-over and the likely closure of most branches.

She and her husband still live in the furnished apartment. It takes time to save a few hundred pounds for the deposit on a house when property prices are rocketing.

That the company failed to express its gratitude by even a modest cash reward revealed only meanness. But to keep her in the same confidential job without buying her loyalty was a sign of plain stupidity.

Most security men are convinced that it is a serious, if not criminal, negligence not to carry out preemployment investigations followed up by irregular periodic checks on the private lives of key personnel. After all, there was nothing wrong with the above French executive when he joined the company.

They believe that employment, particularly in an executive capacity, should be like a partnership in which the partners hold nothing back from one another. "You give up your privacy when you go into business together," an American agent declared. He added that most applicants accepted this condition of employment. "They only begin to holler about intrusion of privacy and all that when, after all those inquiries, they're not hired."

Those who insist on calling themselves "security agents," desperately object to being lumped together with "repugnant bedroom spies." They claim to do no more than United States customs and British social-security snoopers, or than national counterintelligence services that compile thick files of illegally obtained data on nonsuspect civilians including public figures.°

The Roman Catholic priest who wishes to opt out on account of difficulties over celibacy is subjected to an "ordeal by questionnaire"; he must answer in intimate detail questions about his "abnormal" desires, the scandals he was involved in, and his everyday problems with the practice of chastity, so that a security inquiry can examine the moral climate of the seminary where the "weak" priest was trained.

Government agents spend far more time checking staff than seeking out foreign enemy agents, because discontent in vital institutions like the Pentagon have already promoted the

° Sometimes, and quite wrongly, this is regarded as a United States speciality, practiced by the government, the CIA and the FBI. The only real difference is that in most other countries, government agencies have managed to keep more quiet about it. A Rome tribunal, for instance, condemned the Italian counterintelligence service of the 1960's because it had compiled such files on 157,000 personalities including the President and the Pope. "Inquiries were made into circumstances of an intimate character, into economic and into family affairs, into social life, financial activities, extramarital relations or irregular relationships, on the birth of illegitimate children and sexual habits, at times documented with photographs."

insider and his leaks to the press to the rank of "the greatest menace to government."

Security agents will therefore argue that private enterprise should enjoy the same advantages of security as governments or the church. Their favorite example is that malicious leaking of confidential documents by employees of ITT (International Telephone and Telegraph, one of the largest supranational corporations in the world and the eighth largest in America), exposed secret deals with and pressures on the United States government, created a vast international political scandal, and thus damaged not only the ITT image but also national economic interests.

What these agents fail to question is, of course, where in governmental and business practices the dividing line between true protection of secrets and cover-up for inefficiencies and unseemly acts should be.

Another, usually unasked question—Who are the chief supporters of the security-above-privacy lobby?—also helps to reduce the doubtless strength, if not the validity, of the argument that favors preemployment and follow-up prying into private affairs of staff. Because the answer is that this security gospel is most enthusiastically preached by the main beneficiaries: the huge security industry (in London there are more security men than police; the American security business, including guard services, employs about three hundred thousand men, and its annual income is in excess of $2.5 billion); the various security equipment manufacturers (whose sales promotion for safes, fire and burglar alarms, closed circuit television, and so on, now almost inevitably involves "selling the security package" complete with protection philosophy, gloomy predictions, and practical advice); and an army of private detectives (most of whom advertise but few can provide actual industrial counterespionage services).

Private detectives cash in mainly on other people's privacy. Staff background investigations for aggressive or defensive purposes are their most regular connections with the world of industrial espionage and security, and even this work they tend to mix freely with financial fidelity and marital infidelity reporting, new borrowers' credit rating and discredited debtor chasing, snooping for insurers, and legwork for lawyers.

Whether people like them or not, it is a fact that the majority of these agents do an honest day's toil—in San Francisco, a detective's sons refused to join the flourishing business because "it's too much work"—and their efforts help employers, moneylenders, litigants, and the law. But it is beyond doubt that there is an abundance of pitfalls and plenty of elbowroom for crooks in security work.

One of the pitfalls is that success is usually regarded as a must in this trade. I interviewed about five dozen private detectives in a dozen countries. At least the decent ones seemed to agree that a negative finding, a clean bill of moral health for the subject, was just as successful as proof of, say, alcoholism or court convictions. Yet even these admitted that "you can hardly afford to draw a blank—very seldom can you return to your client saying 'Sorry, couldn't find anything,' because there're plenty of others to do the job."

This spirit is reflected by the ambiguous slogan, *Seek and we shall find*, which paraphrases St. Matthew (Seek and *ye* shall find; knock and it shall be opened unto you), and which is the unfortunate choice for the advertisements of a perfectly reputable New York detective agency. There are, however, other agencies which not only imply a promise to seek and find, but also offer a "results or money back" guarantee which can be the most dangerous pitfall in this work because "overambitious reporting"—not to mention outright fabrication—can ruin a man for life without anyone telling him what hit him or giving him half a chance to defend himself.

Most of the basic background information is assembled without the subject's knowledge or approval. This secrecy is thought to be essential particularly in the early stages of preemployment checking, in cases of proposed merger or investment, but the findings can be very damaging. That is why cautious American companies, with more costly experience in this field than their European colleagues, stick a responsibility disclaimer on each report.

The following is such an antilibel label used by Burns International:

THIS IS A CONFIDENTIAL REPORT

> The customer agrees that he shall permit none of the information contained in this report be directly or indirectly revealed to the subject of this report, nor to any other person unless he be in the employ of the customer in a capacity which makes it imperative that he have access to such information for the protection and benefit of the customer. The customer assumes any and all liability for information revealed by him and his employees; and for any action taken by him, based on information contained in this report.

Detectives maintain that it is not for them to evaluate information, select what is and what is not relevant, pass judgment, and make unwarranted remarks or recommendations. But some of them argue that not everything can be turned over to the client.

R. B. Matthews of Management Investigation Services, told me: "I may report verbally everything to the clients, but I don't give them a full dossier. Personnel departments are not always as safe and secure as they should be. If the report fell into the wrong hands, we could expose people to blackmail."

One of his clients, a large public company, had some bad

experience with new board members: personal problems came to light only when it was too late. "So now, when they choose someone as a potential nominee, we run a basic check without the man's knowledge," he said. "If we find nothing against him, the company will inform him that 'he is on a preliminary list of possibles for a board appointment.' It's vital to mention a list even if he's the only one considered, because it's bad luck not to be chosen from among many, but it really hurts to get an outright personal rejection.

"At the same time, he will be told that a certain screening process must be one of the many facets of assessment and his full cooperation is required. Most people submit to this without hesitation, and when we interview them, we explain that if they are to become public figures, they must surrender certain rights of privacy and conduct themselves in such a manner not to be detrimental to the corporate image. We also like to tell them right away, when they are keen to get the job, that as board members they will have to submit to irregular, periodic checking, too. Unfortunately many big companies fail to keep an eye on key men or, which is equally bad, fail to tell them about the security system in advance.

"A thorough screening should also *help* the applicant. The man who knows that he has no secrets from his superiors is practically blackmail-proof.

"Quite recently we did a job like this for the company. While our subject had no idea that he was earmarked for promotion, we discovered that in 1938, when he was a student in Cambridge, he mildly sympathized with the Nazi movement. It seemed just a stupid youthful error. He had never been a party member, and it was all forgotten by the time the war came. There was no indication of any continued political leanings to the right or left. Nevertheless we had to report this to the client. The board considered it, and decided it was no reason to break the man's career.

"So now he was duly informed, and I interviewed him myself. He spoke freely about everything—except Cambridge. It seemed a darker period of his life than we thought. He kept repeating that no, he had never had any political affiliations. I had no choice—this had to be made known to the board. I suggested that the chairman should have a discussion with him about politics in general and, if necessary, challenge him on this point.

"An interview was arranged, and after a few minutes, he came clean voluntarily. The chairman could now tell him that his secret was no secret to us, and that his mistake would not be held against him because his voluntary revelation had made it unnecessary to challenge him. The man then telephoned me to express his gratitude; for the first time in his life, he was out in the open, no longer worried about the dreadful thought of "what if somebody found out."

Well, this man was lucky. Many others were not. I have seen scores of files in which the odd infected remarks, as lightly dropped as a used Kleenex, stood out like massive headstones of individual tragedies:

• The German investment analyst whose bad luck was to have a brother-in-law working for a rival organization. He never understood why he was suddenly cold-shouldered instead of promoted.

• The Swedish "design and development manager" who would never know that the top American job he thought to be in the bag was never offered to him mainly because a young, keen detective, on his first assignment abroad, talked to him in a fashionable suburb of Malmo, offered him a sip from his hip flask, and tried to be funny by saying, "You Swedes do love the odd drop or two." The manager admitted he was no teetotaller and added with a smile, "One needs some defense against all these beautiful Swedish wives!" An innocent joke? The detective's "discovery" grew into this sentence in the report: ". . . reason to believe that subject has certain degree of dependence on alcohol consumed mostly in ill-chosen company, e.g., wife-swappers. . . ."

• The senior planning engineer who lost his most confidential job quite unexpectedly and, unable to find *any* suitable employment in Britain, was forced to emigrate to New Zealand, because his employer had received a report that ". . . some of his financial difficulties may be due to the fact that, unknown to his wife, he is supporting his illegitimate child. . . ." (In this case, the detective discovered, eventually, that the little bastard was not the engineer's and that he acted only as a post office for a friend who was sending the money from Canada. This agent had at least the nerve and decency to inform the client, the man's former employer, about the error—but in view of potential compensation claims, "It was mutually decided not to stir things up."

• The odd-job man in Detroit who became a "security risk" when an agent found scraps of old company notepaper in his garbage can—although it was possible that the man had taken them home for his children to scribble on.

• Or the Dutch sales engineer who lost the trust of the old family firm he had worked for all his life, because after the loss of some confidential information, a routine inquiry revealed that he had a mistress. (The detective who conducted the investigation told me: "Stupid old man blew his something—head? Top—what? He was angry, very angry. No help I told him a mistress can be good thing, keeps the man steady, what? Better than bad marriage, prostitutes, office girls, divorce, another marriage—The mistress can be good for marriage and good for work because happy man work better.")

Yet erroneous reporting, outright falsification against or in favor of the subject (some agents make it quite clear that they are approachable), and sheer carelessness are not very surprising, considering that some detectives charge ridiculously low fees when even the more reliable basic summaries of a man's background are usually quite cheap. It is difficult to compare prices because the meaning of "basic" or "standard" information varies a great deal from country to country and from agency to agency.

American detectives reckon it is not advisable to hire an executive whose security screening is not worth a fee of somewhere between three hundred and five hundred dollars at a minimum, depending on circumstances. For that they will contact previous employers, gain their confidence to obtain off-the-record information, check the man's habits, weaknesses, financial and marital stability, court and criminal record if any, driving history, medical history, and so on, but only locally. To do the same in other states or abroad will, of course, cost more.

Other American agencies distribute detailed price lists which enable clients to specify tailor-made investigations. A preemployment check by the Inter-State Bureau of Investigation of Baltimore, Maryland, "will normally disclose falsification of work and education history, involvement in current or past criminal activity, emotional instability, immorality, alcoholism, narcotics addiction, dishonesty, laziness, chronic absenteeism, and similar undesirable and costly traits."

An elementary package deal—eight-point flat-fee service —Standard Background Investigation costs forty-five dollars in Baltimore and up to 50 percent more when moving farther off within the state. This includes aspects like "current and past neighborhood check for activities (your selection); current and past employment check . . . ; current activities determined through neighbors and employers; criminal/court or driving record (one area or state of your selection); various credit files. . . ."

In the case of an executive, the fee will probably be

increased by additional items such as an "asset search" for $50; criminal/court records, $10 for each area; driving record, $8 per area; special investigations, $9 per hour plus mileage plus expenses; the use of a "special purpose vehicle," $4 per hour plus mileage; "motion picture film [at] 30 cents per foot, minimum magazine charge $15." *

Some investigators quote rates for special inquiries under such headings: work competence/incompetence check, record of company policy violations, involvement in immoral conduct, and distasteful personal habits.

Prices also vary a great deal in Europe but a somewhat meaningful screening usually starts around seventy-five pounds or its equivalent, going up to over two hundred pounds for a kind of "positive vetting" when even the milkman is interviewed, and barmaids in the subject's residential and office area are visited by friendly agents. A really complete record of a man's private and working life, perhaps in several countries, may cost up to two thousand pounds—yet oddly enough, some detectives offer a man's "last five years, residence, social standing, financial standing, jobs and criminal record" for a mere twenty pounds.

Society and authorities are usually up in arms when allegations are made or fresh evidence comes to light about agents obtaining and selling criminal records which, in their countries, are not supposed to be available to the public. Agents who offer such services openly or under a variety of euphemisms usually claim that they will find out only what is legally and freely accessible to anyone. This may be true in most American states. Elsewhere, when hard pressed, they will explain that "it's easy to obtain a man's convictions because these are read out in court."

How do they know where to look?

* By now, these prices have probably been increased.

"Well, it's obvious. Newspaper-cuttings libraries are an excellent source."

But surely, not all cases are reported in the national press.

"No, but we can look through the libraries of local papers."

And so the pointless dispute continues, because few detectives want to admit that it would take ages to uncover a man's criminal record in this way with any degree of reliability—a vast number of man-hours that would never be paid for by the usual five pound or ten pound or even twenty pound fees.

The truth is that any private investigator worth his shoe leather, rich enough to pay his telephone bill, and smart enough to offer such services, has *inside contacts.* Yes, bribery is the name of the game, and in most cases, the ultimate recipient is a policeman. The private detective only adds his modest profit to the not particularly generous bribe. A couple of years ago, a British agent advertised his readiness to obtain anybody's "bank balance with full details" for six pounds and criminal records for four pounds. *The Guardian,* the first newspaper to campaign against this racket, collected evidence that such confidential information was regularly offered for sale at prices ranging from fifty pence to twenty-five pounds.

Due to exposures, and under pressure, the prices have gone up, but still not excessively. To find every crooked policeman and official would demand very extensive police inquiries, but I do not doubt that most agents can—and if they have sufficient trust in the client's discretion, they will—get *any* information they need.

To obtain a person's bank balance is, in fact, easier today than it used to be—thanks to computerization creating a concentration of data. An individual's current bank statement would now be available for about forty pounds, although a company's financial record may cost considerably more.

Private detectives on the Continent are not very specific about the prices, but most of them claim—off the record, of course—that "in today's moral climate it should not create an unsurmountable problem to find the official who can be bribed."

Records of arrests and convictions are freely available for a regular fee in most American states, but not in New York City where the constant demand for such information has created a bonanza for corrupt policemen and other officials. Some of them received just two dollars for a criminal record. Others were on a semiregular payroll at ten thousand dollars a year, and thirty thousand dollar fees were not exceptional. Not only those who received, but also people and companies who paid the bribes were eventually exposed. American Airlines and Trans-Caribbean Airways, brokerage houses, and other companies as well as eight major detective agencies, including well-known names like Pinkerton's and the Wackenhut Corporation, appeared on the list of those obtaining the criminal records of prospective employees. Pinkerton's president answered the accusations with criticism of the local regulations. He contended that criminal records were public information; if the city authorities made intensive use of such information when employing municipal workers, why should they deny private concerns the right of taking similar precautions?

The same argument could be reiterated in Britain and elsewhere every time the police inform professional organizations and government departments about an employee's convictions. They claim to do it in "defense of these bodies" and "for the public good." This attitude, in fact, helps the private detective, who instead of risking outright bribery, cons the information out of banks, various other companies, and government departments.

When, in 1973, the Withers brothers—British private

detectives and bug peddlers—were convicted of conspiracy to effect a public mischief by obtaining confidential information from government departments, Scotland Yard, banks, building societies, and so on, a great deal of indignation was voiced that it could all be done on the telephone by experienced and smooth-talking con men, who could easily impersonate officials *entitled* to receive such disclosures.

Yet should banks and various authorities freely exchange personal data among themselves without the subject's approval and right to challenge the validity of such information circulating about him? ° If, in the name of governmental self-defense, the answer is yes, it will clearly support the security men who maintain that private firms also have "the right to know" because staff background checks are purely defensive.

Allegedly, most private agents scrutinize the purpose of every assignment and verify the bona fide intentions of the client. If the job is to observe representatives calling on customers, perhaps the client wants the sales list of a competitor. If a "preemployment" check is required, perhaps the client only wants to bribe or blackmail the "applicant."

With due respect to well-meaning agents, their honest efforts to verify the client's "right to know" are often doomed to failure, particularly if the assignment comes from a scheming industrial espionage organization—or from a no less ruthless counterintelligence agent who is convinced that aggressive defense is perfectly justified.

° If the proposed German *Datenschutz Gesetz* became law, it would forbid the exchange of personal data even between German police authorities. In America, NCHS, the National Criminal History System is now controlled by the FBI and will provide, by 1975, a central on-line access to criminal records in all states. On municipal level in Long Beach, California and Wichita Falls, Texas, criminal files have been integrated with other sensitive information adding up to detailed individual profiles, and all local government departments have access to these.

Promotion to Death

The defense of industrial secrets can always match the attack, subject to the "what's worth what to whom" Kubik principle which gives the marginal advantage to the spy. Apart from physical security systems, guards, safes that squeal or destroy their contents if the locks are tampered with, shredding machines, strict control of document movements, confidential files treated in an electronic way to raise the alarm if removed, staff screening and electronic countermeasures, the defense has a vast choice of tactics ranging from:

The petty (In accordance with company rules, a London store executive was dismissed by the John Lewis Partnership because she married a department manager in a rival store. It was feared that inadvertently, future plans, supply sources, pricing policy, and other secrets might be passed on to him.)

The cautious (Du Pont, the American chemical giant, which held a virtual world monopoly in nylon production and achieved three and a half billion dollars in annual sales, suffered great losses through industrial espionage; once the company was awarded almost seven million dollars for damages; on another occasion, a foreman stole some plans valued at three million dollars and tried to sell them to a competitor. So when their quest for a new product with the potential of nylon and the prediction of a future leather shortage focused their attention on substitutes, and when their scientists produced a breakthrough—Corfam, the first synthetic leather to "breathe"—they were determined not to let industrial spies interfere with their fantastic prospects.

That is why shoe manufacturers, producing test shoes from the first batches, received visits from Du Pont inspectors who swept up all the scraps of waste to prevent them from falling into the hands of competitors. Although some defense specialists believe that such extreme caution only serves as an appetizer to would-be spies, no Corfam sample was lost, and security remained airtight—right to the moment of crash, when the project was abandoned and eighteen-years research with a hundred million dollar investment had to be written off.)

The overcautious (Many companies, especially when already damaged by espionage, tend to classify almost everything as "confidential"; eventually this not only reduces the care the real secrets receive from the staff, but also lures inquisitive opportunists and professional agents.)

The elaborate (In some merger negotiations, security men deliberately put out such a vast quantity of false rumors that items of true intelligence and leakages already in circulation were completely swamped, and nobody would anymore believe anything.)

The sophisticated (Costly cover operations for important business moves and even "diversion laboratories" to conceal the main line of research have been devised by counterintelligence agents. When Players decided to introduce a new low-priced cigarette, No. 6, with gift coupons, different code names were used by the various departments preparing the campaign, advertising material was designed and produced in four countries, and to mislead anyone who might have noticed an extraordinary amount of activity that would clearly indicate the birth of a new brand, they even launched a dummy novelty, a cigarette in the top price bracket without coupons, only to be withdrawn as soon as the actual frontal attack began.)

The plain (In Japan, it is becoming obligatory for would-be executives to take a four-month course in economic counter-intelligence.)

The whimsical (There is a growing resistance to the employment of ex-military counterintelligence agents for industrial security work because they tend to overcomplicate affairs, overcompensate for the imaginary cunning of the opposition, see an ambush in every lucky break, and believe anything but the plain truth; this is how a leading ship-building firm lost a major contract.)

The range of security measures continues right up to what is sometimes described as aggressive defense, in the name of which many outright espionage operations have been mounted. (A successful specialist in such techniques said: "When a client is attacked by unethical means, depriving him of due profits, unusual methods may be needed to protect him. You can beat guerrillas only by employing their own tactics against them.")

Thriving, bourgeois, stark, stale, stolid Stockholm has shown me many of its faces. Mysterious and frightening, it has never looked to me except once. But then mystery and a protracted sensation of fright were probably my traveling companions all the way to Bromma airport, and from then onward, throughout the cab ride to my hotel in Humlegards-gatan, in the heart of the city, at every corner I anticipated an "accident." In the dipped over headlights of the hotel lobby, a half a dozen massive, modern womblike swivel chairs faced me. From behind them, at their gleaming metal stems, only pairs of feet could be seen. Whom did they belong to? Would anybody take careful note of my allocated room number?

My fears were, of course, totally unfounded. Yet it is easy to grow suspicious and see unknown hazards lurking even in the hot face towels the stewardess distributes with a set smile, when you know that inadvertently, you have been instrumental in the downfall of a spy and the wrecking of a well-organized intelligence operation.

My total involvement in the case was embarrassingly brief and prosaic. Prior to Stockholm, the "adventure" had taken me no farther and to a no more exotic place than the bar in the glass skullcap of the London Hilton, and the "action" was restricted to a chat and a couple of drinks with François Levine, the French business consultant who, as I have already said, gave me one of my first really useful introductions in the land of the double cross.

He is one of the last dandies of the century. He will never be caught dressed in the wrong clothes for the occasion or the time of the day, and if anybody ever shoots him on a private jet flight between Mombasa and Johannesburg, the world will only learn what the right attire for midafternoon death over Africa is. A tall man in his late fifties, with the merest touch of middle-age spread around his waist, he has a slightly puffed face with a bluish tint suggesting that he has just finished shaving. If I did not know that he always used an old-fashioned, long, machete-like razor, and that in his opinion, electric razors are only for suppressing the voice of compulsive bathroom singers, I would have thought that he last shaved on his way up in the elevator with a battery-operated model. And then again only while I did not look for a second.

During that short conversation with me, he mentioned one of his current cases.

Through a contact—presumably, one of his many regular retainers on the payroll of various commercial organizations —he had heard that a Swedish firm was regularly receiving confidential information about research done by a rival. Within twenty-four hours, he had sold this piece of intelligence to the victim from whom he also accepted an assignment for further defensive investigations.

There were no more than a dozen people who might have had access to the leaked information, and Levine's operatives compiled "an in-depth profile" on each.

"We found a scientist who seemed to have some extra income from an apparently mysterious source, but he was soon eliminated," Levine said. "We were then left with a laboratory technician as our main suspect because there were things in his past with which he could have been black-mailed."

"What was that?"

"Um—*things*. Look, my friend, I could invent something and lie to you. Would you prefer that?"

I did not, and settled for *things*.

"The stupid thing was, of course, that the firm, I mean my client, never bothered to find out anything about his background. No screening, nothing. But then Italians can't be bothered."

"So it was an Italian firm."

He laughed. "OK. But ask no more."

It was easy to agree to that. He would not even name the industry in question. Without some further details, it sounded like a rather dull case.

Levine kept the technician under surveillance, and it was soon established that the suspect had regular contacts with an outfit working for the Swedish firm, the recipient of the intelligence. Only one unanswered question remained. How did the technician smuggle the information out?

Apparently the research laboratory was under very strict control. The security arrangements included a complete change of clothes on entering and leaving, and it would have been impossible to hide the great sheaves of papers that seemed to have reached the rival firm.

Levine, an ardent exponent of aggressive defense techniques, planted a man at the rival firm and discovered that the papers they had received were prints from microfilm.

"And that's the puzzle I'm working on right now," he said. "We searched and searched the lab, but couldn't find anything. I swear there isn't any camera in there. I swear the man can't get it in and out of the place regularly. But then, how does he get on with it? Because he does, you know. We were careful not to change anything in the daily routine of the lab. That swine still has the opportunity to photograph things—if he has a camera. But he hasn't."

He was becoming rather agitated, and as I was not particularly interested in hearing more about this routine affair and his headaches, I was not sorry when he dropped the subject.

Staring down on the darkening landscape of London roofs, the conversation drifted toward town planning or rather the lack of it, the loss of flavor and character in buildings or rather the evolution of new, usually less likable ones, and Levine commented on the new tall hotels and office buildings, which he found as unsuitable for old towns as Bermuda shorts for funerals.

We were clearly running out of topics.

To lengthen the agony of the conversation, I said that "only working in them is bleaker than looking at them." Once I had had to do a week's research in one of those blocks in New York. After a couple of days in the perfection of the office and its thoughtful scientific comfort, I began to feel detached from life as if on an endless trip through space. Airtight windows, sealed forever. Sunshine lighting. Tinted glass to keep out the sun. The constant temperature of incubators. Coffee, cocoa, iced water on tap. Paper cups. Paper towels. Music piped in. Fresh air piped in. Specially filtered. I mentioned to Levine what an American designer who worked in that building told me:

"Sometimes we just long for a breath of that lovely, smelly, polluted New York air. We go to the john for a breath of oxygen like the Japanese queue up at slot machines."

Levine jerked to life. "The john? Did you say the john, my friend?"

I nodded. He wanted me to repeat it all. I did. He was halfway to the door when he shouted back: "You could be right, you know!" I imagined him shaving fervently on the way down between the tenth and ninth floors.

A week later he telephoned me. It was a long-distance call but he did not say from where.

"You were right. Thanks," he shouted down the line, giving the impression yet again that in his heart he still could not trust these technological delusions like telephones.

He told me that his men had originally checked all entrances and even airducts, but they had given the sealed windows of the lab only a most cursory look. My casual mention of *fresh* air in the men's room gave him an idea. And they found a tiny window near the ceiling—with the suspected technician's fingerprints on the frame.

Then it was only a matter of waiting. The man was on night duty, and on the third night, an agent watching that window through an infrared viewer spotted him in the men's room. The light came on and went off twice; then a string with a small weight was lowered all the way to the street. A man emerged from the shadows in the street and tied something to the string. Then the package went up.

Some twenty minutes later, the light flashed twice more. The dangling package reappeared through the window. The accomplice in the street untied it, and the string went up again.

"A friend who worked for us in the lab confirmed it that all this time the technician was in the john which was inside the security perimeter where he could have taken and photographed any documents," said Levine rather triumphantly. He added some derogatory remarks about the client's own swollen-headed security adviser who never thought much of Levine and strongly objected to giving the assignment to an outsider: "No, my friend, I won't be a magnanimous victor, I can tell you that. When I'll tell him and his chairman about it all—"

"Don't they know it yet?" I interrupted.

"No. It happened only last night. I wanted to wait until we'd get the photographs and all the proof."

"I'd like to see their faces when you tell them," I said, only trying to be polite.

There was a pause. "It can be arranged," he yelled at last. "Yes, you could be there as my special adviser. I'll let you know."

So there I was now, waiting in the new Anglais Hotel in Stockholm, with a not very enviable but certainly irresistible invitation to be in on the kill.

Levine came to pick me up. At that stage, I thought he was only grateful to me. Which only showed I was yet to learn much about him.

We went for a leisurely drive, then doubled back toward the university, then back again to the hotel, and into the underground parking lot. As soon as we stopped, a chapel-sized solemnly dark station wagon with tinted windows shot into the tight slot next to us. "Come on," said Levine, and he was out of our car and into the other almost in a single swing. I followed him, and the American car took off as if ready to fly through the roof.

We were with two ash-blond, sinewy six-footers—as Italian as Lohengrin. I guessed they were Norwegians. (This was later confirmed by Levine who made no apologies about his original lie, which admittedly had proved him a good liar: he mentioned "Italians" in the Hilton as if it were a slip of the tongue.) They took us on a second sight-seeing tour, and tried not to appear too eager.

One of the two was the chairman of the firm, and the other, at the wheel, the security adviser. Levine quickly cashed in on my presence, introducing me as a specialist he had had to consult in the course of his investigation. He told them a most impressive pack of lies about me, delaying the presentation of his "theory" which he expounded in a hesitant, not-too-convincing manner—only to provoke some sneering remarks from the firm's already hurt security man. Levine let him argue; then casually produced the photographs—and the fingerprints—and the eyewitness's account —and the rest of the evidence.

The chairman was flabbergasted. Our feverishly flushed driver mounted the curb, receiving some most un-Swedish reactions from several pedestrians. As the dialogue between the chairman and Levine continued, I sat in readiness to take over the wheel if our driver had a stroke.

Our hosts spoke to one another in, presumably, Norwegian for a few minutes; then the chairman thanked Levine for his work and told him that full payment would be put through in the prearranged way.

"What's your next move?" asked Levine in a soft voice that made me suspicious.

The chairman planned to fire the laboratory technician personally. The security man would ensure that the man would never in his life get another decent job. Levine smiled and said nothing. The two were discussing legal action against the traitor, the rivals, the Swedish government—and Levine kept smiling. It was impossible not to notice that self-assured, derisory smile. The security man, concentrating on the road, could not see it. But the chairman did, grew silent, and looked more and more uncomfortable as the driver indulged in wilder and wilder plans for retaliation.

We were already out of town, on the road toward Uppsala, when we stopped to meet another car that was waiting to take us back to the hotel. Levine was still smiling, and the chairman asked him if he had anything else to say.

"Well, no, not really. I mean it's not for me to comment—" The chairman virtually had to persuade him to say what he so obviously wanted to.

"It's only that I'd not regard this matter as closed," said Levine, and two minutes later his services were retained for a further indefinite period "on the same terms as before." Then he put the knife into the security adviser. "I listened to your plans, sir, with great interest, but I have to disagree. The worst thing you can do is to fire the man."

The chairman went pale. The security adviser gave a stylish contrast in bright beetroot.

"What I suggest, sir, is to *promote* this most loyal technician of yours."

Levine's idea was a masterly double cross. If the flow of information was now suddenly stopped, and if Levine leaked a few words to the opposition, and if these two moves were accompanied by an unexpected and rather spectacular promotion with a great salary rise, it could have only one meaning: the blackmailed man had been loyal to his employer all the way; he had probably reported everything to the chairman himself, and the material reaching the rivals must have been false and deliberately planted to mislead them. By the time they checked every detail and did all the research themselves, it would cost them just as much in time and cash as if they had never received any intelligence information.

There was a long, long stretch of silence. Then the chairman mumbled something in Norwegian. During a second pause, Levine smiled at me, and now I knew why I was there—to witness the personal triumph of this abominable showman.

"I think you're right," the chairman at last conceded. "But I'll never forgive myself that I'm not punishing but rewarding this—this—cat." (The whole discussion was conducted in English, and probably he could not think of a more damaging word offhand.)

Levine's smile was wiped away. "I wouldn't say that, sir. You will, in fact, punish him rather severely. What I mean is that the opposition will surely understand that this bastard has double-crossed them, and *they* will see to it that he will not enjoy the fruits of his labor. This promotion could be a double-edged weapon—yes, perhaps weapon is the right word."

Before we changed cars, Levine said good-bye and held out his hand to the chairman, who turned away. I wondered whom he despised more, Levine or the traitor?

Standing under a street light, Levine was smiling again. In his own professional eyes, it was a job well done. And he definitely looked quite freshly shaven.

10

Kubik File II

IT WAS A PECULIAR EXPERIENCE to travel without a destination. Without a *known* destination, that is. What made it worse was that it was my choice. If my misgivings about the arrangements grew into an irresistible urge to quit, I was free to terminate the journey at any point. Which, of course, would have made me a bigger coward than I was—particularly on my way to meet Kubik.

The previous night I had had a telephone call: "Mr. Kubik wants to meet you." The man had a strong American accent.

"Does he?" One can ask such stupid questions when confronted with the unexpected. "I mean, when?"

He asked me if I had a valid passport, and also if I was prepared to be away for a couple of days. I said yes to both questions.

"You'll be picked up tomorrow morning at 8:45 sharp." He rang off.

The driver who came to collect me was not exactly the verbose kind. He said he was from a call-a-cab service. With an American accent? Driving a Jaguar?

"Why not?"

"But no radio?"

"Not a radio cab."

End of conversation.

He drove on the M4 toward Heathrow airport. Turning off at the last exit before the airport, we took a short detour, and were back on the motorway once again. Then the turn toward Heathrow. The rotary and then through the tunnel. As we reemerged into daylight, we pulled out of the stream of traffic and stopped, letting all the cars pass. Drove across the road to the gas station and waited for five minutes—without buying juice. Came out at the far side; back into the road leaving Heathrow. Through the tunnel. Another stop at the rotary. The driver was watching the traffic. If any car followed us, he would have noticed. Then again, all the way around, into the tunnel—and to the terminal entrance. The precautions bore the Kubik hallmark, reminding me of New York and Terry-Ann.

"Have a nice trip." The driver gave me an envelope and left me.

It was a ticket to Geneva. Luckily I had only hand luggage and could check in fast—with two minutes to spare.

Throughout the flight, I expected further instructions from everybody who passed my seat. Watched them all avidly. The stewardesses pretended not to notice it; they were used to passengers full of expectations.

Geneva airport. Asked Information if there was a message for me. No. Sat down. Stood up. Walked around. At the gate my London driver appeared. He must have been on the flight with me, although I had not seen him.

"Your car, sir."

I followed him to a Citroën. He drove into town, down to the lake, and up the Quai Wilson, where he dropped me at *Le Président* restaurant.

"You must be hungry. We'll pick you up at three."

He seemed to make a special effort to say that much in one go.

It was an ideal spot to watch me and see if I would make any telephone calls or other contacts. I made sure I did not. At 2:45 I asked for my bill. "It's been settled, sir."

My guide-guard-driver held the door of the car open for me. Did this first polite gesture signal the nearness of Kubik? Drove along the road to Lausanne, but a few miles out of town turned toward France. Were waved on without stopping at border. Three minutes later: Divonne-les-Bains. Holiday resort in an after-lunch slumber. Even the car was snoring as it ground to a halt on the gravel road. We were facing one of the casinos strategically sited on the doorstep of gambling-dry Switzerland.

One should never look at a shrine of gambling in daylight. Without the dreamlike quality of clever floodlights, footlights, spotlights in the crowns of the trees, all that is left is the sumptuous architecture, which emphasizes the European tradition of turning the loss of your money into a solemn and grand occasion.

Inside, however, time stands still. Not quite daytime, not quite night, it is casino time, whatever the clock says. The murmur, the smoke, the croupiers' monotonous announcements, and the direction of the money flow are also constant; only the players vary slightly—in the afternoon, there seems to be a predominance of desperate addicts and hopeful honeymooners. How will Kubik fit into this pattern?

My driver volunteered to "look after" my briefcase and instructed me to amuse myself for a few minutes. It was not all that easy. The atmosphere was clearly anti-James-Bondian with a marked absence of beautiful women and big spenders.

A light tap on my shoulder. "And how are you, *mon cher?*"

Vera Fielding! Just about the last person I would want to meet here and now.

"Small world, *n'est-çe pas?*"

It could not be a coincidence. But what was the reason? The driver was hovering in the background, not near enough to hear the one-sided conversation, not far enough to miss a single move. I felt very uncomfortable.

"Speak up, *mon cher.* Say hello or something and stop looking so guilty. Some people might say it was a minor indiscretion that you sent a word of warning to Kubik about me, but I'm not like that. After all, I was very, very naughty or even nasty when I asked all those questions, wasn't I?"

"Yes, a small world," I mumbled with a total lack of originality but with plenty of conviction. Luckily she was quite capable of carrying on the conversation single-handed.

"And you didn't realize how small it is. But that's forgiven. The indiscretion, I mean. What surprised me was that you broke our agreement. That I didn't expect from you. . . ." She went on and on.

I had only myself to blame for walking into an ambush like this. After years of cautious treading on the thin ice over the deep waters of double cross, I was so keen to meet Kubik that I came along on the strength of a no-nonsense phone call, without checking to see if it really was Kubik who summoned me. It seemed too late to back out. And why should I? If she wanted to retaliate in some way, she would surely choose a better spot than a not too crowded casino.

"What agreement?"

"You promised to leave my husband out of it."

"Vera, please, let's not start that again."

"Why? Don't you believe that I have a husband?"

"It's not that—"

"And don't say you never met him. You talked to him in Zurich at the party. Here"—she reached around my arm, embracing me—"Don't you remember him?"

I spun around. A smallish figure breathing right into my

shoulder blades. A vaguely familiar face, pale fleshy cheeks overwhelming deep-set watery eyes. Angular skull sparsely covered with thinning russety hair. A body seemingly assembled from children's building blocks with short arms hanging loosely from square shoulders. Like a cube. I think I managed not to sound too astonished:

"Pleased to meet you, Mr. Kubik. Or shall we say Blockley?"

"Let's stick to A-square. More befitting," he bellowed, and they both laughed heartily. This speck of microwitticism never ceased to amuse them. "Sorry my wife had to play a little joke on you in Zurich, but I was anxious to find out how much you knew about me and how much you were ready to say."

"No harm done."

"No, Vera came back with a most satisfactory report."

He thanked me for the warning and claimed that he was now ready to "balance the debit side" in his books: "An aye for an aye and a nay for a nay, what?" More belly laughter. "That's my motto. You'll appreciate that, I'm sure." I honestly tried to.

He was still shaking my hand. His freckled white knuckles looked soft and flabby, but his fingers were grinding mine like millstones for ever and ever and ever—which turned out to be yet another of his standard jokes.

The fun of seeing me surprised could not be the reason for this invitation. His gratitude as an inducement could also be discarded. After all, I had warned him about his own, apparently trusted wife.

"Well, *mon cher*, I'll leave you to it. I have an awful lot of losing to do." She walked toward the roulette tables.

Kubik and I were shamelessly studying one another. He looked a sprightly well-preserved sixty-year-old. Later I would learn he was only forty-seven. He wore a plum-blue suit with white shirt, silver tie, and a meticulous white triangle in his breast pocket—a man of elegance left here from the late 1940's when, as he would tell me, his "life-style, ideals, and principles were shaped." Apparently, ever since the moment he could afford it, he always ordered these plum-blue uniforms by the half dozen, and wore them regularly from breakfast to bedtime, changing perhaps twice a day into identical outfits. With a little shine at the elbows, he could have been any old-fashioned bookkeeper—except that the exquisite finish of the suit clearly stated that those shineless sleeves had not been sculpted for skating over somebody else's balance sheets.

He led me toward a small table near the bar at the far end of the floor.

"I never gamble, do you?" he asked, and added without waiting for a reply, "I prefer the dice to be loaded in my favor." He laughed. I felt he could go on amusing himself for hours. "Have a pleasant trip?"

"Yes, thanks to the efficiency of the guide you sent for me."

"Most efficient man, quite right. Quite passable with the gun, too, but he prefers something more quiet as long as it's sharp or pointed."

"I'll send him a pair of knitting needles for his birthday." Which was rewarded by undeservedly roaring laughter from Kubik. Raised eyebrows and shock waves all around did not embarrass him at all.

I ordered a coffee; he demanded a large jug of iced water which he would soon swallow noisily, washing down a variety of vitamin pills to supplement the hydrotherapy he was receiving in Divonne.

"How is the family?" An innocuous question—with the gentle hint that I was no stranger to him.

Instead of answering, I only asked: "And which part of Central Europe do *you* come from? Romania?"

"Right, first time. From Craiova, to be precise. You see, I have no secrets from you." Yet the roof did not cave in on him; tidal waves failed to roll in; and the gods of honesty did not bother to show displeasure.

It was a haphazard, floating, fluttering dialogue. He could not be pinned down on any subject, but sometimes returned to it voluntarily. He talked about several of his failures and triumphs (some of which I have already mentioned elsewhere), but every word was a potential trap for me. He asked many unexpected questions, then switched to another topic, telling me something and watching my reaction. Did I spot his lies? Did I know the cases and people he mentioned? Would I say something about Kam Luang's government contacts? (Then he told me how I had scared this Mr. Fixit of Hong Kong.) What did I think about various people whom, he guessed, I had met?

Then about money. How much there was to be made. A photograph of his yacht. And of his villa in Capri. And the picture of his Tangier house.

"I didn't know that Barbara Hutton had sold her house."

He remained totally unperturbed. "Oh? Perhaps I'm carrying the wrong picture." All right, I had caught him out. So what? Perhaps he wanted to see if I would. "Tangier has changed, yes; everything is changing. I used to enjoy doing economic intelligence work. Now it's less buccaneering, more respectability. Just an ordinary information service. I'm like a market-orientated Reuters. It's only that they sell what they can report, while I find out and report what I can sell. We could have lots of fun together, you and me."

I did not want to set myself up as his judge. I was not there to convey pangs of morality and social conscience. And I knew that it was probably foolish to ignore this last remark and the implied rich rewards. But I could not resist answering him by turning the tables a little. "As an ordinary newsman, why did you hound Mory?"

"Was he a friend of yours?" He was well versed in the art of avoiding answers by asking questions.

"Is that your answer?"

"Did you think highly of him?"

"No." To hell with it. He got me answering his questions instead of the other way around.

"Neither did I."

"Was that a good enough reason for you to see him broke—and possibly dead?"

"I didn't kill him."

"I know. It was suicide. Did you engineer it?"

"His wife thinks so, doesn't she?" It was a tricky question. Did I want to admit that I had met her? I hesitated. He made it easy for me: "I know she does. And I know that you've seen her. You don't have to say it. Where is she now?"

"I don't know."

"And I believe you. I don't know why." There was a pause. His eyes turned gray. Did this little act surpass the best of chameleons? Was he a good enough actor to tune his voice to convincingly warm sincerity? "I want to find and help her."

"Why?"

"She's a civilian casualty of a war that was not her concern."

"It widowed her."

"That's why. I went to see her in San Francisco after the collapse of Mory's Hong Kong copying business. His accident was an odd affair, and the insurers refused to pay up until some strings were pulled. And now, once again I want to help her. I don't want her to think of me as a ruthless enemy. No, I don't even want to find her. It's good enough if you tell her that I'm ready to help."

"Why?"

"I don't like to be hated. Or even disliked. Perhaps in that respect I've become a true American. I fight to win—then I'm ready to lose it all on helping the loser."

"I doubt if she'd appreciate that. Perhaps if. . . ."

"The background?"

"Yes."

He managed to surprise and impress me yet again with his genuine concern about an indifferent, insignificant woman's opinion. Or was there a more sinister motive? Or was I becoming too suspicious? Could anyone be too cautious with industrial spies?

My tape recorder was in the custody of my guide who preferred sharp or pointed objects to guns and who was reading a newspaper a few tables away. I felt sure that there were some tiny peepholes in the pages directed toward me. Kubik had asked me not to make notes: "Why call attention to ourselves?" I wondered if he knew that nature could not possibly have called on me as frequently as it seemed to, and that each time I left him, I scribbled down a few reminders of our talk to support my memory.

Presently he was way down memory lane himself and clearly enjoyed reminiscing.

"I had a spot of trouble with the Germans during the war which took me to Austria, and then a slight conflict with the Russians which landed me and hundreds of others in an eastbound freight train as freight." Mild amusement rather than self-pity colored his voice. "I was weak and starved out, but without scruples on attacking from behind, and so I was able to persuade a guard to let me go. He even gave me his submachine gun as a parting present, which fetched a good price in Trieste."

With that sale he was thrown into postwar Trieste at the deep end, but within a few hours he was swimming as if he had found at last his natural element. He learned to move freely from Zone A (controlled by the Anglo-American forces) to Zone B (administered by Yugoslavia), and after the humble beginnings of running errands for traders in this smugglers' paradise, he soon went up in the world by financing his own gold, currency, and mainly cigarette operations on a modest scale.

"I still looked just a kid, perhaps because of the longish periods of starvation behind me, but this was an advantage. In the harbor, where nobody trusted anyone, I was less suspected than most. Some raids I came through unsearched when my pockets were lined with contraband. Sometimes I held other people's stuff until the raid was over. I took the chance on spec: jail for failure, 10 percent set fee for success.

"Gold coins and gems were the biggest problem. If the police found any of these on anyone, the man was automatically classed as a smuggler and arrested. But I was lucky.

"My special talent was that I could swallow anything fast and without water. At the beginning of a raid, friends would rush to me with gold coins for safekeeping. I think that more napoleons passed through my bowels than through any banks within a thousand-mile radius in those days.

"In the mornings after the raids, I always had the pleasure of shitting in company. People would gather in my room soon after dawn and wait for me to get up. First the books were put in order—who had how many of what in me—then we'd sit around, drinking coffee, waiting for me to give the word.

"Portnoy's father had a problem with relieving himself? I had to relieve half a dozen men at a time. You should have seen them when once I was constipated for three days—while the price of gold was falling, and my clients could not sell!"

Laughter overwhelmed him, and he could not continue his story for several moments. Then he described in detail how the depositors paced up and down like expectant fathers, how they all helped him at long last to remove his pants, how greaseproof paper was laid out as usual in the middle of the room, how they all squatted around him with kind words of encouragement and sympathy, and how they all cheered when results of his labor began to show and the digging for gold and gems could begin.

The charge for this service was 15 percent, and Kubik was very proud that there had never been any argument when the safe was opened.

"Apart from gold, good food began to pass through me regularly, and I learned to enjoy a full stomach," Kubik recalled between two more glasses of water and a colorful meal of vitamin pills. "But one thing you never forget—hunger. Hunger and the half a bar of Hershey chocolate which an American soldier threw at me from a passing lorry on a deserted German road as I was crawling in the dust toward what turned out to be Trieste. Clutching my treasured gun, I was dying and I knew it. That bite of chocolate saved my life. And from then on, I couldn't look at an American soldier without asking myself, Is that him?"

This peculiar constant sensation of indebtedness was, in fact, to shape his entire life.

"Late in 1946, I was in a hurry to make as much as possible because the Italian peace treaty was about to be signed in Paris, and we didn't know how the Trieste Free Territory plan would affect our trade," Kubik said. "Just before Christmas, returning from Cittanuova of Zone B, I walked along the waterfront and went into a café for a nightcap. All the customers were standing in a tight circle, so I knew there must be a fight in the middle. Some friendly elbow work eased me through the circle and gave me a grandstand view.

"The fight was almost at an end. A huge monster of a bleeding sailor was kneeling on another guy's throat, and the one below was about to sound the last rattle. His hands were trying to shift the crushing weight on him, but he had no chance. A knife lay on the floor, near my foot, out of their reach.

"I wasn't terribly impressed. I had seen too many deaths to feel squeamish. Fights and deaths are private matters; you soon learned that in Trieste. Interfere at your peril—even your protégé might kill you for it. Then I noticed something: the guy about to turn his eyes inward was in uniform. American uniform. It was too late to find a patrol somewhere in the docks. I just wanted to run away. You know what kept me there? The crazy thought that the other half of that bar of chocolate might still be in that wretched G.I.'s pocket.

"I shouted for a drink. Everybody looked up. It just wasn't on. To be tough was one thing; to think of a drink while watching death was another. But that one second's consternation gave me a chance to kick the knife. The sailor kneeling sideways couldn't notice it. The G.I. could. Right at the end of his tether he just about managed to plunge the blade into the big back above him. There was only half a groan. By the time we looked back down, the two were lying side by side just about breathing.

"That G.I. was Truman, I mean his nickname was Truman because he looked like the President. He became like a father to me."

"And the sailor?"

"I think he survived. He was alive when they took him away."

With Truman's friendship, a new chapter began in Kubik's life. His trading, smuggling, gold-swallowing continued—the American had access to PX supplies—but he also learned the trade value of a different commodity: information.

Before the war, Truman used to scrape a living from gossip-peddling in Wall Street. He knew many people and gathered up crumbs of information in bars around the stock exchange. He was usually paid for tip-offs, but his best pickings came from deliberately planted information when somebody "posted" false rumors through him.

In Trieste, he worked as a clerk in the zone commander's office and always knew in advance about the work and building contracts to be given to civilians. For the right fee—also allowing for the more and more valuable services of his assistant, contact maker, and negotiator, Kubik—he would not only help a client to the contract but also tell him how much he could charge as a maximum without ruining his chances.

It was, however, Kubik who first thought of a lucrative innovation: he would sell the information to several firms at the same time and collect the first round of rewards; then, as a pattern of informal bidding developed, he would sell one competitor's budgeting to another and collect a second round of fees; finally, as a bonus, Truman would reluctantly accept the praises showered upon him by his superiors for cutting down contract costs and saving substantial sums for Uncle Sam.

Kubik refused to tell me in what year Truman helped him to emigrate to the United States, but by the early 1950's, the partners were in business in New York.

Was that where Mory came in?

"No. He appeared on the scene almost ten years later and in a rather odd way. I only wanted you to understand the special relationship between Truman and me. I saved his life—he taught me everything he knew."

By the end of the 50's, the pair were well established in several parts of the world. Kubik was handling most of the European business which included special assignments, such as wrecking the cigarette advertising campaign, and also the development of clearing houses that led, eventually, to auctions of stolen information. But before the boom came the crash.

"Working on spec, investing our own money, was a new development," Kubik said. "We made serious mistakes, and Truman ran into a spot of trouble in the States. So we switched places, but the financial problems remained. Then he fell ill. He lived in Paris with his daughter who was a classical ballet dancer, and naturally, she wanted him to have the best doctors. I sent them as much as I could, but he also ran up a lot of debts, borrowing mainly from a German friend of his who lived in Istanbul. I met him only once. And I didn't like him. He was a common criminal. No class. But a heart of gold."

Truman died and his daughter disappeared just when Kubik's intelligence operations began to pay off. The square-shaped Romanian lad, by then with a taste for plum-blue suits, took over the business and two responsibilities with it: he resolved to track down and support the Truman girl, and to repay his partner's debts.

"When I had the money, I went to Istanbul," he told me. "I found it safer to travel by boat than overland. And I mean tankers and not luxury liners. I didn't fancy going through airports and customs with a small well-worn plastic bag that contained twenty thousand dollars' worth of Swiss francs in cash—quite a fortune to me in those days.

"The door of the crook's flat was slightly open. No one answered the bell, so I walked straight in. And it wasn't a pretty sight in there, I can tell you that. There was blood everywhere. Then I found where it all had come from. On a sofa lay a naked girl with Truman's crooked friend, also naked, right on top of her. Both were riddled with bullets. A machine-gun job. Just under the shoulder blade, the guy was almost cut in halves. Some of the bullets must have gone right through him into her. She must have expected something different; I mean more of a fluid to go into her. Their faces were still pleased with what they had been doing." Kubik shook with laughter once again.

"Anyway, jokes apart, I wasn't sorry. He was no friend of mine, and I dislike criminals in any case. That's what made me hesitate, but only for thirty seconds. Then I put down the bag with the money and kicked it under the bed. That's what Truman would have wanted me to do. That's what he taught me. Debts must be paid, and I did just that."

To trace Truman's daughter was a more arduous task. Apparently she was drifting around the world without a friend anywhere. She had never met Kubik and did not know what her father's business used to be. For a while she was drinking heavily, and with that her days in classical ballet were over. She worked in cabarets in Paris, then in Cyprus, then in the Middle East, and then in Singapore. . . . I sat up. Kubik's eyes were on me. They were grass-green now. The pause after the word "Singapore" must have been deliberate. His hard gaze tried to pin me to the chair, but his voice remained soft. Too soft, perhaps.

"Yes, it was in Singapore that I ran into Mory for the first time."

"In 1965?" I tried to make it sound casual.

"Come to think of it—yes . . . Is the date significant for any reason?"

It would have been pointless to pretend that it was not. He must have at least an inkling that I had met Mory twice in that same year—probably just before and again soon after the first Kubik-Mory encounter.

"Yes," I said lightly. "I believe it was a significant date in his life."

"Why?"

"Perhaps because when you ran into him you meant to run him over."

"Yes, it was funny." He was not laughing. "How did *you* meet him?" It was now his turn to try to sound casual, but those darkening green eyes told me this question was not put to me at random. His *debt* to me? A vague proposition to join him and his organization? Yes, these might have been additional factors. But I knew it instinctively that this question was the key to my presence in Divonne. I had only made it easy for him by bringing up the subject myself. He had planned the conversation. He had worked out how his stories, selected extracts from his career, would lull me into a mood of sympathy by the time it came to answering this question. Because it was through Vera Fielding's introductions that I met Mory.

He repeated the question. Did my hesitation give him the answer?

"Let me see. . . ."

"I mean we're only comparing notes, aren't we?" He was just a shade too impatient to be convincingly casual. "Perhaps we had several mutual friends. It could form a bond between us. . . ."

"Er . . . I know we met in Beach Road. At a satay stall. The smell of charcoal is again in my nostrils as we talk about it. . . ."

"Yes? Go on."

"I think we met by chance. Yes, there were no introductions if I remember well. . . ."

I had to keep my options open. Perhaps Vera had already told him about it. But then why would he press for an answer?

His voice came from far away, as if through an eiderdown. He spoke about Truman's daughter.

"I found her in Singapore. She was working in a bar

sometimes as a dancer, but mainly as a hostess. That didn't surprise me. She was also working for Mory in the gold-smuggling racket. That surprised me but failed to shock me. What did shock me was that Mory wouldn't let her go. Not even when I offered to buy her out. And she wouldn't leave without his approval or, in fact, permission. She was too frightened. I promised her protection. Wasn't good enough. It had to come from Mory. And he wouldn't budge."

"So you decided to run him out of town. Out of business."

"He gave me no choice. I had to do something for the girl. I even had a heart-to-heart talk with him. Tried to be friendly. And then he said that it was not up to him. There was somebody else . . . I mean above him. . . ."

"Who?"

"I wonder."

"Do you?"

"He wasn't lying. He couldn't yield to pressure. He, too, was afraid. Even when he knew that he was beaten. And because finally he ran for it and disappeared from Singapore without a word, the girl still refused to leave with me. I wanted to arrange what was more or less an abduction. For her sake. And I knew she'd need psychiatric treatment to help her overcome her fears and forget Singapore and Mory who—Oh, yes, my first assignment was a union job!" After an imperceptible pause, his voice suddenly rose above the general noise level of the room. The last half sentence was too unexpected and irrelevant to be meaningless.

I looked up, then turned to follow his eyes—watery blue once again—and saw Vera approaching us. She was riding on air with a combination of light abandon and stiff restraint as if *haute-école*-trained in the Spanish Riding School of Vienna. She must have been either drinking or winning. The latter turned out to be the case.

"Everybody is my guest tonight! I'm starving—How about

you two?" She slowly danced her invisible mount around the table, nodding in rhythm to Kubik's question about her luck. "Every-body is-my guest-to night." She tightened the reins and stopped in front of me. "What were you talking about?"

"Your husband just began to tell me about his first important assignment ever. A union job."

Did I detect relief in those ever-changing eyes? And if yes, who was the real subject of the abruptly ended conversation: Vera or I?

Not by Industry Alone

The lavish dinner at the casino was excellent both as an epicurean experience and as an opportunity to discuss what Kubik described as "the modern applications of intelligence which doesn't live by industry alone anymore."

Both of them seemed extremely interested in noncommercial assignments, and it was, in fact, a political job that had eventually brought them together in a "formal lifelong partnership"—their marriage.

"Love, sex, friendship, and everything else are secondary to such partnerships built on absolute, and I do mean absolute, trust," said Kubik more to Vera than to me. She did not flinch.

I did not relish the prospect of finding myself in the crossfire of the conjugal battlefield when these two nuclear powers of blissful coexistence would bring out the ultimate weapons. So I praised the meal and asked about Kubik's first major assignment.

"Truman had a friend who was involved as a union official in a long-drawn-out strike and wage negotiation," Kubik said flavoring every word of a pleasurable memory. "We were asked to help, and help we did, although in those days, our resources were somewhat limited and so was our experience, too. The union was trying to disguise the fact that their coffer was practically empty and that the strike could not last another week. Truman's friend suspected that the corporation he was up against employed professional agents who must have discovered that the union was scraping the barrel, but he had reason to believe that the bosses were also getting desperate. How desperate? That was the question.

"The decision was to make a last stand at a top-level conference with management. Our friend was to reduce the demand slightly as a sign of goodwill and strength, hoping that it would lead to negotiations on the basis of a vastly improved pay offer. The difference between the parties, if I remember well, was something like three dollars, and the reduction in the demand amounted to ten cents. The trouble was that if we failed, the strikers would have to return meekly and rely on the firm's 'generosity.' A bleak prospect—that much we knew."

The meeting between the two three-man teams was brief and to the point. The reduced demand was flatly rejected and countered with a similarly ludicrous offer.

"I was one of the union team, posing as an observer," Kubik chuckled. "And was I pleased to be there?! It was a dream come true. I didn't give a damn about the outcome of the battle. It was not my war. But I was there! If only people back in Craiova or the traders in Trieste could see me now, playing a silent but key part at a conference with people who controlled millions and millions of dollars.

"Anyway we were in and out in fifteen minutes. We walked to the end of the block, with Truman's friend saying nothing and the other guy repeating, 'If only we knew what they say now, behind our backs.' It was then that I 'discovered' that I had lost my tatty little briefcase. I ran back, apologized humbly to the secretary for causing any inconvenience, but could I please look around, perhaps I left my case in the office. She kindly went into the conference room where the management team were still sitting, and returned with my briefcase, holding it with two fingers in disgust.

"That briefcase contained, of course, the secret tape recording of the conversation in the ten minutes *after* our departure. I had 'accidentally' kicked it under a sideboard during the conference.

"I know today you get much more sophisticated equipment than that, with remote control and acousto-switch for anything from three hundred dollars up depending on the quality of the briefcase, but you now also buy extra suspicion with it. Not in those days. I believe I was the first to use this gadget in a major affair. It was a primitive little homemade job with a cheap recorder, and it was a hell of a job to get it started, but it gave us vital information.

"It told us that the bosses were just as desperate as the union. Within a few days they'd have to give in to anything or close down and pack up for good. On the strength of this recording, our clients could borrow more funds from other unions, and hold out a little longer."

Then Kubik had a long talk with Truman. He was unhappy with the $120 fee they had earned. He also argued that the strike and the breakdown of negotiations was principally due to pride and misunderstanding on both sides. It might be profitable to clear up the confusion.

"The same night I sat sipping brandy in a very grand house outside Detroit. They plied me with cigars although I didn't smoke, and I kept only one for Truman. The vice-president of the corporation appreciated my motives as well as the quality of the recording, and entertained me in style. I also received a five thousand dollar check. And it was real nice to be paid for an act of charity. Because it was just that. Now that both sides knew that the other knew it, too, they could sit down to talk real business. And I'll tell you something. There were no hard feelings on either side. Because I still do quite regular contract work—I mean some of my specialists do it—mainly for unions."

The tape-recorder briefcase became very popular for a while, and was widely used in various sales negotiations where the first few minutes after the departure of the other party brought out the true reactions to, say, a suggested set of prices. Today fewer people would probably fall for it, but "suckers breed fast"—as Vera Fielding remarked with a scornful glance toward Kubik—and the bug peddlers still sell such wares in impressive quantities.

As for intelligence agents in the union versus management war, business is definitely booming. Most of the assignments are parts of long-term contract work for both sides, and that is why operators appear to be particularly reluctant to talk about it. Strictly off the record, however, several of them admitted that "such work would come our way through trusted friends." They usually added that only "defensive assignments" would be acceptable, but the cases they mentioned contradicted this claim.

Executives who use industrial spies maintain that it is sheer self-defense to find the "real problem" behind the alleged causes of industrial unrest, to spot the "troublemaker" in whose excessive demands they seek—and often find—political motivation, and to prevent damaging strikes by timely counteractions.

Union officials (again it is not the organization but the individual who resorts to the use of professional agents) also justify their action in the name of self-defense. They must know the employers' plans if they want to safeguard with foresight their members' jobs; they must know the various pressures on a company to exploit a situation; and they must take into account the financial elbowroom the management has.

Very few of these cases have ever reached the courts, and only a full special investigation could produce detailed evidence, but the indications are clear that a strong subculture of espionage thrives on industrial relations.

In 1956 and 1957 the New York Transit Authority bugged all the meetings of the Motormen's Benevolent Association at the Palm Garden social hall and in the Times Square Hotel. When in December 1957, a decision was made to stage an eight-day strike, an investigator was hiding in a closet watching and identifying the speakers.

The American Teamsters' Union employed bugging and wiretapping artists like Bernie Spindel—while one of the managements they were dealing with had a German remote-control robot camera installed in light fittings above their conference table. (The camera was discovered in the course of routine debugging and can be seen in San Francisco among the successful investigator's trophies.)

Samuel Dash reported in his book, *The Eavesdroppers*, some typical interviews with policemen who did bugging and tapping jobs for industrial disputants in Philadelphia: "Both union and industry want the same thing. They want to know what the other's moves are going to be before they come off. . . ." It was there that pickets were bugged by security men, and police wiretappers reported to union officials the company negotiators' telephone conversations. During a conference, the management team offered to leave and give the union "a chance to talk things over" among themselves in privacy. A bug was hidden in the conference table and the "secret" discussion was monitored. When caught out, the management explained that the idea was "to find out where the real problem lies" so that they could then offer some constructive proposals.

In Italy, the "Fiat scandal" provides a good example. In 1971, one of the numerous former policemen employed by the company to spy on workers and unions was sacked. He claimed that his status as a spy entitled him to white-collar termination pay. The firm insisted on treating him as a blue-collar man, and when he went to court with his complaint, a magistrate ordered the confiscation of Fiat's secret files on two hundred thousand men and the unions involved.

European security men told me that in Germany the elected workers' councils (*Betriebsrat*) are a chief target for management espionage because these, not the unions, negotiate jobs, working conditions, and in smaller industries, sometimes even wages. Only where these councils are represented on board level, too, with participation in economic policy and full access to all relevant facts, does espionage become entirely superfluous.

In Britain, both sides deny most strenuously that industrial relations are espionage-riddled. I could mention a few nonattributable case histories, but perhaps a random selection of recent news items may be more convincing. The Trades Union Congress submitted a memorandum to the government committee on privacy and cited cases of spying on workers: "It may be that it is the regular practice of some companies to plant informers in union meetings whether held on the firm's premises or elsewhere. Some security firms are apparently prepared to provide staff for this very purpose." Equipped with twenty-one unions' answers to a questionnaire, the TUC concluded: "We have information to suggest that this practice is widespread."

On the other hand, the TUC justifiably demands that a

wide range of company information should be made available to unions, which need details about trading and investment plans, work prospects, reorganizations, mergers, pricing, sales, and production costs for "unimpeded wage bargaining." While negotiations about this continued, some unions declared that they would not need professional snoopers. APEX, the clerical workers' union with thousands of well-informed accountants as members, threatened to leak to the press confidential details denied to them, and Clive Jenkins of ASTMS declared with his usual modesty: "We can obtain information [on uncooperative employers] that would send most of the City into a cold sweat." And he was not bluffing. His Association of Scientific, Technical and Managerial Staffs has almost three hundred thousand members who practically control several major finance houses and computer services in key industries.

Empty threats? When in 1972, Henry Ford II became engaged in hand-to-hand fighting with British unions and announced that there was nothing wrong with Ford of Britain, merely something wrong with the country, he could not keep it a secret that his vast multinational organization was slowly transferring work from Britain to Germany. A white-collar workers' union branch at the Merseyside plant produced a comprehensive ten-page document which listed what parts production had been transferred to German suppliers, what the price differences were, and what further plans were being drawn up to the detriment of the British worker. Although many conclusions based on this information could be invalidated, a desperate Ford's spokesman exclaimed: "I don't see why we should be put on the defensive answering our own confidential material."

In order to prevent a similarly embarrassing situation, the Joseph Lucas car-components group tightened office security in Birmingham, and issued special orders that documents must be locked away at night. During the day, if safes were not readily available, staff "going to the lavatory were supposed to take confidential papers with them rather than leave them on their desks." Although shop stewards vehemently denied it, the allegation was that their spies might have searched production papers in unattended offices, and the discovery of company vulnerability due to certain component shortages would help them to decide the most effective pattern of future strikes.

The tactics of such battles were perhaps best demonstrated in the big postal strike of 1971. While it was alleged that some postal executives had precise day-to-day intelligence reports on the union's reserves and its progress in negotiating gifts and loans from other organizations (information that undoubtedly helped to defeat the strike), Tom Jackson, the general secretary of the union, brazenly quoted from a secret telex message that had been sent out by the postal authorities, and which, he said, had come into his possession the night before.

"When you examine more closely many of these skirmishes between unions and management, you often find that money and the fair demand for a bigger share of profits only disguise deeper-lying issues of politics," said Kubik, and swallowed more vitamin pills to supplement his dinner that must have contained a week's adequate supply of calories. Was he still compensating himself for the day when half a bar of manna was dropped to him from the celestial height of a passing lorry?

He claimed that politics was another insatiable customer for the resourceful professional agent. "And I'm not talking about international politics or the menace from the Big Bad Red Bear," he added emphatically. "This is why it's crazy to talk about industrial spies. It's the intelligence-gathering technique that matters, and the methods that never change whatever the subject of an inquiry. Politicians know this, and take advantage of the services available from private organizations to supplement the information provided by the enthusiast, the fanatic, the disloyal, and the dissatisfied—which amounts to the same thing, come to think of it."

Both Vera and Kubik spoke contemptuously about the idealist amateur because, as Vera said, "political sympathies kill company loyalty, but individual aspirations often kill both, and therefore the free-of-charge source should never be trusted."

This is vehemently contradicted by national espionage services, which rate the trustworthiness of ideological bonds much more highly than the services of the intelligence prostitutes because there may always be somebody willing to pay a little extra for the reversal of the information flow. But on the whole, it appears, both kinds are employed indiscriminately when political rivals resort to the full armory of industrial espionage from bribery and blackmail to bugging and theft.

In Britain, the ultra right Monday Club relies on political sympathizers in obtaining confidential policy decisions and plans from the inner circles of the media. The same happens on the left. When Harold Wilson fought one of his biggest personal battles with the BBC—after the Yesterday's Men TV program featured the leader of the opposition in an unfair light—the Labour party published an internal BBC document that had warned producers to "keep faith" with their interviewees. The party's weekly news bulletin raised the question why the confidential ruling had not been applied to that program. Nobody got around to asking how the papers circulated only among BBC staff were leaked to the party.

Election years are always good for political espionage leading to damaging scandals, but 1972 was an exceptionally instructive one.

Kubik mentioned a "colleague"—a partner or his local representative, I believe—who runs a "general information service" in Tokyo and who "earns a fortune on each election." Japanese politicians who want to win a seat in Parliament are expected to buy their supporters' votes. They distribute cash and household gadgets, organize free lunches and outings to the tune of several million dollars' worth of yens. Although reference to these kind gestures as ordinary bribes would be regarded as an uncalled-for insult (the word is *orey*, reward, if you please), the system is illegal, and opponents of the ruling Liberal Democrats like to know and reveal how money from tycoons helps to keep the government in power. Kubik's associate collects and sells such information to propagandists of the four opposition parties, but sometimes he finds it more profitable to accept kindly gifts of no-strings-attached *orey* for not selling his intelligence material. (Judging from the figures Kubik mentioned, in proportion to the almost twenty million dollars spent on the last election, the agent's profit must have been a quarter of a million dollars in 1972.)

Nineteen seventy-two was the year when a former French civil servant obtained and published confidential documents about alleged corruption in high quarters, a potential booby trap for the Gaullists in view of the coming elections in 1973 (eventually won by them with a reduced majority); and also the year when only a couple of months before the German elections, a scandal of leaks, bribes, and spying shook the Bonn government and the opposition alike.

Papers and magazines in the Springer group, very critical of Brandt's *Ostpolitik* and dialogue with the Soviet Union, were not only so well informed that deliberate leaks became obvious, but were also able to publish highly confidential documents that embarrassed the government. The public prosecutor ordered a raid on the offices of *Quick* magazine.

The raid was thinly disguised as a "tax-evasion investigation." (Newspaper payments for information must be described in tax returns, according to the law, as bribes and are as such tax deductible.) The raids discovered, incidentally, some secret documents including contracts with two junior ministers who soon resigned from their posts. They maintained that they had only provided advice on press law, tax questions, and media policy for almost forty-seven thousand dollars a year.

When the government inquiries and pressure on journalists to reveal their sources remained fruitless, and proof of bribing state officials and misusing confidential papers could not be produced, the federal intelligence service was instructed to gather information on publishers and their staff. Eventually this nefarious operation had to be admitted, but, "a dilettantish error by an overzealous employee" was blamed for it.

In Frankfurt, the man who calls himself an "industrial intelligence organizer" and who, in fact, arranged my contact with the former member of the Bundestag and our talk about a German's expulsion from Britain claims that "only the cuticle of the affair had slightly been scratched. There's so much double-dealing going on that even the politically motivated ideological allies distrust one another. So they often insert a professional operator as a go-between who cannot afford to sell out to the opposite sides if he wants to stay in business for a long time. It also means that the pro will make his own exclusive network of sources available to them."

This service is expensive. "My overheads include watching a register of some two hundred important secretaries' birthdays," he said. "The competition is so strong, particularly in Bonn, that the presents cannot be just some candies and bunches of flowers anymore. And there's Christmas and Easter to think of. Some people I know buy tights wholesale.

I find that it pays to be like a good lover, pay a little more in cash and attention, and come up with the personal touch when choosing presents. But then I'm the first to know about lots of things from promotion prospects all the way down to dirty weekends in Brussels under the pretext of business trips to Common Market offices."

He also advocated the use of true professionals, because he argued, "If they're stupid enough to get caught, they will take the rap and keep their mouths shut—at a price."

This principle of the hush-money-operated safety valve failed, however, in the United States—also in the year 1972. After the infamous Watergate operation collapsed, two hundred thousand dollars, the initial price of silence, was immediately made available with promises of eventual presidential clemency thrown in as a bonus by the Nixon reelection campaign committee.

The agents, mostly ex-CIA professionals, who broke into the Democrats' headquarters and were captured *in flagrante delicto* at gunpoint, duly began to plead guilty to the charges brought against them. By that they hoped to prevent lengthy proceedings that would expose their masters to more probing questions and further embarrassment. That was to be the only way to smother the scandal because the affair was obviously too monstrous to be dismissed, along the German lines, as just another haphazard and dilettantish error by an overzealous, solitary minor official.

The scandal, however, refused to die. One man cracked, and then another. After the trial of the Watergate Seven but before they were sentenced, one member of their group broke the silence. The rest is current history: the continuing story of Watergate is set for a record-breaking run to beat any television soap opera. Growing well beyond the bound of a bungled bugging maneuver, the affair is developing into an all-time classic of industrial espionage with one man's politics appearing as another's industry. With eleven separate investigations, including the Senate hearings, in progress, we begin to see the contour of a systematic effort to uncover the weaknesses of the Democrats' presidential campaign and discredit the opposition. It displayed all the unsavory characteristics of a Kubik bonanza complete with burglary, eavesdropping, wiretapping, and photographing private letters and confidential documents held by rubber-gloved hands for the camera. Not only Watergate, but also another two centers of the Democrats were to be bugged. Call girls for pillowtalk and blackmail were to be used. Espionage mercenaries were recruited as election specialists.

The personal aspects of disruptive techniques were not ignored either. Senator Muskie's official campaign stationery was stolen and used for forged letters to make false accusations against other Democrats. A smear file, with handy items like Chappaquiddick, was prepared against Senator Kennedy in case he entered the presidential race. "Details of an intimate nature" were sought about other Democrats' background, sex life, and bank accounts.

A sordid chapter in American politics, no doubt, but private intelligence operators, who supplement their commercial earnings by dabbling in politics, seem to be genuinely amused by the international and particularly by the national reaction of surprise and shock.

"What's the fuss? Why are they so amazed?" the man in Frankfurt asked me. "You can find similar cases, if on a minor scale, in most parts of the world, and espionage is part and parcel of the American political game. Or else, how could McGovern quote from 'top-secret staff reports' and memoranda stamped 'CONFIDENTIAL, Eyes Only,' and so set out to prove that Nixon was planning to turn a national event into a public-relations bonanza for big business? Surely, that revelation also came from intelligence sources, whether these were enthusiastic supporters or paid professionals." °

Unfortunately there is an abundance of examples to support such cynical views. Away back in 1938, a New York private detective was hired in Philadelphia to bug local politicians' discussions in a downtown hotel to help the Republican party in a pending gubernatorial election.

In 1960, burglars tried to find and steal John F. Kennedy's medical records to wield his health problems as political weapons against him and his bid for the Presidency; and allegedly, in 1968, FBI Director J. Edgar Hoover informed Nixon that bugging had been applied against his presidential campaign.

In 1964, during the Goldwater campaign for the Presidency, the Republican Platform Committee prepared an important policy meeting in San Francisco. They rented a conference room in the Mark Hopkins Hotel on top of Nob Hill overlooking the bay, and called in a security specialist to carry out an electronic debugging sweep.

He told me: "They also wanted me to handle all aspects of security. I charged them a pretty steep fee, but that was OK with them. I insisted that I must have full control of the conference arrangements. I wanted to search the room, do the sweep, install and maintain an electronic screen to jam all transmissions around that room, bring in my own boys to guard the doors and check credentials, scrutinize every piece

° The Democratic presidential contender made this speech in September 1972. He did not disclose how the documents had been obtained. He alleged that the President planned to misuse in 1976 the bicentennial celebration of the United States Declaration of Independence; and that McDonalds, the vast hamburger chain which maintains a Hamburger University offering degrees in "hamburgerology," and which is a major contributor to Republican campaign funds, would be a chief beneficiary of this once-in-a-lifetime advertising opportunity.

of furniture, chairs, and tables, and even the coffee and refreshments brought in during the meeting, and give the guards the right to search anybody entering the room at their discretion. And I meant anybody.

"That was the snag. There were governors and senators coming; they said they could not subject them to a search, and to expect any danger from that side was an exaggeration. I argued that I'd rather lose the business than do a bad job, and if I was not given a free hand, I could not guarantee security.

"With that our negotiations broke down. I don't know what exactly happened next, whether they brought in someone else or not, but I do know that ultimately, that meeting was bugged and recorded. Which only proved my point: in jobs like that nothing is an exaggeration."

Timely information about rivals' plans is just as important in politics as in industry.

In 1967, the Nassau County Executive office was held by a Democrat. The head of the citizens' committee supporting the Republican candidate tried to get some plans and campaign literature from a secretary who worked for the Democrats. (His version was that the girl had approached him first, offering information for cash.) Eventually three thousand dollars was to be the fee for answers to a list of questions plus the key to a Democrat's office.

The girl pretended to accept the offer "because I'm a woman and I was curious," but she notified her superiors without delay. She was instructed to continue the deception and try to find out how far the opposition would go. The Democrats' counterintelligence operation also involved the introduction of a student to act as a go-between, allegedly "for the sake of security" but in fact to witness the deal. When the Republican asked to see a copy of the confidential budget prepared by the Democrats, he was given a dummy.

He, in turn, presented it to his boss, the Republican county chairman, who told him: "Whether it's real or unreal, I don't want to see it." The pages were then torn up and thrown into the wastepaper basket—from where the pieces were later recovered "to prevent them from falling into the hands of the cleaning woman."

The negotiations, however, continued, and the secretary taped a telephone conversation. A subsequent press conference heard her ask how the money would be deposited for her.

ANSWER.   "In cash."
SECRETARY. "Oh, OK. Then there won't be any problem?"
ANSWER.   "Oh, no, none at all."
SECRETARY. "Income tax or anything like that?"
ANSWER.   "No, no."

The guilty man had to be disowned, and the Republican candidate commented: "I was shocked at what happened, and I don't condone it. I had absolutely no knowledge of it."

The county chairman, who did not want to see and tore up the "document," was "also shocked," but for the different reason that the opposition "would prepare a fake budget in the hope of making a sale. This is an attempt to entrap myself, our candidate, and the Republican party."

And the compromised official, who resigned his position, also claimed to be shocked: "I feel like a fool. I feel like I was sucked in and trapped."

Kubik gobbled up his second double-portion of dessert and declared that he was the only person in the Nassau affair who was not shocked at all: "I was advising a Democrat throughout—not the party, just a private arrangement with one official without ever asking where my fee came from— and I think we handled it very professionally. And quite frankly, that's all I care about. Internationally I'll support any

American without any hesitation. But at home, I have no politics. Left, right, or center—they're just clients to me."

Most of his political assignments fall into two categories: (1) to find people who can be bribed, who will accept kickbacks (he sees a vast difference between these two kinds of corruption) or will "release" information to unauthorized persons; and (2) to "do some muckraking in campaign funds."

He claimed that this latter line is most profitable in the United States where vast sums are at stake and stunning revelations about buying political appointments and business advantages are the order of the day, especially before presidential elections. He foresaw, however, that such business could soon develop for him in other countries, too.

"Take Britain, for instance. Like in the States, the parties must disclose where donations to their funds come from and what they do with the money. This can be most embarrassing to donors, and that's why some of the biggest companies refuse to support politics. What's that brewery corporation? Watney's? They used to give generously to the Tories, but only until the workers' clubs began to boycott their beer in 1970.° Then they were quick to stop it. On the other hand, the unions support the Labour party with only about a quarter of their income from membership fees and political levies. Don't you think that the Tories would dearly love to know what happens to the other three quarters and how much of that is used to help the party in indirect ways?"

Did he receive any such party assignments in America?

"I have some regular clients."

And in other countries? He refused to give a direct answer, but volunteered some information on another kind of polit-

° The boycott by Labour clubs was, in fact, in 1969, after a large donation to Conservative funds. In 1970, the company gave less than half the previous amount, and nothing in the year after that.

ico-industrial espionage "when ideological and commercial interests happen to coincide." One of his examples concerned the British Leyland Motor Corporation—a case I had heard about from various sources before and after that evening in Divonne.

In 1969, two—possibly three—commercial groups with interests in motor vehicles and spare parts began a battle for expanding markets in the Middle East and Africa. One of these groups was in the copycat business, selling a vast range of "genuine phoney" car and armament spare parts of very dubious quality. Another international group with American, German, and French interests was also deeply concerned about competitors' activities in the target areas.

Kubik told me that he refused to undertake inquiries for them—and I know of another organization that declined the potentially very lucrative assignment—but there were others who went ahead according to the point-blank brief: "find any dirt on competitors." A Japanese and a British investigator traveled widely for at least six months, collecting the information, and their initial budget amounted to several tens of thousand pounds.

For reasons unknown to me, the then newly formed British Leyland (from the merger of BMC and Leyland) became one of the targets. At least one intelligence agent had specific instructions to produce "documentary proof" that, despite denials by everybody concerned, Land Rovers were manufactured and/or assembled in Israel. He was also expected to locate such a plant in Israel, identify shareholders and key personnel, and discover what, if any, dummy companies existed (a) to disguise the delivery of parts or machinery to Israel, and (b) to export Israeli products to certain Arab countries with dummy invoices.

In 1973, the Arab Information Center in London told me: "We don't know what British Leyland's Israeli interests are.

We don't know anything about Land Rovers." At the same time, an Israeli official of the London embassy said: "Land Rovers? You might say that we 'obtained' a large number of such vehicles from Jordan during the 1967 war, but we never manufactured or assembled new ones in Israel."

I do not know what actual secrets the private intelligence sources working on the case discovered—or indeed, what false evidence they fabricated to satisfy the client and justify their considerable expenses. But it is a fact, that at the end of 1969, the Arab Boycott Office examined the position, and from the beginning of 1970, British Leyland was blacklisted in all Arab countries—a move which badly hit their sales, particularly those of Land Rovers.

One explanation offered to me was that Leyland's Triumph cars as well as lorries and buses were admittedly assembled in Israel, and this might have been the cause of the boycott. If so, the timing of the Arab reaction would still remain somewhat spurious. Because the blacklist was started in the early 1950's, and the company's interests in Israel were anything but new in 1969. In fact, their lorry monopoly was *curtailed* in that very year.

Since then, Leyland's Israeli business has gradually been reduced for various reasons. In 1972, it was reported that Leyland began moves preparing an application for removal from the blacklist in order to open up the oil-rich Arab markets once again. In 1973, an Arab Information Office spokesman told me: "Yes, there have been certain moves. . . . No, I wouldn't call them negotiations, perhaps certain discussions, but it's up to Leyland when they come off the boycott list. . . . may take six months or two years, it's up to them. . . ."

It appears that the true or totally unfounded rumors about the Land Rovers have cost the company at least four-years valuable trading in markets for which they now have to fight.

"In my experience," Kubik commented, "the most ludicrous aspect of cases like this is that the victim of such operations is the last to know about it and, what's worse, to take it seriously. I'm sure that if somebody had warned them in 1969, they would have shrugged it off. And the more impressive the names on the opposition list are, the less they will believe what's going on."

We had reached the p.s. of an unabridged French menu, and Vera left us for a couple of minutes to talk to their ubiquitous bodyguard who ate alone at another table an arm's length away. The dexterity of his wielding that pair of cutlery was not a reassuring sight. Kubik immediately lowered his voice and stared at me hard. "When you're dealing with well-known politicians and the greatest potentates of international business, you cannot afford to be associated with dubious characters such as—er—how shall I say—sex traders?"

Vera returned, and we had a brief argument about my airfare. I insisted on repaying it, and Kubik would not hear of it. Finally Vera took the money, offering to settle the dispute at the roulette table. "Go easy on your cognac, *mon cher*; you might have to bail me out."

Kubik followed her with his eyes, which were watery blue once again. The penetrating stare was gone. His face began to go through a most astonishing visible process of aging, shriveling by the second like a hot-air balloon under which the fire had gone out. Yet another his spectacular performances? If so, his voice now soft and guttural was a perfect match for it.

"I'm tired, you know," he announced quite needlessly. I half rose to leave, but he held me back. "N-no, it's not that. It's not a good night's sleep that I need. . . ." His empty gaze climbed down my shoulder, under the table, and came to rest on the left toe of his shoe.

He lifted his fistful of brandy as if it weighed a ton, rolled it around the glass, and put it down again without drinking. "And I'm slipping, you know. Beginning to find time for aimless chats like this."

I tried to look impassive.

"All right, all right, I wanted to ask a few questions, and some of them you answered, but there were times when it wouldn't have been all that important. And if it was, I would have sent a couple of persuasive men to visit you and get the answers, all the answers, one way or another. Not anymore . . . well, not automatically—"

We were interrupted by a waiter who delivered two small bundles of money, one for each of us. A neat solution of our air-fare argument. Vera made the casino pay for the ticket.

"A resourceful woman," I said.

"And very ugly, too," he laughed. "Don't worry, she knows it. But that has nothing to do with our partnership. Luckily she's not interested in sex. Not in her own, I mean. She's fascinated only by other people's sex life. Why, she's even offered to supply me with girl friends. And I might take her up on that. That's what I mean when I say that I'm slipping. Finding time for idle chats in my club—yes, I'm a member of one of the most famous clubs in London where I was approached with the Leyland job by a true blue-bloody aristocrat—blue-bloody, that's how I describe him, isn't that good?—and finding pleasure in traveling without an assignment, just for fun, and all of a sudden, finding out that I have an eye for beauty and all the things I've always thought of as signs of weakness and a waste of precious time that could be used for making money."

"Perhaps you feel you've arrived."

"Is that what you call it? Arrived? That I don't want to go back to Craiova anymore just to show them how much money I've made? That I'm bored with flying alone in my private—well, perhaps I'd better not say what, but it's a jet, all to myself, yet I book in on ordinary flights, sometimes not even first class, just to chat up whoever sits next to me? That all of a sudden I find making money greater fun than having it? Is that what it means to have arrived?"

"Perhaps in your case, yes."

He downed all his brandy in one noisy gulp, and refilled our glasses in a hurry as though horrified by the vacuum in a vessel where something consumable could be stockpiled.

"And does it mean nostalgia? And the joy of reminiscences about Trieste when a ride in a military police jeep was the utmost in luxury but one could count on friends like Truman? Did Vera introduce you to Mory?"

It was my turn to get busy with the brandy. "Do you honestly expect me to answer that?"

"Why not?"

"Do you think I'd tell her or anybody else for that matter whether you did or did not give me an introduction to, say, Terry-Ann?"

For a flash his eyes turned green again with a speck of yellow in the center, and his back was hunched as his chin jutted forward aggressively. For a fraction of a second "Danger! Watch out! Danger!" was scrawled all over his white-tight cheekbones and knuckles. Then he relaxed. "OK, I'll buy that." He smiled. "About the only answer I will buy—Want to know why? Because Truman would have probably said the same. And I respect that."

A sentimental outburst was what I least expected from him, but there was more to come. He knew I was working on a book and asked me not to write about this conversation, not until he gave me the go-ahead—if ever. I promised.

·He spoke about the loneliness of his trade, reassuring me several times that he was not giving me just a sob story.

"You don't get into my business by answering an ad and

certainly not on the advice of a career-guidance counselor. You drift into it on the waves of opportunity, and learn the technique of survival from your own experience as you go. And if you survive long enough, the first thing you learn is to change your name to Mr. Lone Wolf. Which is all very romantic. Kind of buccaneering. At first. And you learn that a secret remains a secret if it's known only to one—Mr. Number One—alone. Which again is very romantic. To be in the know. And cash in on it. And laugh at all the ignorant fools. But then it becomes too much. I mean what you know. You feel like bursting at the seams. To tell someone. A laugh is a laugh only if you share it. I mean a joke is always for two, what? I'm sure you'll appreciate that."

I managed to do that, nodding diligently. "Is that how your partnership with Vera came about?"

"Right, first time. She has a good sense of humor, you know, and it was great to share things with her. And she's very resourceful, as you said, and ambitious . . . a little too ambitious. . . ."

"You mean she likes to be top dog. The Top Dog."

He ignored that remark. "The trouble with her is that she can't let anything that's hers go. I mean I knew her old sex business—nothing wrong with that—but once we reached the stage of respectability, dealing with really top people and supranational organizations, you just have to drop certain sides of the business. I mean expert safemen don't pick pockets. And she promised to stop. . . ."

There was a seemingly absentminded pause, enough for me to blurt out some information, but he never asked for it.

"Then there was something else. Mory. Truman's daughter had disappeared; I couldn't do anything about it, and I had finished with Mory. But Vera hadn't. She kept turning up fresh information about him. That he double-crossed one of our friends in Hong Kong. That he might still know where the girl was. That Truman would turn in his grave if he knew that I had only half dealt with the bastard. That did it, I suppose. Kam Luang fixed him soon enough. But I never wanted him to die. That was his own doing. I wanted him to live with his misery. Anyway that was that as far as I was concerned."

After another large brandy and a little more, he began digressing more and more into his personal philosophy, but the gist of it was that only a few weeks before our meeting, he had received a telegram urging him to go to Beirut. Truman's daughter was there. She had jumped out of a sixth-floor window, reached the hospital alive, asked a doctor to contact Kubik—and died by the time he arrived there.

"I made some inquiries. She used to be in a rather dirty racket. She was kept under very strict control—to put it mildly. Even after Mory's death. By an organization headed by a woman . . ."

"Vera?"

"What makes you ask that?"

"Your own story."

"Oh. Well, I don't know the answer. Do you?"

"No."

"Pity. Because I find it odd that Vera was so much after him. So relentlessly. Until his death. As if she wanted to remove the only clue I could stumble on one day, the link between herself and the girl. . . . Oh, well, I was hoping that you'd join me in asking her a few questions. Tonight. . . ."

After a long minute's tight-lipped silence, he finished his drink and stood up. "Let's see how she's doing."

Our shift was coming to an end. We had talked for more than eight hours. Without a dinner break.

The croupiers, waiters, and players had all been replaced by fresh ones. Only Vera was her same old self, galloping furiously with inexhaustible energy from table to table, picking up winnings, placing her stakes, tipping generously, sputtering scalding remarks about everybody in sight without anybody missing her attention.

"Did you say horrible things about me?" she asked without turning toward us.

"Charming!" Kubik thundered jocularly. "You must have had our table bugged!"

"No, *mon cher*, it's just that you had that silly yellow flicker in those beautiful majolica-blue eyes. Besides"—she turned to me with a sickly sweet smile—"he's getting into the habit of spreading nasty tales about me. I only hope you didn't believe everything he said."

"That wasn't very subtle, darling," retorted Kubik in his softest voice. "These days, when diplomats are turning into spies, intelligence operators ought to learn a little more diplomacy."

The big guns were beginning to blaze again, and that made me look forward to a cozy trip with the taciturn knifeman back to Geneva.

Four months passed before the familiar, though still not endearing, American voice was on to me on the telephone once again.

"Kubik wants you to know that now you're free to do anything you like with that chat you had in Divonne."

"Did he say why?"

"Nope."

"I can write about it."

"That's what he said."

"Where is he now?"

"He didn't say. But there's another message."

"Yes?"

"His wife won't be around for a while."

"That's the message?"

"Yeah. She's gone cruising. Around the world and down to places like the Great Barrier Reef in Australia. That's all, I guess."

He rang off. And left me wondering from which side she would be watching the glass bottoms of the boats that float over those filigree coral formations.

11

The Game Nations Play

HYBRID BAD GODESBERG IS AN OVERFLOW of Bonn. The glorified beer crates of ministries and other modern government buildings seemed to have drifted like jetsam against the current to be deposited on the bank of the Rhine and form this satellite, industrious enough to look like a ghost town during office hours, affluent enough to give the impression that it had more cars than drivers on some of its fine thoroughfares in rush hours, and small enough to retain olden comforts for its bureaucrats who could ignore staff canteens and the like by snatching easily a midday meal—and a twenty-minute nap, I suspect—in their homes without ever exceeding the meticulously observed lunch hour.

The latter aspect of Godesberg life I would have never discovered had my appointment not been at 11:30 A.M. In connection with some other research, I had to see a couple of civil servants in one of the more remote outposts of the German federal health ministerium. The outpost nature of the building was signified not only by its location but also by the emphatic lack of lush green plants in the lobby and the chummy manners of the porter.

At about 12:25, both my hosts began to grow increasingly

fidgety, and I took the hint. I proposed a beer and sandwich, but was kindly advised that Bad Godesberg could offer the visitor a decent selection of not too expensive restaurants where they would gladly have a meal with me if only their wives had been forewarned.

I had parked the car on the forecourt of a building next door—surprise, surprise, yet another government outpost—and as I put my briefcase in the trunk, I was approached by two youngish milk-reared civilians whose sensible shoes and somber faces conjured up visions of undercover traffic wardens. All right, I had committed a minor parking offense. I was ready for them with my me-foreigner no-understand line of justifiable self-defense.

The senior in bulk and presumably rank introduced himself as Herr Gebhardt and addressed me politely by name. His creaking accent sounded like an Erich von Stroheim imitation but, as in the Hollywood movies, his English and his manners were conspicuously impeccable.

He flashed a card and mentioned a four-inch word of *Bundes* something or other. I suggested that this was going a little too far, but he smiled away my misgivings with a reference to Landau and other "mutual acquaintances in the know, so to speak." With apologies for the odd arrangements —it just so happened that they had heard that I would be here at that time—he suggested that we both might benefit from a brief discussion to be held in the privacy of a tiny office he had borrowed, conveniently but purely at random, in the health ministry building for this most fortuitous encounter.

"It's so much more private than a restaurant or even one's own office," he said.

"Particularly if one is not very keen on advertising where one's office is," I added, and he acknowledged it with a straight extended nod.

His backer-up, who never bothered to give me a name—or any of his thoughts, for that matter—marched into the building ahead of us, went to the porter's glass cage, and bodily ensured that the two of us could walk in quietly behind him. We crossed the lobby, rounded a bannister, and took the stairs to the basement, and the endless door-lined corridor where the too slippery tiles would have certainly justified the cancelation of an ice-dancing championship. Which was most embarrassing to me. Not because I was there to prove how good I was at skating, but because it is a distinct disadvantage to rely on two rubber-soled strangers' arms for ordinary stumble-free walking.

The office was small, just like the one I had left a few minutes earlier, and Gebhardt's light conversation easily filled it. Chatting about the value of economic intelligence was his opening gambit, and it was no good. Clearly, small talk was not his forte. But then he produced a grainy photograph. Vera Fielding's.

"What's this? A murder inquiry or something?"

It was a stupid error, and I knew it. Too late to take it back.

"What would make you ask that?"

"B-film experience. That's how they do it. Anyway the face looks familiar. What's the question?"

"Only familiar?"

"It's a very bad picture. Obviously a blowup from something quite inadequate for this much enlargement."

"Would it help to see the original?"

"Of course. Especially if you have a magnifying glass."

"Fortunately, I can accommodate you with both. Here—"

It was a large cocktail-party crowd, and it took me some time to spot Vera among all the figures in the distant background. The faces in the foreground were much more fascinating in any case. I noted at least two five-star generals of industry, one distinctly and a few vaguely familiar politicians, and a couple of waiters who, I believe, used to belong to De Gaulle's personal corps of bodyguards.

"Recognize her?"

"Yes, Vera Fielding."

"Is that her real name?"

"You tell me. To make the benefit mutual."

"Let's put it this way. Do you think that Fielding is her real name?"

"It's the only one I know."

"You think she's dead?"

"No, not really."

"You mentioned a murder inquiry."

"I was referring to the present situation. Our meeting by chance. The lucky coincidence that you happen to carry a photograph and other paraphernalia. The way you sprang it on me."

"I'm sorry. You must accept my apologies."

That did it. I remembered the advice an old lag gave me. Beware of the polite policeman. Were these policemen? Or from counterintelligence? At a later stage, Gebhardt volunteered some vague answers. He talked about economic information services and "a natural interest in people who are interested in us." I found it judicious not to press him too hard with my excessive interest in his official position. In return he spoke of the growing German concern about "foreign competitors who are desperate enough to try almost anything in order to break into the strong German market and also to undercut German exporters whose position is already weakened by the strength of the Deutsch-Mark."

"Our industry needs and deserves some government assistance in their defense from, shall we say, foreign aggression," he said, but admitted with a trace of despair "that certain politicians are still reluctant to subscribe to this view, and some sections of the diplomatic service still regard it as something way below their dignity to provide economic information that is useful only to individual firms. They don't see, what you and I know, how formidable the opposition can be."

"Such as Vera Fielding?"

"If you like."

He mentioned two examples. Both were international bidders, one of them on an Italian multimillion project. He had "reason to believe that information obtained by this lady" helped to defeat the German bids.

I had to admire Kubik. These were typical high-level operations which he thrived on. He would plan them shrewdly with foresight, moving his puppets with great precision while retaining his own obscurity and, if necessary, focusing the gebhardts' attention on vera-fieldings.

"Do you know who she works for?"

"Difficult to say." I wondered if he knew.

"Not more difficult than to catch her."

"Catch her? For what? I don't think she can be classified as a criminal."

"You're telling me!" His voice was hoarse with sheer exasperation. "If only there was a law for it!"

"But there isn't."

"No." And after a pause, an old ruse—or was it a rare moment of truth? "Look, we, I mean our department, we're sort of novices at this game. It might help us if you told me a little more about her. If you don't mind telling me, that is."

Was he suspecting me of involvement beyond a reporter's interest?

"Ask anything you like. I have no secrets from you."

Which was true. Well, more or less. After all, most of what I knew had been given to me freely and intended for publication—by one party or another.

His questions clearly indicated increasing German uneasiness about the signs of more and more serious threats of foreign espionage onslaught. He recognized that in the trade wars—ranging from seemingly trivial little skirmishes to full-scale international confrontation—the combatants fought for their economic survival, and that the cumulative effect of a series of isolated industrial defeats could have disastrous consequences on a national level.

Although on that day in Bad Godesberg, I had nothing but Gebhardt & Co. for lunch—and I had a bellyful of it within the precise limits of the obligatory midday break—the effect was quite nourishing, because in return for my cooperation, he dished out two lessons to me: (1) that the Germans—probably together with other Europeans and the Americans—seem to scoff at the foreign intelligence menace as long as it comes "only from the Communists and the Japanese because one sort of expects it from them"; and (2) that the German government is about to join the students of Japanese international sales techniques, which are spearheaded, invariably, by a costly, time-consuming, almost ceremonial espionage operation.

Espionage? The mere mention of the word was twitchingly resented by the Japanese official who wished to remain anonymous when, following Gebhardt's advice, I met him in one of the several restaurants that cater to the fast-growing, already two thousand strong, Japanese colony in Düsseldorf.

"Unfortunately, we're misunderstood by the world," he informed me. "People still talk about the legendary Japanese businessman who visited a Swedish safety-match factory and dropped his hat into some chemical container only to get the mixture analyzed when he returned home. But why should he do that? Couldn't he get the match heads analyzed?

"Anyway today it's more likely that a British bowler hat would be dropped into Japanese chemicals."

He had spent four years in America and, by now, more than two years in Germany. He claimed that "Japanese officials came to acquaint themselves with Western customers, learn languages and perhaps golf, which teaches us to play the course, not the competition. But we're newcomers in the field; we want to learn all we can about the course and find out how good we need be to take on the best players. What's wrong with studying Lee Trevino's results and watching his technique?"

Yellow Peril versus Cookie Pushers

The results of "studying and watching" are well known. Japan is approaching the annual trade surplus of three billion pounds a year, and the yen is becoming too strong even for its own good.

This is not the place to analyze the Japanese sales techniques verging on dumping, the protective barriers around their home market, price cutting, inducement to retailers, the flood of television sets, transistor radios, transistorized anythings, steel, cars, and ball-bearings, the service, the efficiency, the ingenuity, the hard work into the night, and the business communications network that is third in the world only to those of the Pentagon and the leading international airlines. But it is a fact that the 30, 40, or even 56° percent annual growth of Japanese exports to current target countries is not unique; that hidden or half-disguised government subsidies to exports are something Japanese industrialists can count on; that more than half the world's market for shipbuilding has already been captured by Japan

° To Britain, in 1972.

(a bulk carrier that costs ten million dollars in Japan can be produced for fifteen million in Britain and seventeen million in Germany); and that Japanese car sales in Holland increased almost tenfold in three years, not only because each vehicle is a cache of free gadgetry, but also because a Dutchman gets twice the average trade-in price for his old jalopy if he wants to buy Japanese instead of an Italian, French, or German model.

The Germans have come to call it the "yellow peril." They should know. Only ten years ago in the United States, the world's richest market, they used to supply a third of all foreign electrical goods. Now they control about 5 percent, and Japan has more than half the market.

The vanguard of such offensives is a squad of men from JETRO (the Japanese External Trade Organization), which working closely with MITI (the Ministry of International Trade and Industry), sizes up the markets all over the world and spots the gaps for phenomenal Japanese sales penetration.

Many of their successes are due to dogged attention to detail. They noticed, for instance, that British cutlery manufacturers had to pay crippling wage increases in the late 1950's and early 1960's. Cutlery prices were bound to reflect this, and ridiculously cheap Japanese knives—and forks and spoons—were immediately held to the throat of Sheffield. By 1966, the value of imports was approaching the two million pound mark.

In the meantime, the Japanese also had a cutlery bonanza in America, to the tune of some fifty million dollars a year. In 1971, American protectionism caught up with the sharp sales. Imports were to be restricted to eleven million dozen—twenty million dollars worth of surplus eating irons had to find new mouths to feed. Britain was already protected from a further vast assault by a trade agreement, so a JETRO squad stepped in and spotted the new suitable gap in Germany. Now it was Solingen, the famous German counterpart of Sheffield, that faced the threat of annihilation. And by the beginning of 1973, several German manufacturers—like makers of other traditional German goods before them—came to terms with the enemy; they imported semifinished Japanese cutlery and stamped their own trademarks on them, to keep at least the old German names going.

Another classic, perfectly legitimate operation demonstrated sheer ingenuity. Who but a man from JETRO would have recognized that although America never suffered from chronic shortage in barber chairs, there might be room for some hairy competition from copycats.

This most unlikely, cozy little business relied on the hundred thousand American barber shops that bought about ten thousand new chairs a year and forked out ten million dollars for the benefit of a few specialist firms like Paidar of Chicago. It is claimed that Mr. Yoshikawa, founder of an old Osaka factory, thought about breaking into this American market in the course of one of his daily prayers. Some Americans are convinced, however, that it was a JETRO official who helped him see the light by slipping a memo into his prayer book. Further assistance was given to him by some sample purchases, which enabled him to copy, religiously, the most popular American model. His most competitively priced chairs enjoy the full backing of an efficient on-the-spot service because the necessary spare parts of the American and Japanese products happen to be completely interchangeable.

Japanese-style intelligence, however, can be somewhat more adventurous than the short back and sides, and less upright than the crew-cut. On such occasions, JETRO officials recede from the limelight, leaving the assignments for the more elaborate coiffures—with the wig, false moustache, cloak and dagger thrown in for good measure—to razor-sharp practitioners of intelligence.

The least objectionable of these techniques is the goodwill visit to factories. Over a period of, say, twelve months, two or three groups are shown around the target plant. It is all arranged by reputable trade delegates—and cunningly planned by spies. The visitors flatter their hosts with open admiration and innocent questions. The innocent answers add up to not so innocent conclusions.

When an African country invited bids for a large quantity of a precision engineering product of military importance, delivery dates and quality rather than price were likely to be the decisive factors of the successful bid. Two group visits were arranged to the main plant of the American company with the best chance to win the contract. None of the visitors in the groups had any overt connection with the Japanese firm intending to bid. After the damage had already been inflicted, American security men traced the pattern of the intelligence jigsaw.

The first group of visitors duly marveled at the American machinery used for testing the quality of the final product. They inquired about the hourly volume of output of each unit. To note the number of units did not require any questions. They asked, however, about the number of shifts worked in that section.

The second group showed particular interest in storage facilities. They listened sympathetically to the complaints of a junior executive about the crippling cost of storing finished products, and to his boasts about a system of production for prompt deliveries rather than stock.

An examination of the American samples—purchased via a merchant acting as middleman—showed that in quality, the Japanese had little if any extra to offer. But the answers received by the visitors revealed the American weakness:

production could not be stepped up significantly without plant expansion—and there were hardly any reserve stocks for an "emergency" like winning the contract. The Japanese bid, at competitive quality and prices, offered therefore guaranteed early deliveries.

The Scottish shipbuilder who "grumbled that he wasn't simply competing against rival Japanese shipyards but against *Japan Incorporated*" ° meant the combined effort of Japanese government and industry. He might as well be the spokesman for the French, Italian, and British bidders who lost a seventy million pound Argentinian railway modernization contract to the Marubeni-Irida bid, which was backed by an all-out Japanese drive for business in Latin America, featuring a national intelligence effort, intense pressure, and top-level trade missions to Argentina, Chile, and Brazil. And he might have spoken for the pharmaceutical companies everywhere that will soon feel the effects of the growing presence of the Japanese Drug Information Marketing Intelligence Corporation.

At the low end of the scale come the assignments that are unacceptable even to several experienced German agents who are no strangers to business intelligence.

"I had two offers from Japanese officials," one of them told me in Munich. "The first job was worth something in the region of twenty thousand dollars, the second considerably more. In Düsseldorf, you could pick up at least one a month at up to fifty thousand dollars each. The trouble with them is that once you get into that racket, you're hooked for life. Once people think that you work for the Japs you don't get other work."

This retired German army intelligence officer agreed with several others that "such assignments have full government

° *The Observer*, June 18, 1972.

approval and backing," even if they come from a private company or from some "marketing men or business consultants who often act as 'cutouts' safeguarding the anonymity of a government official. The proof of this is that the Japanese must not import goods or services without a license from the government. An assignment like this is, in fact, importing a service that must be paid for abroad in foreign currency— with the bank's permission. Whenever I was offered a job, I was told that the fee would be paid from Tokyo to my bank account in any country."

He knew, of course, that official support to industrial intelligence efforts and shady deals abroad was not merely a Japanese speciality. Allegedly the Israeli Vered Water Research and Development Corporation paid almost two and a half million pounds in bribes to various African leaders and officials to win contracts. Right-wing opposition parties revealed in an unsuccessful no-confidence motion that in 1966 an African was bribed with a hundred thousand pounds—in vain, because the man was assassinated before the deal could go through—and that the treasury's foreign-currency department had authorized the payment as "brokerage money."

In North Africa, a French engineering company won a major battle over other competitors by leaning heavily on a diplomatic crutch. A relatively junior man of assistant attaché rank had so singularly intimate personal contacts that he not only discovered the competitors' terms, but also engineered a specially extended closing date for the French bid, which could thus be adjusted like a bet today on yesterday's Grand Prix.

In Vienna, during the scandalously conducted international design competition for the hundred million pound United Nations City, several intelligence outfits cashed in handsomely on obtaining details of supposedly secret proposals. How this might have influenced the outcome of the competition—an affair that shook the government—could be a tale in itself to tell one day. But it is a fact that diplomatic circles were buzzing with intelligence activities throughout to help various interested parties. When, for instance, Austrian officials refused to give the British designer an opportunity to examine and comment on a secret hostile report knocking his entry, then the clear favorite, it was a British diplomat who came to his assistance by obtaining a copy "from private sources."

With millions of jobs and a nation's prosperity at stake, the increasing governmental involvement marks the beginning of the "cool war," as opposed to the cold war, to use the former Bundestag member's expression I mentioned earlier. In this World War III, the so-called Western allies fight one another, although they try to maintain a cool common front against Russian or Czech "trade delegations."

While in March 1973, the Institute for the Study of Conflict alerted Western businessmen to Russian economic intelligence and claimed that almost three quarters of the thousands of Russian diplomats and trade officials were spying mainly on science and technology,° no such open warnings have been issued, as yet, against non-Communist nations' industrial spies.

A totally embittered American corporation security agent exclaimed when we met in Washington only three years ago: "At least one in every ten American companies is seriously hit by industrial espionage, and we may be losing anything from half a billion dollars upward annually only because we're left exposed to every Tom, Dickovsky, and Mata Hari who can stick a CD plate on his bugging device. We, on the other hand, continue to staff—and I mean stuff—our em-

° "The Peacetime Strategy of the Soviet Union."

bassies with snobs who buy the jobs and professional cookie pushers."

All this has already begun to change. Diet breaking by plying drinks, tasty tidbits, and cute little canapés at cocktail parties may still remain a vital diplomatic duty, but the refreshment pushers now receive their guests with open ears, as well as open arms, to pick up gossip and fragments of information with the devotion of the Spanish ambassador at the court of Queen Elizabeth I.

The rewards of such diplomatic endeavors could be invaluable, but only if early warnings of business opportunities and tip-offs from "usually reliable sources" reached all the big and small interested companies in their countries without delay. That is why several governments issue economic news sheets or, in a more organized fashion, Japan publishes an *Industrial Project News*, India and France send regular information bulletins to industry and export organizations, and the United States operates a computerized service to answer sporadic inquiries from American firms.

Britain was the first to set up—and is still the only one with—a vast export intelligence service for industry and commerce.

The incoming flood of news was first published twice a week and then, since 1962, daily. The value of these bulletins can be measured not only by the thousands of subscribers' growing interest, but also by the length to which foreign competitors were willing to go to obtain copies.

Both the desired and unwanted popularity were understandable. The bulletins were full of export leads, contacts, chances for contracts, market reports, market "pointers" often from confidential private sources cultivated by cookie pushers in disguise. There were also periodic market analyses that evaluated the entire political and financial climate of a country from a business point of view. These would pinpoint export opportunities in, say, an electioneering speech that demanded "better coastal protection for the nation"—meaning potential future demand for ships, weapons, port installations, electronic gear, even road building.

Initially, it was easy for anybody to benefit from the supposedly exclusive British information service. When public libraries received copies every day, it was noted that many foreigners had become avid readers overnight. With the introduction of restrictions, foreign embassies were known to have latched on to the service, and a number of countries as well as larger companies set up dummy offices in London to serve purely as listening posts.

By 1970, the service had grown into a hardly manageable mammoth. It had already published 176,000 calls for bidding, 53,000 export opportunities, and thousands of other reports from all over the world. The 200 British commercial posts abroad were filing more than 40,000 items a year. Diplomats were specially trained to provide such economic intelligence via cable or the use of the confidential diplomatic pouch. The operation had to be switched over to a more selective computerized card service geared to the interests of individual firms, so that only the largest general merchant houses would require blanket coverage.

The number of subscribers is now approaching the six thousand mark. Under six thousand headings of specific commodities, about sixty thousand items of information are available to them each year.

In addition to the regular services, special inquiries are also carried out by obliging diplomats, who evaluate and generally indicate their sources but may withhold the names or positions of their informers. When a British firm is approached by, say, a most imposing Global, International and Worldwide Trading Corporation of Saudi Arabia—writing grandiloquently on handmade paper with embossed print—a diplomat may pay a casual visit to Global's head office, which may turn out to be a tarpaulin shack housing a goat and its proud owner—not exactly an inducement to extending largish credit facilities.

In view of obvious foreign interest in the service, security was tightened yet again, but complete security was never even envisaged.

Each new subscriber's application is scrutinized. Strange company names receive special attention. The list of directors is reviewed, and foreign names are noted. All this is, of course, more a game of let's pretend than serious security, and it cuts out, at its best, only the most naïve foreign agent who would apply for information under the inconspicuous name of Mr. Kosygin from the Kazakhstan-Great Britain (KGB) Ltd.

A more professional grade of vetting applicants concerns their turnover. It is unlikely that a brand new one-boss-with-part-time-secretary firm, with $235 as capital, should want to register as "general merchants," pay crippling subscription fees, and be genuinely interested in all areas from Austria to the Comoro Archipelago and in all commodities from jade statuettes to paper-cup dispensers—unless there is an ulterior motive.

Although batches of computer printouts are always sent to selected individuals or to a particular room number, the cards are seen by several people in most offices, and it is known that information has been privately peddled abroad to competitors. This may be done by the opportunist or the bribed official or the professional plant—criminals whose motives are comprehensible to counterintelligence agents.

What does baffle security men and will send them scurrying to migraine clinics is a comparatively new phenomenon—a serious loophole in Britain's Export Intelligence Service—called "corporate loyalty" that overrides patriotism among the staff of huge supranational organizations. When I mentioned the British service to a "multinational executive" in Holland, he pulled out a batch of cards from a drawer and asked without any trace of embarrassment: "Is that what you're talking about?"

Executives of these companies have the power to negotiate with prime ministers as equals and, as Professor Wedderburn of the London School of Economics told the American Bar Association in 1971, their weight is reducing national governments to the status of "parish councils."

"British reports? We use them mainly to cross-check our own information received through other channels," said the man in Holland, and indicated that he regarded his own sources superior to the entire British network of embassies and trade missions. "Yes, we did hear that the States and Sweden have closely studied the British system and considered setting up something similar. I hope they'll follow the lead. Every bit helps us, you know."

Within these organizations, industrial espionage becomes totally superfluous. They simply transfer information. American labor unions openly blame the multinationals for a large chunk of the country's trade deficits as well as for exporting jobs, know-how, and technology to their foreign plants, but there is a ready-made answer for them: firms like ITT, IBM, or Dow Chemical collect almost half their profits from those foreign outposts, and that ensures their freedom from national control on both sides of the Atlantic.

Beyond the bounds of a supranational company there is, however, tremendous scope and demand for economic intelligence and industrial espionage—and the carrot dangled before the professional agent is cast of pure 24-carat gold with the diamond-studded stalk thrown in free for his labors.

The menace is fully appreciated by all these giants, and their defenses are fortified accordingly—as can be demonstrated by the not-too-widely advertised roles of just two men.

John A. McCone is a director of ITT, the eleventh biggest multinational in the world with interests in seventy countries. In March 1973, his widely varied duties included an appearance before a Senate subcommittee investigating truly top-level, surreptitious activities. When the late Salvador Allende was about to take office as the first Marxist president of Chile, ITT offered a million dollars to support any plan the United States government might have to stop him. The offer was made, understandably, through McCone's CIA connections. He is, of course, well versed in covert operations, and his contacts are of the highest order. He himself is a former head of the CIA.

In September 1972, Britain's ICI, the biggest chemical company in Europe, decided that their security had to be reviewed. They appointed Sir Martin Furnival Jones to guard the company against espionage, protect their investment secrets and patented discoveries, look after the wealth stored in their expanding computer data banks, and arrange better screening for their 180,000 employees in Britain and Europe. Sir Martin, the model for "M", James Bond's fictitious boss, used to be head of the former MI5. As director general of Britain's security, one of his greatest triumphs was the first British mass expulsion of foreign diplomats for commercial espionage. By the time the Tupolevs had left Heathrow airport, Sir Martin must have been clearing up his desk in preparation for his retirement in April 1972.

With security appointments like these and with increasing national involvement, has the once so fiction-flavored industrial espionage come of age?

This was just one of the questions we were discussing with several detectives and a few old friends among them at the seaside hotel in Brighton, where the Council of International Investigators held its eighteenth annual convention in August 1972.

It was a relaxed, jolly gathering of busy businessmen from all over the world, with a marked absence of dirty macs, upturned collars, well-greased trilbys, and dark glasses. There was not a bug in sight, and only miniature cameras were drawn from their shoulder holsters during the Grand Banquet when visitors had the pleasure of watching the Traditional Roast Beef Ceremony, participating in the Loving Cup Ceremony, and eating fish and chips with their fingers from newspaper in ye Olde English style.

Cabaret was provided by Her Majesty's Band of the Grenadier Guards, and it was bang in the middle of the drums rolling across the bridge on the River Kwai that a waiter called me out to the lobby.

Kubik's fetch-and-carry bodyguard was there.

"Wanna see the chief." It was a statement rather than a question. His knife must have been too blunt to smooth the edges of his manners.

I just nodded. "When?"

"Tonight. It may be at dawn. Don't go to bed."

The old pattern. I was determined to suppress an upsurge of questions. What was Kubik doing in Brighton? How did he know I was there? Why did he want to talk?

I did not particularly like the arrangement and toyed with the idea of inviting one of the tougher banqueteers to shadow me. That, of course, might have led to the cancellation of the meeting—and curiosity got the better of me yet again. So I settled for talking to one of the Americans who, I knew, was trying to sell nonlethal weapons of self-defense to Scotland Yard and was absolutely bristling with samples of CS gas dispensers. The result was that he let me borrow a mouth-organ-sized contraption for the night.

"The magnet is to stick it under your seat in the car; the clip is to wear it on your belt," he explained. "Press the white button—that's the torch—pretty strong to let you see where the stuff goes. You operate the black knob with your thumb. One click—that's the safety catch off. Click two—don't do it here unless you want to evacuate the bar—that's the actuator of the aerosol with the active ingredient. One little spray keeps the enemy away, as we say. The name is Chemical Lance, and when you use a Lance, you've got the best chance. It makes the opposition cry—and perhaps vomit and convulse—but it will not cause any permanent aftereffects."

The fervent sales talk made me hesitate, and only my distrust for Kubik's messenger persuaded me to keep the bulky container in my pocket when he called at last, and we left the hotel at three o'clock in the morning.

Antishadowing precautions were applied as usual. First we had a half an hour up and down The Lanes, those quaint little streets of antiques and curio dealers where we would have had to walk sideways to allow others to pass if there were a single soul in sight. My companion was not the ideal choice for such a late night stroll. I was constantly ready to find some of his cutlery in my back, and the unnerving effect suddenly taught me how easy it must be to use a gun—if you happened to have one on you. Eventually we reemerged from the maze in North Street, near the Royal Pavilion, where a Jaguar car picked us up.

After a transfer to a small but fast boat at Hove, it was at a quarter to four that we approached an ocean-going yacht that looked like the picture Kubik had shown me in Divonne—but then, all expensive boats look somewhat alike to me.

Once aboard, I was asked to wait in a comfortable saloon that bore every mark of the aftermath of a rather protracted conference where at least ten people must have been busy emptying glasses and filling up ash trays. I sat with my hand on the gas gun in my pocket.

"Hi, honey . . . come on, say hello or something . . . Why do you look so surprised whenever we meet? Have you forgotten Vera Fielding?"

She looked fresher, more cheerful, and slimmer than in Divonne. "Surprised? Er—well, it must be the accent, I suppose."

"What accent?"

"Yours. The French one is gone, you almost sound like a Texan."

"Good for business. I mean if you're dealing with non-English-speaking people on the old Continent."

"What brought you to Brighton?" I asked rather rashly.

"That's not you, honey, to ask direct questions like that."

"Nothing wrong with asking. You don't have to answer."

"I had to meet someone who was at the same conference as you were."

I had a shrewd guess who it might be, but it seemed pointless to ask her for verification. "That's how you heard that I was here?"

"Let's settle for that version. Sorry about the inconvenient hour, but we had a very important negotiation here which went on and on."

"And it shows."

"Yeah. Wanna Bourbon?"

"Thanks. I'll settle for a Scotch. I'm not a client from 'the old Continent,' you know."

"That's good. I like that," she said, filling a tumbler overgenerously to the brim.

She kept chattering until I understood what she did not spell out—that it was for me to ask about Kubik.

"Is he here?"

"Who?"

"Your husband. Remember? You had a husband who invited me here tonight."

"Oh, him, sure I remember. But we've separated, and the invitation came from me."

"I'm sorry to hear about the separation."

"Don't be. It's for the best. He's retired from the business, you see. He was getting old. And tired. And his nerves, yeah, his nerves couldn't take it any more. It's too much, really."

"But not for you, I suppose."

"No, not for me, honey. It's a sad story, really."

"He must be missing his yacht."

"I wouldn't say that. He was after the quiet life. Had enough of all the hanky-panky. Perhaps because he felt out of his depth. The business has grown; we must deal with real bigwigs, top-level negotiators. He lacked class and style, you know. So he opted out."

"And where is he buried?"

"What a stupid thing to ask! He's not dead. Just resting. Sailing, in fact, around the world. Tahiti, Bali, Great Barrier Reef—that sort of thing. Relaxing. Knowing that the business is in good hands."

"That's what you wanted me to know?"

"Yeah, you could put it that way. And also that it was a straight-forward agreement between us. No hard feelings at all."

I tried hard, but in vain, to imagine the maneuvers leading to the "straight-forward" deal that put him out of business.

"Would you tell me something in return, honey?"

Too preoccupied with my thoughts, I merely nodded.

"Did he ever mention Truman, his friend?"

"Why do you ask?"

"Or Truman's daughter and Mory and Singapore? Not that it matters, really, but I wanted you to know that I had nothing to do with it."

"With what?"

"Whatever sob story he might have told you about them." She clearly enjoyed showing off the amount of information at her fingertips. About me, about Kubik, about the skeletons in some large corporations' vaults.

In hospitals they must have been distributing early-morning cups of tea when I finished my drink and the audience was over. The small boat was to take me back ashore, and just as we were saying good night—or rather good morning—she asked if I was still contemplating writing this book. "You can, of course, say what you like, honey, but I must warn you that I have some of the best bespoke legal advisors who can tailor outstandingly good libel suits."

I was delighted to hear that she had not wasted all those years in Kubik's company. At least his personal brand of humor lived on.

The Jaguar was not waiting for me. It was the first time that I saw this knifeman grin. "Nobody told me to drive you back, sirree. . . ."

So I walked. A chilly breeze chased me, and the penultimate in nonlethal self-defense gave me no protection against it.